W9-AOO-430

DOG BREED GUIDE

THE COMPLETE REFERENCE TO YOUR **BEST FRIEND FUR-EVER**

T. J. RESLER & GARY WEITZMAN, D.V.M.

President and CEO of the San Diego Humane Society

NATIONAL GEOGRAPHIC
WASHINGTON, D.C.

CONTENTS

WHAT IS A DOG?

DOG BREED GUIDE

PICKING A PUP

FOREWORD
BY DR. GARY WEITZMAN

I love dogs. To me, dogs are the most fantastic creatures on the planet. I can't even imagine a world without them! I pride myself on knowing dogs, inside and out. I've spent my entire professional career making sure I understand their behavior, what makes them tick, and what keeps them healthy. I thought I knew most of the breeds that make up the enormous panorama of dogs with whom we share our planet. Turns out, I only knew a fraction of the incredible variety of dog breeds out there; after working on the *National Geographic Kids Dog Breed Guide*, I realized how many more there are to know!

From the Chesapeake Bay retriever to the Peruvian Inca orchid to the Alaskan klee kai, this book will introduce you to some dogs you've heard of—and lots you haven't. Of course, all dogs share some common traits: two eyes, two ears, four legs, and a tail. Some are small and fluffy; others are big and wirehaired. Some love a good lap; others are born to run. Some are patient and great with kids; others are better with experienced owners. You'll discover how these and other characteristics come together to make different breeds of dogs unique animals. Some of the dogs in this book are familiar-looking pups you may see on your block, while others are rare creatures that live on the other side of the world. But no matter where they roam or how unusual they are, dogs share one very special trait: They want to be with their people, whether it's as a pet getting and giving affection or doing the job they were bred to do. Dogs look to us for direction and care. What we get back is loyalty, love, and protection. When you finish this book, you'll not only be more of a canine admirer than you started out, you'll also be on your way to becoming a genuine dog aficionado. After all, who else would know that the Slovakian rough-haired pointer has amber eyes or that the Large Munsterlander has been around since the Middle Ages? Only a true global dog expert!

🐾 I've been caring for dogs my whole life. At the San Diego Humane Society, where I'm the president and also a veterinarian, we take care of tens of thousands of dogs and puppies. My job, and my organization's mission, is to protect animals and ensure that every canine companion gets a new home or the chance to stay in the home she has. We offer training classes and veterinary care, including vaccinations, microchipping, and other services to help people take great care of their dogs. Good pet care is the most important thing you can do as an animal admirer and advocate.

OUR CANINE COMPANIONS

You've heard the expression: Dogs are our best friends. From the towering Irish wolfhound to the tiny Chihuahua, these social animals are part of our pack. They play with us, snuggle up to our sides, greet us with wagging tails—and sometimes gnaw on our slippers or swipe our food when we're not looking. (When you invite a descendant of wolves into your heart and home, you might get a bit of mischief!)

Dogs have been part of our lives for so long that they probably changed the course of human history.

Long before we figured out how to plant corn or raise chickens, our canine companions were tagging along by our side, helping us catch our dinner and protecting us. Our first domesticated animal, dogs probably helped our ancestors survive, even in harsh environments. Dogs adapted wherever we went, and along the way, they learned how to read our expressions and moods and become our best buddies.

Dogs are the most diverse species to walk the Earth, but it's been only in the past couple centuries that we've had such an assortment of differently sized and shaped pooches. Some diversity happened naturally, but people also created new breeds through careful, selective breeding. At first, we focused on qualities that would help us get work done, breeding dogs to become even better hunters or guards. But then we just bred dogs to become cuddly lapdogs, elegant show dogs, and our best friends. No matter their shape or size—or if they're purebreds or mixes—we love our dogs.

In the following pages, you'll become a dog expert. You'll meet the dog family and learn how dogs evolved—along with some human help. You'll also be introduced to the results of all that diversity, learning how subtle changes in ears, noses, heads, bodies, and fur resulted in more than 400 distinct dog breeds. You'll find out the background of each of those breeds, along with quick facts that provide important information, including size, coat, the amount of grooming the breed requires, its exercise needs, and how easy it is to train. Among those hundreds, see if you can find the half dozen "top dogs"—the biggest, brightest, and tiniest breeds.

Along the way, you'll meet some amazing pooches at work and play—canine stars and heroes—and learn about pooch professionals, the people who work with dogs on a daily basis. If you're ready for your own pup, you'll find some tips for picking the perfect pet for you, and you'll learn the basics of caring for your new best friend.

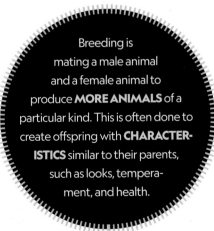

Breeding is mating a male animal and a female animal to produce **MORE ANIMALS** of a particular kind. This is often done to create offspring with **CHARACTERISTICS** similar to their parents, such as looks, temperament, and health.

THE DOG FAMILY TREE

The adorable pup cozying up by your side has an impressive scientific name: *Canis lupus familiaris,* the domestic dog. Dogs and other canine species, including wolves and coyotes, are part of a larger family, called the Canidae or canids, which includes related species, such as foxes. Like your own cousins, dogs are more closely related to some family members than others—in their case, wolves. Scientists use genetic evidence to figure out the relationships, and they're making new discoveries every day about when one species branched off from another. The large canid family includes about three dozen species (34 to 38, depending on whom you ask). This diagram will introduce you to some of your dog's wild cousins.

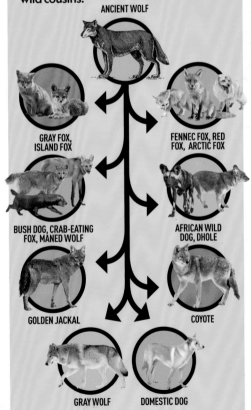

ANCIENT WOLF

GRAY FOX, ISLAND FOX

FENNEC FOX, RED FOX, ARCTIC FOX

BUSH DOG, CRAB-EATING FOX, MANED WOLF

AFRICAN WILD DOG, DHOLE

GOLDEN JACKAL

COYOTE

GRAY WOLF

DOMESTIC DOG

FROM WOLF
TO WOOF

A toy poodle and an Afghan hound hardly look like wolves (or, for that matter, like each other!). But don't let their appearances fool you.

All dogs—from the waddling pug to the graceful greyhound—are thought to be descendants of a line of wild wolves that is now extinct. Dogs were the first domesticated animal—the first to be tamed and to live with people. (Yes, way before cats!)

But just when dogs first became domesticated is a matter of scientific debate. For a long time, scientists thought it happened about 15,000 years ago, but now they think it was probably more like 20,000 to 40,000 years ago. Before they became completely domesticated, early dogs crossbred so often with wolves and with each other that their genetic makeup got mixed. And scientists are working with dogged determination to sort out the when and the where.

What we know for sure is that the transformation from wolves to dogs was a breathtaking evolutionary leap. Scientists used to think we humans got the credit for taming wolves, but now most believe it happened in a more amazing way: Dogs domesticated themselves.

Here's how: Our ancient ancestors would hunt animals to survive. After devouring the meat and using whatever other animal parts they needed, they'd throw the rest of the animal carcass away. Some clever wolves realized that our ancestors' leftovers would make an easy meal. The wolves who came closest to people got the prize.

Not every wolf dared to go near people, of course. The wary ones stayed away from humans—and remained wolves. But the ones enjoying our scraps got more and more comfortable hanging around humans. Over time, they bonded with our ancestors, gradually becoming less wild and eventually becoming dogs.

The tamer the wolves became, the more they changed in appearance. Wolves are designed for hunting. They're large and have long, powerful jaws to take down big prey. Early dogs adapted to be our companions: Over many generations they grew a bit smaller, so they could survive on our scraps, and their snouts shortened because they didn't need jaws with killing power.

Most remarkably, dogs learned to understand our body language, facial expressions, and spoken words, and they could do things that were difficult for us to do alone. They protected us and helped us hunt. They scrambled up rocky mountains to herd sheep. They hauled our stuff on sleds into the wilderness and helped us live in some of the most unforgiving environments on Earth.

When wolves transformed into dogs, they didn't only change their lives. They changed ours, too.

SLY AS A FOX

Foxes are wild animals that are highly alert and nervous around people. But a long-running Russian experiment has turned foxes into playful, doglike pets—and it showed us a lot about how animals become domesticated.

Starting in the 1950s, Russian geneticist Dmitry Belyaev traveled to fox farms and picked the tamest foxes—those that didn't cower in the corner of their cages or snarl when people approached. He bred them together and raised fox cubs. When the offspring grew up, he picked the tamest to become parents to a new generation.

After only two to three generations, the foxes no longer cowered or snarled around people. By the fourth generation, the fox cubs wagged their tails and got excited to see people. In fifty generations—a short time in evolutionary terms—they acted just like dogs. They played with people and picked up on human cues. They barked more like dogs instead of howling and screaming like wild foxes. They even began to look more like dogs. Their ears flopped, their tails curled, and their coats came in new colors, sometimes with big black and white patches.

Those spotted coats, curly tails, and floppy ears are common in domesticated animals—but not in their wild cousins. It's something scientists, including Charles Darwin, noted long ago. What the Russian fox experiment revealed is that the adorable "domesticated look" is also linked genetically with tameness. The Russian researchers selected foxes based only on their behavior. But as they bred the foxes for tameness, they got all the other domesticated doggy behaviors and looks, too. They turned wild foxes into domesticated pets—and gave us a glimpse of how wolves transformed into our adorable pups.

DOGS DEBUT

It's hard to pinpoint exactly when and where wolves transformed into dogs and how they spread through the world.

Scientists have found archaeological and genetic evidence pointing to different times and places, and they're making new discoveries all the time. Recent research indicates that dogs probably became domesticated sometime between 20,000 and 40,000 years ago. But dogs also migrated with people, so their ancestry gets complicated really fast. Where exactly dogs first became domesticated is still unclear. Based on the available evidence, scientists have proposed Europe, Southeast Asia, Central Asia, and the Middle East. To solve the mystery, researchers are comparing the skulls and genetic makeup of today's dogs and the ancient dog remains they've found in archaeological sites around the world.

NORTH AMERICA

SOUTH AMERICA

AMERICAS

Ancient American dogs, descended from Asian dogs that arrived with people thousands of years ago, disappeared after European colonists came with their dogs in the 15th century. The colonists' dogs may have brought a disease that wiped out the first descendants.

EUROPE

Dogs were in Europe more than 15,000 years ago, probably before Asian dogs migrated there. This puzzling evidence makes some scientists wonder if dogs became domesticated twice, both in Asia and in Europe.

ASIA

Dogs today trace most of their ancestry to Asian dogs. But that doesn't necessarily mean all dogs originated in Asia, only that the Asian dogs thrived and probably moved into other regions.

EUROPE

A S I A

ON THE MOVE

Asian dogs migrated westward with people sometime between 5,500 and 14,000 years ago. After the Asian dogs arrived, the original European dogs may have largely disappeared.

AFRICA

Proposed area where dogs were first domesticated

The best archaeological find isn't **TEETH** or **LEG BONES,** it's a bone that curls around the **DOG'S EAR.** It's the best at preserving **GENETIC** evidence.

AUSTRALIA

PEOPLE
LEND A HAND

Dogs may have domesticated themselves, but people took it from there.

Starting back in ancient times, our ancestors noticed that some of their canine companions stood out from the pack in a special way. Maybe they ran faster, followed the scent of prey a little farther, or rounded up sheep effortlessly. Those dogs were especially valuable to people who relied on herding sheep or hunting to survive. So they kept those supertalented pooches and raised their puppies.

By breeding dogs with the traits they valued most—a practice called selective breeding—our ancestors made sure those traits were passed on to puppies and strengthened over the next generations. Over time, they created new dog breeds.

At first, people emphasized traits that would help them get work done or stay safe. They bred dogs to become good guards, trackers, herders, or sled dogs. But then, society changed—and dogs along with it.

In the 18th and 19th centuries, the industrial revolution transformed society in Europe and America. Factories became common, drawing workers from farms to the city. The increasing availability of machine-made goods fueled trade, shipping and railways, and all kinds of businesses. This gradually gave rise to a new, urban middle class of business people,

doctors, lawyers, and teachers. In England, where people traditionally had been born either into the wealthy aristocracy or low-income working classes, the Victorian era saw a new middle class that found it had enough free time and money to pursue hobbies. They found a new hobby in an unusual way.

In 1860, British and French troops, at war with the Chinese Empire, plundered the Summer Palace in Beijing. They destroyed many Chinese treasures and brought others home with them, including a handful of Pekingese dogs, considered sacred in China. The British troops presented Queen Victoria with the smallest Pekingese, a pet dog petite and docile enough to hold on her lap.

Queen Victoria's Pekingese created a sensation in British society. Soon, owning a lapdog was a symbol of status. People started breeding dogs to create various tiny "toy" breeds. Others bred dogs to get certain looks, like different colors or types of fur. "Dog fancy"—a charming term that captured their love of dogs—became a passion of the middle classes in England and soon in other countries. People no longer bred dogs simply for what they could do. They bred dogs for appearance. It wasn't long before people met to show off their prized pooches in the first organized dog shows. In 1873, the world's first kennel club formed in London to govern these shows. Over the next 150 years, people developed more than 400 dog breeds.

DOG DESIGN

Centuries of selective breeding have created dramatic differences in dogs' looks. But at their core, they all have the same basic anatomy: a build inherited from their wolf ancestors. Like those wild ancestors, dogs are carnivores (meat-eaters), designed to find and catch prey. These days, they're happy to have you serve them dinner. But you'll still see the instincts of a hunter when they chase down a ball you throw.

MUZZLE

Powerful jaws are designed for a predator.

NOSE

A dog's nose is specially designed to have an outstanding sense of smell.

TEETH

Four large, spiky canine teeth can grab and hold prey. Shorter jagged teeth tear apart tough foods, such as meat.

EARS

Sensitive ears pick up sounds that people can't hear. They can also move to detect sounds from any direction.

EYES

Eyes are set apart to allow a dog to judge distances well.

HIPS

The hip joints on most breeds allow a large range of movement, enabling big strides.

PAWS

Pads on the paws cushion a dog's weight.

CLAWS

Claws on long, powerful toes keep a dog from slipping.

DOG DIVERSITY

Dogs' breathtaking variation can be seen especially in their different head shapes, ear types, and coat varieties and colors.

Each dog breed has a certain "look"—a characteristic head shape, similar ears and coats—and all members of that breed will share that look. It's the result of selective breeding over the past couple of centuries. Some breeds, such as Airedales or West Highland white terriers, have one standard style. But others, such as poodles or dachshunds, come in a variety of colors—anywhere from a couple to many—a couple coat types, and maybe even different sizes. But they still have a characteristic look. No one is going to mistake a dachshund (no matter what color, size, or coat type) for an Airedale!

HEAD SHAPES

Dogs' heads come in three basic shapes, with variations on each. Key differences are the length of the muzzle and the degree of the "stop," the dip from the skull to the muzzle.

Medium
Most dogs have a head of medium proportions—both length and width—with a significant stop, or dip, from the skull to the muzzle. The formal term for this is mesocephalic.

Long and Narrow
Typical of sight hounds, a long and narrow head—formally called a dolichocephalic head—has a much less noticeable stop between its skull and muzzle.

Short and Broad
This impressive head type—called brachycephalic—is typical of bulldogs, Pekingese, and shih tzu. The skull is almost as wide as it is long and has a deep stop.

EAR TYPES

All dogs' ears originally stood up like little triangles on top of their heads, similar to wolves' ears. But centuries of selective breeding have created a large variety, and ears now help distinguish one breed from another. In general, dogs' ears fall into three main types: erect (standing up or pointy), semierect (standing up with part tipped over), and drop (hanging down in some fashion). Within those broad categories are many variations.

Button Ears
Semierect ears with tops that fold forward, almost in half, with the front forming a V-shape.

Bat Ears
Broad, erect ears with broad bases and round tops. These ears naturally face forward.

Erect Ears
Ears that stand up and open toward the front.

Candle-Flame Ears
Naturally erect ears that are broader at the base and taper to a point at the top.

Folded Ears
Long, drop pendant ears that fall in folds, with the lower parts curling.

Butterfly Ears
Large, erect ears that slant out and move like the spread wings of a butterfly.

Pendant Ears
Long, drop ears that hang down, common on hounds. They come in many variations.

Rose Ears
Semierect ears that fold in such a way to resemble the folds of a rose.

COAT VARIETIES

Like their wolf ancestors, most dogs have a double coat, with a softer, dense insulating layer covered by an outer coat of different length and texture.

Some short-coated breeds don't have an undercoat, and a few breeds don't have a coat at all! Most dogs shed their coats, but some have hairlike coats that keep growing until you take them for a trim. Thousands of years ago, dogs' coats adapted to their surroundings, with dogs acquiring thick coats in cold climates and short coats in hot areas. But these days, dogs' coats depend on the breed, not the climate.

COAT COLORS

Dogs' coats come in many colors and patterns specific to the breed. Some breeds have only one color coat, but many others come in a few colors. Some may be a dominant color but also have markings, like patches, stripes on their noses, or "socks" on their legs. Feast your eyes on some of these canine fashion statements.

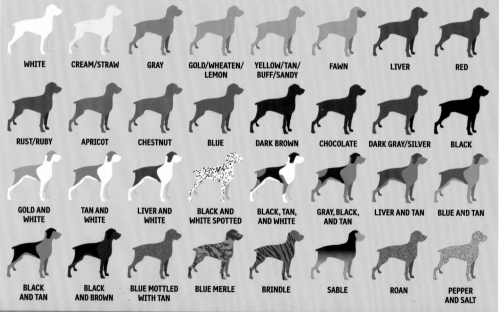

WHITE	CREAM/STRAW	GRAY	GOLD/WHEATEN/LEMON	YELLOW/TAN/BUFF/SANDY	FAWN	LIVER	RED
RUST/RUBY	APRICOT	CHESTNUT	BLUE	DARK BROWN	CHOCOLATE	DARK GRAY/SILVER	BLACK
GOLD AND WHITE	TAN AND WHITE	LIVER AND WHITE	BLACK AND WHITE SPOTTED	BLACK, TAN, AND WHITE	GRAY, BLACK, AND TAN	LIVER AND TAN	BLUE AND TAN
BLACK AND TAN	BLACK AND BROWN	BLUE MOTTLED WITH TAN	BLUE MERLE	BRINDLE	SABLE	ROAN	PEPPER AND SALT

COAT VARIETIES

Wirehaired
A hard, coarse, wirelike texture to the coat.

Long
A straight coat with long hair. Some are silky, but others are hard coats.

Smooth
A short coat that lies smoothly on the dog.

Corded
A coat that hangs in long, tightly matted strands, much like dreadlocks.

Powderpuff
A double soft and silky coat that fluffs up off the body.

Standoff
A fluffy coat with a soft, dense undercoat and with longer hair puffing out.

Short
A dense coat that covers the dog's entire body.

Curly
A compact coat formed of spirals or ringlets.

Hairless
Either no or a small amount of hair.

Full Double
Two-ply coat, with a soft undercoat that provides warmth and waterproofing and a harder outer coat that protects against the weather.

WHAT'S A BREED?

 The exact number of dog breeds in the world is a matter of debate.

That's because when people talk about dog breeds, they're usually referring to breeds recognized by an official regulatory body or kennel club, and these organizations don't agree on the number of dog breeds. When "dog fancy" swept Europe and America in the late 1800s and early 1900s, dog lovers got together and formed these kennel clubs to develop consistent rules for dog shows and to ensure that prize dogs lived up to certain standards of appearance for their breeds. Individual dogs that belong to recognized breeds can be registered with those organizations and trace their family trees, or pedigrees. You may hear them called "purebred" or "pedigreed" dogs.

The thing is, these organizations have slightly different processes for recognizing breeds, and they add new breeds every year. So, while the American Kennel Club (AKC) recognizes fewer than 200 breeds, Europe's broadest kennel club, the Fédération Cynologique Internationale (FCI), recognizes more than 340. This book profiles more than 400 dog breeds—the breeds recognized by the AKC, the FCI, the Canadian Kennel Club (CKC), and the Kennel Club (KC) in the United

French bulldog

Kingdom—plus a few other popular breeds that aren't officially recognized (yet).

Animals get grouped in a lot of ways, including in scientific classifications such as species and family. You already know that the dog species, *Canis lupus familiaris*, is part of the Canidae, or canid, family. (If you've forgotten that bit, flip back to page 9.) A "breed" is a designation made by kennel clubs, not a scientific classification—hence, the disagreements. The kennel clubs don't even agree 100 percent on the standards of appearance that pedigreed pooches must meet. A dog that's technically an inch too tall for his breed's standard in the United States may fit the European standard. Even more contentious is how dog breeds are grouped together. Each kennel club puts breeds in groupings related roughly to the dogs' function. If you watch a dog show, you'll see the dogs competing in these groupings. But there's even less agreement about dog groupings! Each kennel club uses its own system—and so do books—and different clubs may put the same breed in different groups.

This book divides dog breeds into groups based on their origins, characteristics, and what people bred them to do. But even these groupings don't include all dogs! Many, many dogs aren't purebreds—and so, not recognized by kennel clubs—but they may be perfect, playful pets.

CROSSBREEDS

These puppies are born from parents of different breeds—a practice geneticists call crossbreeding. These designer dogs—such as puggles, cockapoos, or labradoodles—show a mixture of their parents' traits (see p. 204).

MIXED BREEDS

Many dogs are mixes of so many breeds that it's hard to pin down their exact lineage. No matter. They still can be excellent pets. Mixed breeds are sometimes called "mutts"—a term many people find adorable but some don't like. In general, pedigreed dogs have more records, not only of their

Labradoodle

lineage but also the personality and health information of their ancestors. With mutts and mixes, you're less sure of what you're going to get. But many people believe that mixes tend to be heartier since they're more genetically diverse.

BREAKING IT ALL DOWN
For each of the breed profiles in this book, you'll find a quick-fact box with information to help you decide if that's the dog for you.

FROM:	UK/Scotland
HEIGHT:	14–15 inches (36–38 cm)
WEIGHT:	14–37 pounds (6–17 kg)
COAT:	Sable, black and tan, black, blue, with white; thick and long
GROOMING:	(combs)
EXERCISE NEEDS:	(balls)
K-9 QUALITIES:	Devoted and fun-loving

From: Where the breed as we know it today was developed.
Height and Weight: How big the dog will get when fully grown.*
Coat: Colors and varieties characteristic of the breed.
Grooming: How much effort it takes to care for the dog's coat. One comb means a brushing about once a week; three combs means multiple times each week; and five combs means a serious daily grooming routine.
Exercise Needs: How much exercise the dog needs every day. One ball means a 20-minute walk or romp in a yard; three balls means several long walks or play sessions; and five balls means a couple of hours of daily exercise.
K-9 Qualities: A quick snapshot of the breed's general characteristics.

* Variations in metric conversions are the result of rounding.

PRIMITIVE
DOGS

If you go to a museum and see ancient art and artifacts depicting dogs, you'll spot noble animals with ears perched upright on their heads and muzzles that taper almost to a point. These ancient dogs, which share many traits with their wolf ancestors, aren't found only in museums! Several breeds today resemble the dogs captured in the art of ancient civilizations. These are the "primitive breeds," dogs that may trace their lineage back to those ancient canines. Besides their appearance, they share other traits with their wild ancestors: They can have only one litter of puppies a year—unlike most pet dogs, which can have puppies twice a year. Most amazingly, some of these breeds don't bark, like other dogs do! They howl and make other melodious noises. You won't ⸺ a dog show with special classes for primitive dogs; it's too hard to ⸺ out which dogs really trace their lineage to ancient dogs, and ⸺ experts don't group any dog breeds together as "primitive." ⸺ genetic evidence scientists find, the more we realize that fe⸺ any—have an unbroken line to those first domesticated wo⸺ breeds probably come the closest, and they're so awesome t⸺ to give them a shout-out.

XOLOITZCUINTLI

This rare breed (pronounced show-loh-etts-KWEENT-lee), the first dog in the Americas, was named after the Aztec god Xolotl (plus the Aztec word for dog, *itzcuintli*). Art depicting "Xolos," also known as Mexican hairless dogs, has been discovered dating back more than 3,000 years. Archaeologists believe Xolos traveled with early humans when they first migrated to the Americas. Long ago, in Mexico, these dogs were sacred, believed to guard homes from evil spirits and intruders. Xolos are prized as a hairless breed, but some puppies are born with fur. They're mellow at home but enjoy long walks and hanging out with their people. A lot! They're sensitive, and won't be happy if they have to spend the day alone. If not trained properly, Xolos—especially the small ones—can get bossy, and they do better around older kids who know how to play gently.

FROM: Mexico

HEIGHT: 10–14 inches (25–35 cm) for toy; 14–18 inches (36–45 cm) for miniature; 18–23 inches (46–60 cm) for standard

WEIGHT: 5–15 pounds (2–7 kg) for toy; 15–31 pounds (7–14 kg) for miniature; 24–40 pounds (11–18 kg) for standard

COAT: Dark gray, black, or bronze skin for hairless; red, liver, brindle, bronze, fawn, brown fur

GROOMING:

EXERCISE NEEDS:

K-9 QUALITIES: Loyal and good-natured

In remote Mexican and Central American villages, **XOLOS AND PERUVIAN HAIRLESS** dogs have a reputation as healers. People hold their warm bodies close to **CURE AILMENTS** such as joint pain, toothaches, and even sleeplessness.

PERUVIAN HAIRLESS

Like Xolos, these dogs have a recessive gene that produces some hairless puppies. But even the hairless pups may have wisps of hair, including a crest on their heads that looks a bit like a cool hairdo. If you have one of these pups, be prepared to apply sunscreen in the summer. In the winter, a sweater or cuddle will keep them warm—but they only want that from their own families. They can be wary of strangers. Lively and graceful dogs, their roots go back more than 900 years in South America.

FROM: Peru

HEIGHT: 10–16 inches (25–41 cm) for miniature; 16–20 inches (40–50 cm) for medium; 20–26 inches (50–65 cm) for large

WEIGHT: 9–18 pounds (4–8 kg) for miniature; 18–26 pounds (8–12 kg) for medium; 26–55 pounds (12–25 kg) for large

COAT: Brownish gray skin with pink patches; blond, dark brown, black fur

GROOMING:

EXERCISE NEEDS:

K-9 QUALITIES: Affectionate and energetic

PERUVIAN INCA ORCHID

An important dog in Inca civilizations, from the 1400s to 1500s, the Peruvian Inca orchid's true origins are unknown. These colorful hounds, which come in hairless and coated varieties, often tuck their tails under their bellies. Usually, dogs do that when they're worried or scared, but "PIOs" do it even when they're perfectly content—and they usually are! These loving little pets are happy, even a bit clownish, around their families.

FROM: Peru

HEIGHT: 20–26 inches (50–65 cm)

WEIGHT: 26–51 pounds (12–23 kg)

COAT: Pink skin with mottling or spots in a variety of colors

GROOMING:

EXERCISE NEEDS:

K-9 QUALITIES: Playful and well-behaved

CANAAN DOG

The national dog of Israel, Canaan dogs trace their history in the Middle East back thousands of years. Intelligent and athletic, they were bred to be watchdogs and herding dogs, so they have a protective—but not usually aggressive—nature. They may be better with older kids than little tots because of their watchdog instincts and their need for firm but gentle handling.

FROM: Israel

HEIGHT: 20-24 inches (50-60 cm)

WEIGHT: 40-55 pounds (18-25 kg)

COAT: Sandy, white, black, red and white spotted, black and white spotted, all shades of brown, solid or with white markings; dense

GROOMING:

EXERCISE NEEDS:

K-9 QUALITIES: Affectionate and protective

PHARAOH HOUND

These are some of the oldest domesticated dogs. Believed to have originated in ancient Egypt, they were brought by traders to the Mediterranean island nation of Malta, where they survived for more than 2,000 years. Pharaoh hounds have an unusual trick: They "blush" when excited, their noses and ears turning a deep rose color. These goofy hounds—always happy to dash off after a small animal—are affectionate with their families, but they may be too rambunctious for young kids.

FROM: Malta

HEIGHT: 21-25 inches (53-63 cm)

WEIGHT: 44-55 pounds (20-25 kg)

COAT: Tan; short and glossy

GROOMING:

EXERCISE NEEDS:

K-9 QUALITIES: Friendly and devoted

TAIWAN DOG

Taiwan dogs, formerly called Formosan mountain dogs, probably trace their roots to the semiwild dogs once used to hunt in the interior of the island of Taiwan. This breed is rare, even in Taiwan. With enough training to keep their hunting instincts in line, they make loyal family dogs—but it's best not to trust them with your pet cat.

FROM: Taiwan
HEIGHT: 17–20 inches (43–52 cm)
WEIGHT: 26–40 pounds (12–18 kg)
COAT: Variety of colors; short, hard

GROOMING:
EXERCISE NEEDS:
K-9 QUALITIES: Intelligent and docile

THAI RIDGEBACK

This rare breed, believed to be one of the world's first dog breeds, originated in the remote islands of eastern Thailand as many as 4,000 years ago. Isolated and virtually unknown outside of Thailand until the 1970s, the dogs didn't crossbreed with others, so their purebred lineage goes way back. In the past, Thai ridgebacks were used for hunting and as guard dogs, but now they're mainly companions. Naturally protective, they can be suspicious of strangers and other dogs, and they need proper training and socialization to make sure they don't become aggressive. They get their name from a ridge of hair that runs down the dogs' backs and lies in the opposite direction from the rest of their coat.

FROM: Thailand
HEIGHT: 20–24 inches (50–60 cm)
WEIGHT: 35–75 pounds (16–34 kg)
COAT: Black, fawn, red, blue; short and smooth

GROOMING:
EXERCISE NEEDS:
K-9 QUALITIES: Loyal and watchful

27

FROM:	Central Africa
HEIGHT:	16–17 inches (40–43 cm)
WEIGHT:	22–24 pounds (10–11 kg)
COAT:	Chestnut red, black, brindle, black and tan or chestnut, all with various white markings; smooth and shiny
GROOMING:	
EXERCISE NEEDS:	
K-9 QUALITIES:	Independent and affectionate

A Basenji **CAN'T BARK** because its larynx (voice box) is shaped differently from the **LARYNX** of most other dogs.

BASENJI

 If you get a pet Basenji (pronounced ba-SEN-jee), don't expect your pup to greet you at the door by barking.

This ancient breed, depicted on the tombs of the pharaohs as far back as 3600 B.C., can't bark. But that doesn't mean they're silent. Basenjis, also known as African Barkless Dogs, express themselves by yodeling, howling, crowing, chortling, and screaming! Basenjis are built to be expressive. They carry their tails in tight curls over their backs, and when they perk up their ears, their foreheads wrinkle. It looks like they're deep in thought.

Fun-loving and devoted, basenjis are popular family pets in many countries. But they also still help people hunt in the remote forests of central Africa, where they flush out game and drive it into nets strung from trees. Their agility and keen sight and sense of smell make them equally skilled at canine sports, such as, rally (an obedience sport), tracking, and competitions where they chase fake prey (called lure coursing). Like Canaan dogs (p. 26), Basenjis are considered a "pariah" breed, descended from dogs that ran free and survived on scraps that people threw away—like the earliest dogs.

Basenjis are curious and energetic, with minds of their own. Those qualities can lead the dogs into mischief, so it's important to keep them mentally and physically stimulated with work and play. Otherwise, you may discover they make their own fun!

POOCH PROS: DOG ORIGINS RESEARCHERS

Some of the great mysteries related to dogs are how early they spread throughout the world and exactly where they became domesticated. Various researchers work to find those answers. Some of them, including archaeologists and paleontologists, take to the field, digging up artifacts and other evidence—such as ancient artwork, fossils, and even human and canine skeletons—that provide an understanding of dog evolution and how important dogs were to our ancestors. Other researchers, such as genomicists and geneticists (scientists who study genes and heritage), take bone and blood samples into their laboratories, where they examine the genetic makeup of ancient and modern dogs and make connections between them. If you work as a dog origins researcher, you may help make the next big discovery in dog evolution!

PRIMITIVE BREEDS OF THE MEDITERRANEAN

Thousands of years ago, traders sailed the Mediterranean Sea, transporting goods from Egypt and North Africa to Sicily, Sardinia, Spain, and Portugal. Among their precious cargo were agile hunting dogs, probably mixes of Egyptian hunting dogs and working dogs from other areas. Hardy and compact, the dogs adapted to their new homes and stayed relatively isolated, developing into new breeds.

CIRNECO DELL'ETNA

These lively and curious pets love spending quality time with their people—especially if it's active play or dog sports. Cirneco (pronounced cheer-NAY-ko) dell'Etna dogs, also known as Sicilian greyhounds, thrived for thousands of years on the Italian island of Sicily, where they were portrayed in mosaics and on coins. They're named after the famous volcano Mount Etna.

FROM: Italy
HEIGHT: 17–20 inches (42–52 cm)
WEIGHT: 18–26 pounds (8–12 kg)
COAT: Fawn, light to dark tan, or chestnut, with white markings; short and glossy
GROOMING:
EXERCISE NEEDS:
K-9 QUALITIES: Independent and affectionate

PORTUGUESE PODENGO

FROM: Portugal
HEIGHT: 8–12 inches (20–30 cm) for small; 16–21 inches (40–54 cm) for medium; 22–28 inches (55–70 cm) for large
WEIGHT: 9–11 pounds (4–5 kg) for small; 35–44 pounds (16–20 kg) for medium; 44–66 pounds (20–30 kg) for large
COAT: Fawn and white, yellow and white, sometimes black or brown with white; smooth or wirehaired
GROOMING:
EXERCISE NEEDS:
K-9 QUALITIES: Playful and loyal

Featured in the art of Portugal, these hunting hounds, also known as Portuguese warren hounds, developed in size to match their prey. The knee-high Podengos hunted rabbits, which they'd stalk like a cat, often digging in rocky terrain or jumping straight up above dense brush to find their prey. These athletic antics make them lively and amusing pets, but they need tall fences to keep them from chasing squirrels and rabbits.

CANARIAN WARREN HOUND

FROM: Spain/Canary Islands

HEIGHT: 21–25 inches (54–64 cm)

WEIGHT: 44–55 pounds (20–25 kg)

COAT: Shades of red, white, or red and white; short and dense

GROOMING:

EXERCISE NEEDS:

K-9 QUALITIES: Energetic and outdoorsy

Also known by the name Podenco Canario, these hounds originally hunted rabbits on the Canary Islands, off the northwestern coast of Africa. Like pharaoh hounds (p. 26), they "blush" when they're excited—and they're excited a lot. A Canarian warren hound is better suited to hunting and outdoor activities than to a quiet life as a house dog.

IBIZAN HOUND

Named for Ibiza, one of the islands off the eastern coast of Spain, these hounds resemble a painting on the sarcophagus of an Egyptian pharaoh. On their home islands, they were pack hunters, working as a team to chase down rabbits. These days, the pink-nosed pups, nicknamed "Beezers," are playful, charming, and even silly pets who are always on the move. And if your fence isn't tall enough to contain their jumping, they may be moving far from home.

FROM: Spain

HEIGHT: 22–29 inches (56–74 cm)

WEIGHT: 45–50 pounds (20–23 kg)

COAT: White, red; short and smooth or wirehaired

GROOMING:

EXERCISE NEEDS:

K-9 QUALITIES: Affectionate and good-natured

THE WILD SIDE

Only a quarter of the world's dogs are pets. Most dogs are feral—domesticated dogs that have become wild—and others are truly wild canines. Here's a sampling of wild dogs from around the world.

NEW GUINEA SINGING DOG

Also called New Guinea highland wild dogs, these feral dogs, most often seen in the wild and in zoos, "sing" by varying the notes of their howls.

DINGO

These Australian dogs are probably descendants of Asian dingoes brought to the continent 3,000 to 4,000 years ago. They live and hunt alone or in packs and roam great distances in search of food. Dingoes also howl like wolves!

AFRICAN WILD DOG

Also known as Cape hunting dogs or painted dogs, these long-legged dogs live in packs and roam the sparse woodlands and open plains of sub-Saharan Africa.

SHORT-EARED DOG

Sometimes called small-eared zorros, these elusive canines live around rivers and creeks in the Amazon rain forest in Peru, where they eat a lot of fish. They're well suited to their diets; they have webbed feet to help them swim.

DHOLE

Also known as Asian wild dogs, these foxlike dogs are efficient pack hunters. Dholes (pronounced "doles") have a wide range of vocalizations, including high-pitched whistles, screams, clucks, and mews.

CAROLINA DOG

Also called American dingoes, these dogs roam the southeastern United States. Their ancestors probably were brought by early settlers from Asia.

SPITZ-TYPE DOGS

It's not hard to see the wolf's influence in the spitz breeds. From their alert, pointy ears to their coloring, these breeds wear their heritage out in the open. It's possible that all spitz breeds can trace their ancient ancestry to early domesticated dogs in East Asia. More recently, as their fluffy double-layer coats attest, many of the spitz breeds developed in the Arctic or Siberia, with others coming from Asia. Though the spitz breeds are capable hunters and herders—and great pets—their claim to fame is as sled dogs. Many of these breeds are ideally designed for pulling sleds, with stiff backbones that transfer the push of their legs into pulling power. Big enough to move heavy loads but small enough to get by on little food—just snow and seal blubber—these pack dogs are true endurance athletes. Many sled dogs can run the equivalent of five marathons in a day, making them the fastest animals over long distances. Experts believe that people living in harsh Arctic climates would not have survived without these dogs. Spitz senses allow them to navigate in blindingly white or gray conditions where people can't see where the snow ends and the sky begins. The dogs even sense subtle changes in the snow underfoot, keeping people safely away from thin ice or crevices.

NORWEGIAN ELKHOUND

These sturdy dogs probably rode the high seas long ago with the Vikings. Back on land, they herded flocks and protected farms and families in Norway and throughout Scandinavia for centuries. And, yes, they helped hunt—and still do—but not necessarily elk. (The breed's name in Norwegian, *elghund*, actually means "moose dog"!) These days, elkhounds are popular, friendly pets, with a bold and playful attitude. When these affectionate dogs grow up with kids, they're great playmates. They're also willing to tackle all kinds of work, including as service and therapy dogs.

FROM: Norway
HEIGHT: 19–20 inches (49–52 cm)
WEIGHT: 44–51 pounds (20–23 kg)
COAT: Gray with black tips; thick and double-coated

GROOMING:
EXERCISE NEEDS:
K-9 QUALITIES: Energetic and independent

KARELIAN BEAR DOG

A hardy dog bred to withstand the harsh climate of northeastern Europe, the quick and fearless "KBDs"—a type of laika—are a national treasure in their homeland of Finland, where they originally hunted and protected people from big brown bears. They're not ideal house dogs. They're fine with people, but their instincts to challenge other animals can cause trouble in the neighborhood.

FROM: Finland
HEIGHT: 20–22 inches (52–57 cm)
WEIGHT: 44–51 pounds (20–23 kg)
COAT: Black and white; thick and harsh

GROOMING:
EXERCISE NEEDS:
K-9 QUALITIES: High-energy and loyal

THE BRAVE HUNTING LAIKAS OF RUSSIA

Laikas have lived in northeastern Eurasia for thousands of years, pulling sleds and herding reindeer in polar regions and Arctic tundra zones. Others have lived a little farther south, hunting in the northernmost forested areas of Eurasia. Laikas take their name from the Russian word *layat*, which means "to bark." And, yes, that means they're good watchdogs.

WEST SIBERIAN LAIKA

FROM: Russia

HEIGHT: 20-24 inches (51-62 cm)

WEIGHT: 40-50 pounds (18-23 kg)

COAT: Sable, sandy, variety of colors; straight and thick

GROOMING:

EXERCISE NEEDS:

K-9 QUALITIES: Loyal and protective

These strong and confident hunters, which originated in northwestern Siberia, have exceptional endurance and have been one of the most popular hunting dogs in Russia. They're loyal to their families, but their strong hunting drive makes it hard for them to live happily as house dogs.

EAST SIBERIAN LAIKA

Originating near Lake Baikal in eastern Siberia, these friendly laikas are a bit larger than their cousins and can live happily around livestock and other pets. They're natural hunters and good watchdogs, but with training and exercise, they can live as house dogs.

FROM: Russia

HEIGHT: 21-25 inches (53-64 cm)

WEIGHT: 40-51 pounds (18-23 kg)

COAT: Black, white, black and white, brown and black; straight and thick

GROOMING:

EXERCISE NEEDS:

K-9 QUALITIES: Friendly and calm

RUSSIAN-EUROPEAN LAIKA

FROM: Russia

HEIGHT: 19-23 inches (48-58 cm)

WEIGHT: 44-51 pounds (20-23 kg)

COAT: Black and white, white, black; harsh-textured

GROOMING:

EXERCISE NEEDS:

K-9 QUALITIES: Protective and a bit excitable

Used mainly for hunting and guarding, these steady and eager workers are loyal to their people and, with the right socialization and training, fit into family life—if the family likes to hike and do a lot outdoors. But they're happiest as hunting companions.

ALASKAN
MALAMUTE

These incredibly strong and athletic arctic dogs, named for the native Mahlemut people of Alaska, U.S.A., are perfectly built for pulling sleds over harsh terrain and in brutal climates. People have relied on them for basic transportation, polar expeditions, and sled-racing competitions for centuries. But "Mals" aren't only working dogs. They enjoy romping with big kids, competing in dog events, and doing anything outdoors.

FROM: U.S.A.

HEIGHT: 23–28 inches (58–71 cm)

WEIGHT: 84–123 pounds (38–56 kg)

COAT: Gray and white, black and white, shades of sable to red; thick and coarse, woolly undercoat

GROOMING:

EXERCISE NEEDS:

K-9 QUALITIES: Friendly and strong-willed

Chewbacca—the loyal and brave sidekick of Han Solo in the **STAR WARS MOVIES**—was inspired by producer George Lucas's pet dog, **INDIANA,** an Alaskan malamute who'd always sit next to him, even when he drove his car.

SAMOYED

With a heritage stretching back thousands of years, these fluffy white dogs were well adapted to survive in the harsh and cold climate of northern Russia. Used to pull sleds and guard and herd reindeer for the native peoples of northern Siberia, Samoyeds (sam-a-yed) also were a central part of family life, curling up in their families' tents in the evening. They still love being at the heart of family life, joining in outdoor activities and playing with kids. Samoyeds' mouths, when open, sweep up into a friendly grin, earning the breed the nickname "smiling Sammie."

FROM:	Russia
HEIGHT:	18–22 inches (46–56 cm)
WEIGHT:	35–66 pounds (16–30 kg)
COAT:	White; thick and soft

GROOMING:	
EXERCISE NEEDS:	
K-9 QUALITIES:	Easygoing and sociable

ALASKAN KLEE KAI

Bred to be smaller versions of malamutes or huskies, these fluffy bundles of energy are a great size for apartments as well as houses. Families make the perfect pack for them.

FROM:	U.S.A.
HEIGHT:	Up to 13 inches (33 cm) for toy; 13–15 inches (33–38 cm) for miniature; 15–17 inches (38–44 cm) for standard
WEIGHT:	Up to 9 pounds (4 kg) for toy; 9–15 pounds (4–7 kg) for miniature; 15–22 pounds (7–10 kg) for standard
COAT:	Gray and white, black and white, shades of sable to red; dense and moderately long
GROOMING:	
EXERCISE NEEDS:	
K-9 QUALITIES:	Loving and energetic

VERSATILE SCANDINAVIAN SPITZ DOGS

The chilly northern areas of Scandinavia have produced a variety of versatile spitz breeds. With ancestry going back to the traditional small laika-spitz hunting dogs of the region, these dogs became skilled at hunting different types of animals. But they became even more valued for their friendly, energetic natures, which make them great pets.

BLACK NORWEGIAN ELKHOUND

A smaller, rarer version of the gray-coated Norwegian elkhound (p. 36), these dogs have all the skills of their close relative: herding, tracking game, guarding, and even pulling sleds. Add to that list "fantastic family companion," and you have a very versatile pup!

FROM: Norway
HEIGHT: 17-19 inches (43-49 cm)
WEIGHT: 40-60 pounds (18-27 kg)
COAT: Black; thick
GROOMING:
EXERCISE NEEDS:
K-9 QUALITIES: Affectionate and strong-willed

NORWEGIAN LUNDEHUND

FROM: Norway
HEIGHT: 13-15 inches (32-38 cm)
WEIGHT: 13-15 pounds (6-7 kg)
COAT: Reddish brown or black with white markings, white with dark markings; dense
GROOMING:
EXERCISE NEEDS:
K-9 QUALITIES: Independent and energetic

These acrobatic hunters, also called Norwegian puffin dogs, can scramble up rocks to reach precariously perched puffin nests. Their athletic prowess is aided by a unique feature: They have six toes on each paw!

FINNISH SPITZ

Finland's national dog loves to play. While still used for sport, these agile dogs are now also popular family pets. They are related to laikas from central Russia (p. 37) and originally were bred to hunt small prey. In some countries, they're affectionately nicknamed "Finkies."

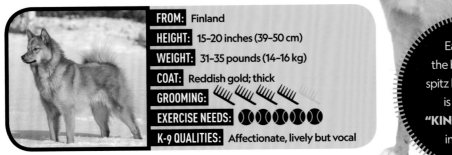

FROM: Finland
HEIGHT: 15–20 inches (39–50 cm)
WEIGHT: 31–35 pounds (14–16 kg)
COAT: Reddish gold; thick
GROOMING:
EXERCISE NEEDS:
K-9 QUALITIES: Affectionate, lively but vocal

Each year, the best Finnish spitz hunting dog is crowned **"KING BARKER"** in Finland.

NORDIC SPITZ

One of Sweden's national dog breeds, these sweet spitzes are not well known outside their homeland. And that's a shame, because they're lively and loving household pets, always up for a romp outdoors. Originally hunting and farm dogs, they almost died out in the early 1900s. But breeders worked hard to bring them back, and they now number in the thousands.

FROM: Sweden
HEIGHT: 17–18 inches (42–45 cm)
WEIGHT: 18–33 pounds (8–15 kg)
COAT: White with tan or black markings; short and straight
GROOMING:
EXERCISE NEEDS:
K-9 QUALITIES: Playful, affectionate, and energetic

SWEDISH ELKHOUND

FROM: Sweden
HEIGHT: 20–26 inches (52–65 cm)
WEIGHT: Up to 66 pounds (30 kg)
COAT: Dark gray with light markings; dense
GROOMING:
EXERCISE NEEDS:
K-9 QUALITIES: Affectionate and protective

Another of Sweden's national dog breeds, these large, agile dogs—also known as the Jämthund or moosehound—hunt large game, work with Sweden's military forces, and also make good family dogs that like kids. But watch them around other animals.

SIBERIAN HUSKY

If you wanted to harness a sled team to tackle the grueling 1,049-mile (1,688-km) Iditarod Trail sled-dog race across Alaska, you probably couldn't choose better companions than Siberian huskies.

Developed by the native Chukchi people of northeastern Siberia, these strong dogs have gained an international reputation for being amazing endurance athletes. In the early 1900s, Alaskans heard about the sled dogs of Siberia. They imported some Siberian huskies and raced them against Alaskan malamutes (p. 38) twice their size. The huskies dominated the sled races for the next decade.

Siberian huskies are ideally designed to be sled dogs. Their shoulder width, back length, and hip angle let them take long strides, and their slightly smaller size keeps them from overheating. Unlike greyhounds (p. 123) and other sprinters that leap through the air as they run, huskies keep one paw on the ground at all times, which helps them to pull a sled forward. And unlike other dogs, their paws have thick fur on the bottom to keep them warm. They even stay warm sleeping in snow! They curl up in a ball and wrap their fluffy tails over their noses so they breathe warm air.

Siberian huskies aren't just great endurance athletes. They're also playful and sociable, qualities the Chukchi knew were key to the sledding teams working well together. Those same qualities make them fun and loving pets for families—their new packs.

HERO HOUNDS

In 1925, the town of Nome, Alaska, U.S.A., was threatened with a deadly outbreak of diphtheria. Back then, before the creation of the vaccination we use today, infected people had to be treated with an antitoxin serum—and Nome didn't have any. The nearest supply was 674 miles (1,085 km) away, and there seemed to be no way to get it to Nome; most transportation had been shut down by the harshest winter in two decades. Nome had but one hope: dog sleds. It would have normally taken dog sleds 25 days to go that far, but they had only six before the antitoxin would be ruined by the extreme cold. They had to act fast. Twenty dog-sled teams lined up on the route to relay the lifesaving serum. By the time the serum reached dog musher Leonhard Seppala and his husky team, only two days were left. To make it in time, Seppala would have to take a shortcut across an inlet of the Bering Sea and watch for any patches of water that weren't frozen. His team set out, and a blizzard blew in! Seppala couldn't see anything in the whiteout, so he had his lead dog, Togo, figure out where to go. Togo led the team safely across the water, and they handed off the antitoxin to the final team. The husky teams got the serum to Nome with half a day to spare, saving 10,000 lives.

FROM:	Russia
HEIGHT:	20–24 inches (51–60 cm)
WEIGHT:	35–60 pounds (16–27 kg)
COAT:	Variety of colors from black to pure white, with markings
GROOMING:	🖌🖌🖌🖌
EXERCISE NEEDS:	⚫⚫⚫⚫⚫
K-9 QUALITIES:	Friendly and sociable

The **IDITAROD TRAIL** sled-dog race commemorates the heroic effort of the 1925 husky teams that transported a **LIFESAVING SERUM** to Nome.

GREENLAND DOG

Despite its name, Greenland can be a very chilly place. Located north of the Arctic Circle, much of the island nation is covered by a permanent ice sheet. No surprise, then, that Greenland dogs are designed to live and work in a cold climate. These powerful dogs have pulled sleds and helped Arctic people hunt for years. The only native dogs left in Greenland, these hard workers are probably best for owners experienced at training strong-willed dogs.

FROM: Greenland
HEIGHT: 20–27 inches (51–68 cm)
WEIGHT: 60–106 pounds (27–48 kg)
COAT: Variety of colors, often darker on top; thick

GROOMING:
EXERCISE NEEDS:
K-9 QUALITIES: Good-natured but stubborn

CHINOOK

Don't let Chinooks' floppy ears fool you, these dogs can haul sleds just like all their spitz relatives. (Yes, they have spitz in them.) In the early 20th century, Americans developed this breed by crossing Greenland dogs (above) with a mastiff-type farm dog and German (p. 62) and Belgian (p. 60) shepherd dogs. Chinooks got a lot of the best traits of all those breeds, including power, endurance, and speed. Gentle and fun-loving, these working dogs—the official state dog of New Hampshire, U.S.A.—make excellent family companions.

FROM: U.S.A.
HEIGHT: 22–26 inches (55–66 cm)
WEIGHT: 55–71 pounds (25–32 kg)
COAT: Sandy; medium-length

GROOMING:
EXERCISE NEEDS:
K-9 QUALITIES: Playful and good-natured

CANADIAN ESKIMO DOG

Also called Inuit dogs, these dogs are one of the oldest sled-dog breeds in the world. Sturdy and thick-coated, they can survive in harsh conditions, and they love to run with a pack. To be happy family members, these rare dogs need work to do—and may be better with experienced owners.

FROM: Canada
HEIGHT: 20–28 inches (50–70 cm)
WEIGHT: 40–88 pounds (18–40 kg)
COAT: Variety of colors, including black and white; thick, coarse, and short

GROOMING:
EXERCISE NEEDS:
K-9 QUALITIES: Friendly and energetic

AMERICAN ESKIMO DOG

Despite their names, these little fluff balls have no ties to Eskimo culture (as far as anyone knows). They probably came to America in the 1800s with German immigrants, who bred them from white German spitz dogs (p. 51) and Nordic dogs. Too little for dog-sled races, "Eskies" are still spitz dogs through and through. And they're great companions—though they may not like tight hugs from little kids.

FROM: U.S.A.
HEIGHT: 9–12 inches (23–30 cm) for toy; 12–15 inches (30–38 cm) for miniature; 15–19 inches (38–48 cm) for standard
WEIGHT: 6–11 pounds (3–5 kg) for toy; 11–20 pounds (5–9 kg) for miniature; 20–40 pounds (9–18 kg) for standard

COAT: White; long
GROOMING:
EXERCISE NEEDS:
K-9 QUALITIES: Playful, smart, and loving

HARDWORKING NORDIC SPITZ DOGS

With their intelligence and work-loving natures, it's no surprise that several spitz breeds from the chilly Nordic region have branched into all kinds of work—and play. These versatile dogs have adapted to lives herding animals, guarding homes, and being pets—but they need jobs to do to keep them happy.

FINNISH LAPPHUND

Descended from the dogs kept by the native Sami people of Scandinavia, the bright, agile "Lappies" helped people hunt but adapted quickly to new roles as reindeer herders. These days, these friendly, loyal dogs are popular family pets—and not just in Finland. They're playful, smart, and calm—a winning combination for families of all sizes.

FROM: Finland
HEIGHT: 17–19 inches (44–49 cm)
WEIGHT: 33–53 pounds (15–24 kg)
COAT: Variety of colors, with lighter markings; long and thick
GROOMING:
EXERCISE NEEDS:
K-9 QUALITIES: Affectionate and adaptable

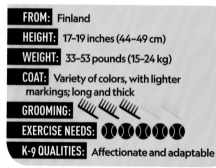

LAPPONIAN HERDER

FROM: Finland
HEIGHT: 18–20 inches (46–51 cm)
WEIGHT: Up to 66 pounds (30 kg)
COAT: Black, dark brown, with lighter markings; dense, short
GROOMING:
EXERCISE NEEDS:
K-9 QUALITIES: Calm, energetic, and friendly

These reindeer herders were created by crossbreeding Finnish Lapphunds (above) with German shepherd dogs (p. 62) and herding collie breeds. They're mainly working dogs, but their calm and friendly nature makes them good candidates for becoming house dogs.

ICELANDIC SHEEPDOG

Iceland's only native dogs, these smart pups probably arrived on the island nation with Viking settlers in the ninth and tenth centuries. By the 15th century, they became popular in England—both as sheep herders on farms and pampered pets of the upper class. These days, the lively and playful dogs are most happy as pets. They love people, especially kids.

FROM: Iceland
HEIGHT: 17–18 inches (42–46 cm)
WEIGHT: 20–31 pounds (9–14 kg)
COAT: Tan, gray, chocolate brown, black, with markings; long or short
GROOMING:
EXERCISE NEEDS:
K-9 QUALITIES: Agile, hardy, and possibly noisy

NORWEGIAN BUHUND

FROM: Norway
HEIGHT: 16–18 inches (41–46 cm)
WEIGHT: 26–40 pounds (12–18 kg)
COAT: Wheaten, red, black, sable, with markings; long, thick, harsh
GROOMING:
EXERCISE NEEDS:
K-9 QUALITIES: Energetic and possibly noisy

The skeletons of Norwegian buhunds have been found in Viking burial mounds—evidence that Vikings believed they'd need the dogs on their journeys to the afterlife. Rare today, these agile dogs once were common farm dogs in Norway. They're lively and affectionate pets that do best with outdoorsy families who aren't bothered by barking.

SWEDISH LAPPHUND

Like their Finnish relatives, Swedish Lapphunds originally worked as reindeer herders alongside the native Sami people, who once lived nomadic, wandering lives. These friendly dogs are popular pets in Sweden but uncommon elsewhere. But if you can find one, you'll have a loving family companion.

FROM: Sweden
HEIGHT: 16-20 inches (40-51 cm)
WEIGHT: 42-46 pounds (19-21 kg)
COAT: Black, brown, black and brown; dense
GROOMING:
EXERCISE NEEDS:
K-9 QUALITIES: Friendly but a bit restless

POMERANIAN

These bright-eyed puff balls—the tiniest of the spitz breeds—weren't always the toy dogs we see today.

"Poms" were selectively bred from dogs three to four times their size to become smaller and smaller during the "dog fancy" years of the 19th century. But they kept all the bold personality and energy of much bigger spitz working dogs.

Pomeranians are popular pets around the world, and it's easy to understand why. The clever little spitzes are cute, spunky, and lovable. They're happy trotting along next to you and keeping busy, but they'll also curl up in your lap and return all the love you give them. Poms can adapt to life on a ranch as easily as in a high-rise apartment building. Their fluffy, double-layered coats—perfectly adapted to the chilly northern climates of their origins—need regular brushing but actually aren't difficult to care for. Poms are hardy but, like all toy breeds, a bit too delicate for rough play. That means they're not great choices for families with young kids.

Despite their small size, Pomeranians are great watchdogs—a role they've had from their earliest days. Originating in Pomerania, a northern European region now split between Germany and Poland, these dogs once sailed the Baltic Sea on the boats of local traders, keeping the crew company and protecting the cargo. If thieves approached, they'd alert the traders with their sharp barks. On land, they were versatile working dogs, herding livestock, pulling carts, and protecting their homes and families. Credit for the Pomeranian's popularity goes to the British royal family. In the 1800s, Queen Victoria fell in love with the Pom, ensuring its place in fashionable society.

⭐ PUP STARS

Perhaps no other dog shows off the Pomeranian's athleticism better than Jiff. The talented little pooch, who looks more like a cuddly toy than a canine, really struts his stuff—literally. He holds records for being the fastest dog on two legs. Yes, two! He's equally talented at walking on his front legs as on his hind legs—and has broken records doing both: On his hind legs, he covered 10.9 yards (10 m) in 6.56 seconds. And for the more challenging feat of walking only on his front paws, he covered 5.5 yards (5 m) in 7.76 seconds. But Jiff isn't only an athlete. He's also a celebrity! He's starred in television commercials and in a pop star's music video, and more than 4.5 million adoring fans—presumably, people—follow him on social media.

FROM:	Germany
HEIGHT:	9–11 inches (22–28 cm)
WEIGHT:	4–6 pounds (2–3 kg)
COAT:	Variety of colors; soft and fluffy
GROOMING:	
EXERCISE NEEDS:	
K-9 QUALITIES:	Loving but possibly very vocal

SUPER SMALLS

Poms have hung out with great artists. **MOZART** dedicated a musical aria to his pet, Pimperl, and **MICHELANGELO'S** pet Pom kept him company while he painted the Sistine Chapel.

KEESHOND

As friendly as they are fluffy, keeshonden are great choices for families with kids. They like attention and always seem to be smiling. Keeshonden (the breed's name is pronounced KAYZ-hund) traveled with merchants on the waterways of northern Europe. Natural guard dogs and affectionate companions, these dogs—sometimes called Dutch barge dogs—protected the merchandise and provided the merchants with companionship. On land, they became favorite farm dogs, too.

FROM: Netherlands
HEIGHT: 17–18 inches (43–46 cm)
WEIGHT: 33–44 pounds (15–20 kg)
COAT: Gray and black shades, with cream markings; long and thick

GROOMING:
EXERCISE NEEDS:
K-9 QUALITIES: Playful and affectionate

GERMAN WOLFSPITZ

Considered the same breed as the keeshond (above) in some places—such as the United States—this breed varies more in size. Many people think the German wolfspitz came first and is one of the ancestors of the keeshond.

FROM: Germany
HEIGHT: 17–22 inches (43–55 cm)
WEIGHT: 60–71 pounds (27–32 kg)
COAT: Gray and black shades, with cream markings; long and thick

GROOMING:
EXERCISE NEEDS:
K-9 QUALITIES: Affectionate and energetic

GERMAN SPITZ

FROM: Germany

HEIGHT: 9–11 inches (23–29 cm) for small; 12–15 inches (30–38 cm) for medium; 17–20 inches (43–50 cm) for large

WEIGHT: 18–22 pounds (8–10 kg) for small; 24–26 pounds (11–12 kg) for medium; 38–40 pounds (17–18 kg) for large

COAT: Variety of colors; long and thick

GROOMING:

EXERCISE NEEDS:

K-9 QUALITIES: Watchful and affectionate

These lively, independent, and cheerful pups are great pets for people of all ages—as long as you remember to train them. Sometimes mistaken for their Pomeranian (p. 48) relatives, German spitz dogs share their heritage going back to dogs of native Arctic people. In some places, they're considered the same breed as the keeshond and German wolfspitz.

VOLPINO ITALIANO

These playful and alert little dogs fit into almost any family, and they're popular pets in Italy. In the past, they were favorites of both the nobility, who kept them as pampered pets, and farmers, who used them as watchdogs. When trouble was afoot, the volpinos (pronounced Vol-PEEN-oh) would bark to alert bigger watchdogs.

FROM: Italy

HEIGHT: 10–12 inches (25–30 cm)

WEIGHT: 9–11 pounds (4–5 kg)

COAT: White, red; long and dense

GROOMING:

EXERCISE NEEDS:

K-9 QUALITIES: Fun-loving and adaptable

EURASIER

These affectionate dogs form close bonds with their families, and they love kids. True to their name, these good-natured pooches have serious international credentials. German breeders created the Eurasier in the 1960s by breeding their German wolfspitzes (p. 50) with chow chows (p. 55) from China and Samoyeds (p. 39) from Russia.

Eurasiers were originally called **WOLF CHOWS,** but they were renamed in the 1970s to reflect their roots in both **EUROPE AND ASIA.**

FROM: Germany

HEIGHT: 19–24 inches (48–60 cm)

WEIGHT: 40–71 pounds (18–32 kg)

COAT: Variety of colors, with a dark face; long and harsh

GROOMING:

EXERCISE NEEDS:

K-9 QUALITIES: Calm and watchful

BRAVE ASIAN SPITZ BREEDS

Most of the dogs on these pages developed in Japan, often as hunting dogs (bold enough to tackle bears and other large animals), but there are native Korean and Chinese spitzes, too. They remain popular dogs in their homelands, and some are gaining admirers around the world. True to their heritage, most of these breeds have strong hunting instincts—so it may be best to keep them away from your pet kitty or hamster.

HOKKAIDO

Named after the Japanese island of the same name, these hunting dogs arrived with the native Ainu people. There isn't much that intimidates Hokkaidos (pronounced ho-KIE-doe), so they're good watchdogs and, with proper socialization, they can be good family companions.

FROM:	Japan
HEIGHT:	18–20 inches (46–52 cm)
WEIGHT:	44–66 pounds (20–30 kg)
COAT:	Variety of colors; thick and harsh
GROOMING:	
EXERCISE NEEDS:	
K-9 QUALITIES:	Brave and loyal

JAPANESE SPITZ

FROM:	Japan
HEIGHT:	12–15 inches (30–37 cm)
WEIGHT:	11–22 pounds (5–10 kg)
COAT:	White; thick and long
GROOMING:	
EXERCISE NEEDS:	
K-9 QUALITIES:	Energetic and intelligent

These little white puff balls of energy are popular pets not just in Japan but in many other countries, and they get along great with kids. Though they look like mini Samoyeds and are just as charming, the two breeds probably aren't related.

KAI KEN

These athletic hunting dogs (pronounced KIE-ken) are used to running in packs, and they won't feel comfortable living as house dogs without patient training from an experienced owner. One of Japan's oldest native dog breeds, they've been given the official status of national treasure. Born almost solid black, their coats change to brindle as they grow older.

FROM:	Japan
HEIGHT:	19–21 inches (48–53 cm)
WEIGHT:	25–55 pounds (11–25 kg)
COAT:	Range of red brindles
GROOMING:	
EXERCISE NEEDS:	
K-9 QUALITIES:	Loyal and lively

SHIKOKU

FROM: Japan
HEIGHT: 18–20 inches (46–52 cm)
WEIGHT: 35–57 pounds (16–26 kg)
COAT: Sesame (white-black mix), red sesame, black sesame with white; thick
GROOMING:
EXERCISE NEEDS:
K-9 QUALITIES: Energetic and devoted

When you earn a Shikoku's trust, you have his love forever—but that's not going to stop him from chasing your cat! These agile dogs (whose name is pronounced she-KOH-ku) still have the strong hunting instincts that they developed in the remote mountain regions of Japan, where they used to go after wild boars.

JINDO

These loyal dogs are happy to play—but even happier to chase after another furry creature. With an independent and strong-willed nature, they need good training and socialization. Originating on the Korean island of Jindo, which gives the breed its name, Jindos are popular in their homeland but fairly rare elsewhere. These intelligent dogs are incredibly loyal to their owners and make great family pets if you have the time to train and interact with them.

FROM: Korea
HEIGHT: 18–21 inches (46–53 cm)
WEIGHT: 20–50 pounds (9–23 kg)
COAT: Fawn, red, white, black and tan; standing away
GROOMING:
EXERCISE NEEDS:
K-9 QUALITIES: Lively and affectionate

KISHU KEN

These rare dogs are calm, loyal, and affectionate. But if they set their minds on chasing other animals, it's hard to persuade them to stop! Another national treasure of Japan, Kishus (pronounced KEE-shoo) probably came from the mountainous Kyushu region, where they hunted large game.

FROM: Japan
HEIGHT: 18–20 inches (46–52 cm)
WEIGHT: 29–60 pounds (13–27 kg)
COAT: Red, white; short and coarse
GROOMING:
EXERCISE NEEDS:
K-9 QUALITIES: Faithful and strong-willed

Many spitz dogs aren't big fans of **SWIMMING**—or baths! It may be because getting wet was **DANGEROUS** in the frigid Arctic areas where they first lived.

AKITA

Developed in 19th-century Japan, Akitas take their name from the rugged and chilly mountainous area of the same name. Their loyalty is legendary—pairs of these brave, powerful dogs would trap an animal between them until hunters arrived—a trait that won them fans across the ocean. Akitas brought to the United States in the 1930s and 1940s became the founders of the American Akitas. Slightly smaller Akita inus, or Japanese Akitas, are considered a distinct breed outside of America. Wherever they live, Akitas are prized for their courage and devotion.

FROM: Japan

HEIGHT: 24–28 inches (61–71 cm) for American; 23–28 inches (58–70 cm) for Japanese

WEIGHT: 65–115 pounds (29–52 kg) for American; 78–99 pounds (34–45 kg) for Japanese

COAT: Variety of colors with white markings (and possibly black faces for American only); harsh, standing out

GROOMING:

EXERCISE NEEDS:

K-9 QUALITIES: Independent and faithful

HERO HOUNDS

Perhaps no dog deserves the title of "man's best friend" more than an Akita named Hachikō. In 1924, a Japanese professor adopted the golden brown puppy as a pet. Every day, Hachikō and the professor would walk to Shibuya Station, in Tokyo, Japan, where the professor would take the commuter train to his job. At the end of the day, Hachikō would greet the professor at the station and they would walk home together. One day in 1925, the train arrived at Shibuya Station, but the professor didn't get off. Unknown to Hachikō, his professor friend had suffered a terrible stroke that day and died. But Hachikō never gave up on him. Every day for the rest of his life—almost 10 years—Hachikō met the evening train and waited for his friend, only to leave alone. Hachikō's loyalty and devotion still are honored in Japan. His life inspired books and movies. A bronze statue of Hachikō sits outside Shibuya Station (above).

SHIBA INU

Shiba Inus (SHEE-bah EE-noo) may be the smallest of Japan's native spitz breeds, but they make up for it with plenty of bold personality. Brave and lively, the foxy-looking dogs have all the courage of the larger Japanese spitz dogs and were used to hunt in the past. Their ancestors arrived with Japan's earliest immigrants, around 7000 B.C.

FROM: Japan
HEIGHT: 15–16 inches (37–40 cm)
WEIGHT: 15–24 pounds (7–11 kg)
COAT: Red, sesame (white-black mix), black and tan, with whitish markings; coarse

GROOMING:
EXERCISE NEEDS:
K-9 QUALITIES: Independent and clever

CHOW CHOW

Chow chows look like big teddy bears, but they're actually not into hugs and cuddles. They're loyal pets—sometimes more devoted to one family member—but they like their independence. Nicknamed the "emperor of dogs," chow chows' origins are unknown, but they probably originated in the high mountains of Mongolia. Similar looking dogs were depicted on pottery and sculptures going back to the Han dynasty some 2,000 years ago. Chows have a unique look, with teddy bear–like fur, blue-black tongues, and large heads circled with a lionlike ruff of fur.

According to Chinese legend, Chow Chows got their **BLUE-BLACK TONGUES** by licking the blue paint God used to paint the evening sky.

FROM: China
HEIGHT: 18-22 inches (46-56 cm)
WEIGHT: 46-71 pounds (21-32 kg)
COAT: Gold, cream, blue; rough and thick or short and dense

GROOMING:
EXERCISE NEEDS:
K-9 QUALITIES: Independent and protective

HERDING DOGS

Quick-footed and cunning, sheepdogs and cattle dogs* are among the most intelligent and capable of working dogs. With natural instincts fine-tuned over years of selective breeding, these extraordinary pups are ready to go to work herding livestock and protecting them from predators. Also known as pastoral dogs because they work in fields or pastures, they've developed a variety of ways to get their jobs done. Some herding dogs bark to get sheep, goats, or cattle moving, while other dogs nip at the livestocks' heels. Some have mastered the skill of stalking and glaring at their charges to keep them in line, and a few even body-slam the livestock to get them moving! Sheepdogs and cattledogs are a diverse group. There's no one particular look that stands out—evidence of the differing regions, terrains, and climates where these dogs developed. Many herding dogs make excellent watchdogs and family pets. Eager to please and highly intelligent, they are easy to train and love taking on new challenges—whether it's in agility competitions or learning to catch Frisbees.

* NOTE: Despite their names, you won't see Swiss cattle dogs in this section. They're really more like mountain dogs and mastiffs (p. 88), so you'll learn about them there.

AUSTRALIAN CATTLE DOG

These brave, intelligent herding dogs from the land down under have amazing endurance and mental toughness, a necessity for driving stubborn, free-roaming cattle across Australia's vast grazing lands. Ranchers developed the energetic "ACDs" in the 1800s from Highland collies (p. 70) and dingoes (p. 33), later crossing them with kelpies (p. 59) and Dalmatians (p. 168). Their stamina and intelligence mean you have to provide plenty of exercise and jobs for these eager dogs. Herding competitions, search and rescue, and flyball (a relay race over hurdles) are great outlets for their energy, but ACDs also love to play with kids or go for a run. They're friendly and devoted pets—as long as you teach them that they shouldn't herd you!—and they also make good watchdogs.

FROM: Australia
HEIGHT: 17–20 inches (43–51 cm)
WEIGHT: 30–40 pounds (14–18 kg)
COAT: Blue or red speckled; short and straight
GROOMING:
EXERCISE NEEDS:
K-9 QUALITIES: Active and loyal

An Australian cattle dog named **BLUEY** holds the record for being the **OLDEST DOG EVER.** Born in 1910, he lived almost 30 years!

AUSTRALIAN WORKING KELPIE

These energetic dogs, created by crossing collies (p. 70) and other herding dogs (and possibly dingoes, p. 33) are capable and independent working dogs. Developed around 1870 to herd sheep in the vast expanses of Australia, kelpies can run across the sheeps' backs to move them through tight places. Vigilant watchdogs, they sometimes stand on their hind legs to look around!

FROM:	Australia
HEIGHT:	17–20 inches (43–51 cm)
WEIGHT:	24–44 pounds (11–20 kg)
COAT:	Variety of colors; short, thick

GROOMING:	
EXERCISE NEEDS:	
K-9 QUALITIES:	High-energy and alert

NEW ZEALAND HUNTAWAY

A mix of several breeds, including German shepherd dogs (p. 62), Rottweilers (p. 107), and border collies (p. 76), New Zealand huntaways are agile and dedicated herders, driving sheep with their loud, deep barks. Prized working dogs since the late 19th century, the smart pups are becoming popular pets, too—though they're a bit too friendly to make good watchdogs. Huntaways are happy putting their energy into chasing balls and playing with kids, but they need to be taught that barking is better for herding sheep than kids.

FROM:	New Zealand
HEIGHT:	20–24 inches (50–61 cm)
WEIGHT:	40–65 pounds (18–29 kg)
COAT:	Black with tan markings, tricolor, dark brindle; short and thick
GROOMING:	
EXERCISE NEEDS:	
K-9 QUALITIES:	Devoted and good-natured

BELGIAN SHEPHERD DOGS

In the late 1800s, it was popular in European countries to develop dog breeds with regional identities. Luckily for dog lovers everywhere, Belgium developed four types of Belgian shepherd dogs. With wildly different coats, they each have distinctive looks, but they share other characteristics. All are big enough to be good guards but small enough to be agile herders. Intelligent and loyal, they have the stamina and determination to take on all kinds of work. During World War I (1914 to 1918), they carried messages, accompanied ambulances, and even pulled machine guns. Since then, they've worked as police and guard dogs. They're also popular companions for people with active lifestyles. Early socialization and training help them fit well into families.

BELGIAN MALINOIS

The short-haired Malinois (pronounced mal-in-WAH), which hail originally from the Belgian village of Malines, are popular police and military K-9s. They're also lively and playful and can be socialized to fit into families, but they need to be trained not to chase kids.

FROM: Belgium
HEIGHT: 22–26 inches (56–66 cm)
WEIGHT: 60–65 pounds (27–29 kg)
COAT: Fawn, gray, red with black "mask" and ears; short and straight
GROOMING:
EXERCISE NEEDS:
K-9 QUALITIES: Energetic and protective

HERO HOUNDS

Seven-year-old Belgian Malinois Brin works as a conservation detection dog in South Africa. Most of her expertise is put to work searching for the critically endangered geometric tortoise since its camouflaging black and yellow patterned carapace—which it uses for defense against predators—makes it difficult for humans to find.

BELGIAN SHEEPDOG

FROM:	Belgium
HEIGHT:	22–26 inches (56–66 cm)
WEIGHT:	50–75 pounds (23–34 kg)
COAT:	Black; long and straight
GROOMING:	
EXERCISE NEEDS:	
K-9 QUALITIES:	Active and intelligent

A long, black coat sets versatile and beautiful Belgian sheepdogs, developed in the village of Groenendael, apart from their cousins. With a playful and loyal nature, they can be good pets for active, outdoorsy families willing to devote time to training and socializing them.

BELGIAN TERVUREN

Developed in the Belgian village of the same name, Tervuren (ter-VYOO-run) love to be with their people and crave work and new challenges. These quick-learning pups like to be part of all family activities. "Tervs" can be good with kids if they're raised together.

FROM:	Belgium
HEIGHT:	22–26 inches (56–66 cm)
WEIGHT:	40–65 pounds (18–29 kg)
COAT:	Fawn or gray with black; rich and long
GROOMING:	
EXERCISE NEEDS:	
K-9 QUALITIES:	Protective and loyal

BELGIAN LAEKENOIS

With their distinctive wiry coats, Laekenois (lak-in-WAH) shepherd dogs were a favorite of the Belgian royal family in the late 1800s. They had two main jobs back then: herding sheep at the Royal Castle of Laeken and protecting the valuable Belgian linens drying outside. Little-known today, they're protective and affectionate pets when raised in a family.

FROM:	Belgium
HEIGHT:	22–26 inches (56–66 cm)
WEIGHT:	55–65 pounds (25–29 kg)
COAT:	Reddish fawn; wiry
GROOMING:	
EXERCISE NEEDS:	
K-9 QUALITIES:	Loyal and calm

Belgian shepherd dogs are taking the jobs once held by German shepherds. The spunky Belgians have gained great reputations as **POLICE DOGS** and even **MILITARY PARACHUTISTS.**

GERMAN SHEPHERD DOG

There's little that German shepherd dogs can't do.
Developed in the late 19th century from older breeds of herding and farm dogs, German shepherd dogs—or "GSDs"—originally herded sheep. But they proved to be so extremely adaptable that they soon took on all sorts of jobs. They're still capable herders on farms and ranches around the world, but they also succeed in a variety of roles, as guide and assistance dogs, search-and-rescue dogs, on military and police K-9 units, and as therapy dogs. Why are they so good at so many things? Part of the answer is how they're built: Their long, slightly sloping hindquarters help create maximum push power with minimum effort. These dogs can trot for hours and climb or jump over barriers. But most of the reason they are so versatile is because they're smart. GSDs are one of the most intelligent and most easily trainable dog breeds.

They are also wonderful companions that stand out for their loyalty and for their willingness to protect their people. When adopted from reputable breeders and raised with a family, these dogs are faithful pets that love the family's kids and are always up for some active play. They're one of the most popular breeds in the world—and with good reason.

CANINE EINSTEINS

FROM: Germany
HEIGHT: 23–25 inches (58–63 cm)
WEIGHT: 49–88 pounds (22–40 kg)
COAT: Black with tan, sable, black; thick and short or long
GROOMING:
EXERCISE NEEDS:
K-9 QUALITIES: Intelligent, brave, and devoted

KING SHEPHERD

Despite their resemblance, king shepherds aren't just supersized German shepherd dogs. Breeders developed King Shepherds in the 1990s by crossing German shepherds, Alaskan malamutes, and Great Pyrenees. The result was a big, calm working dog that fits in well with a family. They're friendly and get along great with kids of all ages.

FROM:	U.S.A.
HEIGHT:	25–29 inches (64–74 cm)
WEIGHT:	90–145 pounds (41–66 kg)
COAT:	Tan, sable, black with markings; smooth or rough
GROOMING:	
EXERCISE NEEDS:	
K-9 QUALITIES:	Easy going and eager to please

HERO HOUNDS

Orient, a German shepherd, was trained to guide his blind owner, Bill Irwin, safely around a city. Whenever he encountered an obstacle more than two inches (5 cm) high, Orient stopped so Bill wouldn't trip. So, in 1990, when the pair stepped out onto a hiking trail, Orient obediently stopped at the first large rock on their path. But Bill encouraged him to "hop up" and keep going. After all, they had 2,144 miles (3,450 km) to cover! Bill had decided to hike the entire Appalachian Trail from Georgia to Maine, U.S.A., and Orient had to guide him. It was a new experience for Orient, but he adapted to the trail, learning what sort of obstacles Bill could handle. Orient would change his pace, hesitating when the going was tough and hopping over stones and branches. He led Bill up rocky mountain paths, through snow and forests, and across freezing-cold streams. The dog followed the scent of other hikers to keep them on the trail, and Bill believed Orient even learned to identify trail markers: white paint marks on trees and piled rocks. It was a difficult journey, with Orient carrying a 20-pound (9-kg) pack and suffering injuries that forced them to shelter along the way to recover. But after eight months, they had hiked the entire trail—the first blind person and guide dog to do so.

SCHIPPERKE

Though they look like spitz dogs, schipperkes (SKIP-per-kees) were bred down in size from black sheepdogs as far back as the 1600s. Sometimes called Belgian barge dogs, they were faithful companions to Flemish riverboat men, hunting rats and protecting their barges from robbers. In the cities, they also served as mascots to tradesmen. Schipperkes make great search-and-rescue dogs, maneuvering where larger dogs can't go. Sturdy and always on the go, they're good companions for kids of all ages, if raised together—and they've kept their watchdog instincts. But that means they can bark a lot.

FROM: Belgium
HEIGHT: 10–13 inches (25–33 cm)
WEIGHT: 13–18 pounds (6–8 kg)
COAT: Black; dense
GROOMING:
EXERCISE NEEDS:
K-9 QUALITIES: Intelligent, lively, and slightly mischievous

TORNJAK

Tornjaks (torn-YAHKS), which were saved from extinction in the 1970s, trace their heritage back nearly a thousand years to the mountainous regions now part of Croatia and Bosnia and Herzegovina. These large, woolly mountain dogs are calm and protective. With the right training and socialization, they're friendly and devoted family pets.

FROM: Croatia, Bosnia and Herzegovina
HEIGHT: 24–28 inches (60–70 cm)
WEIGHT: 62–110 pounds (28–50 kg)
COAT: White with black and tan markings; coarse, thick, and long
GROOMING:
EXERCISE NEEDS:
K-9 QUALITIES: Gentle and watchful

CROATIAN SHEPHERD DOG

FROM: Croatia
HEIGHT: 16–20 inches (40–50 cm)
WEIGHT: 29–44 pounds (13–20 kg)
COAT: Black; wavy or curly
GROOMING:
EXERCISE NEEDS:
K-9 QUALITIES: Active and vigilant

Croatian shepherd dogs, which trace their ancestry to the 14th century, may be smaller than some other shepherd dogs, but they have big-dog abilities: They can round up and drive sheep and cattle. Excellent watchdogs, they do best with experienced owners who can train and socialize them from an early age, and they're probably better as working dogs than pets.

CURSINU

Known on the island of Corsica since the 16th century, Cursinus' numbers declined in the mid-20th century, but they are making a comeback. Brave, traditional herders, they also hunt small game and even wild boars! With consistent training, the loyal and obedient Cursinus can make good companions for outdoorsy individuals, but they're not the best family pets.

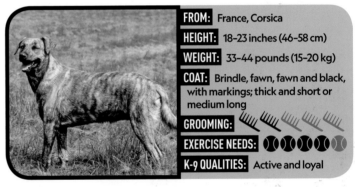

FROM: France, Corsica
HEIGHT: 18–23 inches (46–58 cm)
WEIGHT: 33–44 pounds (15–20 kg)
COAT: Brindle, fawn, fawn and black, with markings; thick and short or medium long
GROOMING:
EXERCISE NEEDS:
K-9 QUALITIES: Active and loyal

HELLENIC SHEPHERD DOG

Brought to Greece many centuries ago by Turkish migrants, Hellenic shepherd dogs have strong protective instincts. These natural guardians are skilled workers and great watchdogs, but they're probably better companions for experienced dog handlers than for families.

FROM: Greece
HEIGHT: 24–30 inches (60–75 cm)
WEIGHT: 71–110 pounds (32–50 kg)
COAT: Variety of colors; long or short
GROOMING:
EXERCISE NEEDS:
K-9 QUALITIES: Strong-willed and brave

One out of five dogs in the United States have popular **"PEOPLE NAMES,"** often the names of fictional characters, stars, or athletes.

ON THE JOB

Dogs have exceptional skills. They're hardworking, they can get places humans can't, and their sense of smell is phenomenal. They're also tuned in to our moods—and even our health—and they're eager to please us. Take all those natural talents and add some specialized training, and the result is a dog that can tackle jobs that are beyond most human abilities. Here are some tremendous tasks dogs perform for us every day.

POLICE AND MILITARY K-9s

K-9s such as Hertz, the German shorthaired pointer (p. 174), assist law enforcement or the military in the line of duty. They provide protection and perform other tasks, such as tracking people, scouting out safe areas, or detecting threats. Police dogs, such as Nick Carter, the bloodhound (p. 134), also chase down suspects who flee from the law.

DETECTION DOGS

Sniffer dogs—or, more formally, detection dogs—put their noses to work in a variety of places. Some make sure that travelers don't bring in forbidden substances—such as ivory, plants, or illegal drugs—from other countries. Some dogs such as Brin, the Belgian Malinois (p. 60), protect endangered wildlife by helping to track and find animals that are difficult for humans to find on their own. Other dogs keep us safe by finding explosives. Sniffer dogs can even detect cancer in people, probably by smelling the unusual biochemical scents cancer cells give off.

SEARCH-AND-RESCUE DOGS

Using their excellent senses, endurance, and tracking ability, some dogs, such as Barry, the St. Bernard (p. 99), work to find missing people. Sometimes the people have gotten lost, or they may have been buried by an avalanche or in the rubble of a collapsed building.

THERAPY DOGS

Therapy dogs, such as Ricochet, the golden retriever (p. 195), are trained to provide emotional support to people in all sorts of circumstances. Some therapy dogs go into crisis areas, like emergency responders, to provide comfort to victims. Others, such as Smoky, the Yorkshire terrier (p. 245), visit hospitals, nursing homes, schools, or libraries to give a lift to someone's day. Some work with injured or sick people as they recover.

SERVICE DOGS

Service dogs are the constant companions of people who need assistance of some kind. They are specifically trained to work or perform specialized tasks to help their owners in many crucial ways. Service dogs, such as Orient, the German shepherd dog (p. 63), work with people who are blind, hearing impaired, or restricted in mobility, to help them get around safely. Others, such as Holly, the sheltie (p. 77), alert their people to oncoming seizures, anxiety, or other health issues. Some provide support for people who have suffered trauma, such as military veterans.

OLD ENGLISH SHEEPDOG

Dogs like Old English sheepdogs show up in literature as far back as the late 1600s and in art a century later. In the early years, they were working dogs, driving sheep and cattle to market. But by the late 1800s, these beautiful dogs were favorites in the show ring. Their distinctive look requires a lot of care to ensure their coats don't become matted messes. (Some people clip their hair shorter so it's easier to manage. Even the shepherds would shear these dogs along with the sheep.) Under that shaggy coat is the core of a herding dog: athletic, smart, and eager to please. These dogs love their people. They're happy to go on long walks or play with kids, whom they absolutely adore. They're big and strong, ready to roughhouse with older kids. Though they love kids of all ages, their energy and size may be too much for little tots.

FROM: UK/England
HEIGHT: 22–24 inches (56–61 cm)
WEIGHT: 60–90 pounds (27–41 kg)
COAT: Shades of gray or blue, with white; very thick and shaggy
GROOMING:
EXERCISE NEEDS:
K-9 QUALITIES: Sweet and intelligent

Old English sheepdogs have really **LONG EYELASHES,** which lift the hair from in front of their eyes. That's how they can see through that shaggy coat!

BEAUCERON

FROM: France
HEIGHT: 25–28 inches (63–70 cm)
WEIGHT: 65–85 pounds (29–39 kg)
COAT: Black and tan, or gray, black, and tan; short and coarse
GROOMING:
EXERCISE NEEDS:
K-9 QUALITIES: Smart but stubborn

Hailing from the flatlands of central France, these versatile, energetic, and athletic herding pups (whose name is pronounced BO-sur-ahn) make excellent watchdogs. They do best with experienced dog owners who can provide the early socialization and consistent training to manage their guarding instincts.

BRIARD

FROM: France
HEIGHT: 23–27 inches (58–69 cm)
WEIGHT: 70–90 pounds (32–41 kg)
COAT: Fawn, gray, black; thick, long, and slightly wavy
GROOMING:
EXERCISE NEEDS:
K-9 QUALITIES: Protective and devoted

Few dogs are as distinctive-looking as the briard (BREE-ar), with its beard and long eyebrows. Since the eighth century, they've been all-purpose farm dogs. Now they're mainly family companions, but they need plenty of training and socialization to manage their guarding instincts. They can be sweet, watchful companions for older kids.

PYRENEAN SHEPHERD

The smallest of the French herding breeds, Pyrenean shepherds have big personalities. They are great companions for active people and families, but they can get into mischief if they're bored.

FROM: France
HEIGHT: 15–19 inches (38–48 cm)
WEIGHT: 15–30 pounds (7–14 kg)
COAT: Fawn, blue, gray, black, black and white; long or semilong, rough or smooth face
GROOMING:
EXERCISE NEEDS:
K-9 QUALITIES: Active and loyal

BERGER PICARD

The oldest of the French sheepdogs, with ancestors going back to 400 B.C., these rare, scruffy dogs—also known as Picardy sheepdogs—can be trained to be good family dogs and playmates for kids. (Their name is pronounced bare-zhay pee-CARR).

FROM: France
HEIGHT: 22–26 inches (55–65 cm)
WEIGHT: 51–71 pounds (23–32 kg)
COAT: Fawn, dark gray, brindle; thick and harsh
GROOMING:
EXERCISE NEEDS:
K-9 QUALITIES: Headstrong but charming

PUP STARS

Hollywood used a team of berger Picards to play the dog in the 2005 movie *Because of Winn-Dixie.* With their tousled coats, they passed for a mixed breed.

COLLIE

These gorgeous dogs, also called rough collies, trace their origins to working shepherd dogs in the Scottish Highlands. Mentioned in writings dating back to the 14th century, versatile and athletic collies adapted to multiple roles. Some guarded sheep in pastures, while others herded the sheep to market. Both jobs required quick responses, a willingness to work in new surroundings, and an ability to understand what people wanted. Collies may have remained the humble companions of shepherds had it not been for a royal vacation. In the 1860s, Queen Victoria of Britain, who often relaxed at Balmoral Castle in Scotland, fell in love with the breed. Her enthusiasm caught on among the wealthy classes in British society—and soon in the United States. The same traits that made collies great herders also make them excellent family pets. Gentle and intelligent, they can understand people's moods. They bond with every member of the family and love to play with kids. They still have herding instincts and may try to round up kids by nipping at ankles, if not properly trained. They're not the best choice for those wanting a watchdog—collies are just too friendly!

FROM:	UK/Scotland
HEIGHT:	20-24 inches (51-61 cm)
WEIGHT:	51-75 pounds (23-34 kg)
COAT:	Sable and white, black, tan and white, or blue merle; long, dense, and harsh
GROOMING:	
EXERCISE NEEDS:	
K-9 QUALITIES:	Proud, sensitive, and devoted

PUP STARS

No other dog did more for a breed's popularity than Lassie, the collie star of stories, novels, movies, radio and television shows, and even comic books. The fictional character—inspired by a half-collie crossbreed named Lassie who saved the life of a British sailor during WWI—faced down any challenge and constantly rescued her human companions from trouble. Lassie is one of a few animals (or fictional characters) to have a star on the Hollywood Walk of Fame.

SMOOTH COLLIE

Smooth collies have all the sweet personality and athletic abilities of their long-haired cousins but in a short-haired package. They're so similar, in fact, that in the United States, smooth collies and rough collies are considered the same breed.

FROM: UK/Scotland
HEIGHT: 20–24 inches (51–61 cm)
WEIGHT: 40–65 pounds (18–29 kg)
COAT: Sable and white, black, tan and white, or blue merle; short, dense, and harsh
GROOMING:
EXERCISE NEEDS:
K-9 QUALITIES: Devoted and active

BEARDED COLLIE

Looking more like Old English sheepdogs than collies, "beardies" are the descendants of Highland collies and Polish dogs that were traded for Scottish sheep back in the 16th century. Affectionate family members, they love giving kisses and playing, but they may be a bit too rambunctious for small kids.

FROM: UK/Scotland
HEIGHT: 20–22 inches (51–56 cm)
WEIGHT: 45–55 pounds (20–25 kg)
COAT: Gray, blue, black, sandy, or red-brown; long
GROOMING:
EXERCISE NEEDS:
K-9 QUALITIES: Active, outgoing, and independent

BOLD LITTLE HERDERS

From the looks of these short pooches, you might suspect they herd only ducklings or other little creatures. But you'd be very wrong! These spunky dogs, known as heelers, nip at the heels of any size animal—even cattle—to get them moving. And they're short enough to duck any kicks from their annoyed charges. The petite pups got their short legs from a genetic mutation—and as a result, are called dwarf breeds—but they were selectively bred to continue the useful trait. Their size also makes them wonderfully adaptable, as happy to live in apartments as on ranches—as long as they're with their people. Active and outgoing, these loving pups want to be involved in any family activity, including hiking or playing with kids. Their herding skills mean they're great at chasing balls.

PEMBROKE WELSH CORGI

The more popular of the Welsh corgi breeds—probably thanks to the admiration of Queen Elizabeth II of Britain—the Pembroke's ancestry goes back to the spitz-type dogs of the Vikings. Brought to Wales around a thousand years ago, Pembrokes worked on farms and became valued family companions. These happy working dogs still need jobs and new challenges to tackle, or they might create their own. Corgis want to do whatever you do—playing, learning tricks, taking long walks—and maybe even be in charge of it!

In Welsh lore, **FAIRIES** rode corgis into battle and used them to pull their carts and carriages. So how did the dogs end up as human helpers? As gifts, from **FAIRIES** to two human **CHILDREN.** If you look closely, legend says, you may notice the outlines of **FAIRY SADDLES** on corgis' backs.

FROM:	UK/Wales
HEIGHT:	10–12 inches (25–30 cm)
WEIGHT:	20–26 pounds (9–12 kg)
COAT:	Black and tan, red, fawn, or sable, with white markings; thick, medium-length
GROOMING:	
EXERCISE NEEDS:	
K-9 QUALITIES:	Fun-loving and watchful

CARDIGAN WELSH CORGI

FROM: UK/Wales

HEIGHT: 11–12 inches (28–30 cm)

WEIGHT: 24–37 pounds (11–17 kg)

COAT: Variety of colors; thick, medium-length

GROOMING:

EXERCISE NEEDS:

K-9 QUALITIES: Outgoing and playful

Brought to Wales around 1200 B.C. by the central European Celts, Cardigan Welsh corgis are one of the oldest breeds in the British Isles. Versatile and smart farm dogs and companions, they traditionally drove cattle and watched over children. These days, they fit into any home. They're good-natured and affectionate pets, active and sturdy enough to keep up with any kid.

LANCASHIRE HEELER

Lancashire heelers may be the descendants of Welsh corgis that herded cattle from Wales to northwestern England and Manchester terriers (p. 231) living near the English markets. Hardy and versatile, these working dogs are also energetic and affectionate pets for families.

FROM: UK/England

HEIGHT: 10–12 inches (25–30 cm)

WEIGHT: 9–15 pounds (4–7 kg)

COAT: Black, liver and tan; short

GROOMING:

EXERCISE NEEDS:

K-9 QUALITIES: Playful and work-loving

SWEDISH VALLHUND

FROM: Sweden

HEIGHT: 12–14 inches (30–35 cm)

WEIGHT: 26–35 pounds (12–16 kg)

COAT: Gray shades, red, with lighter markings; dense, and harsh

GROOMING:

EXERCISE NEEDS:

K-9 QUALITIES: Alert and active

These ancient herding dogs, saved from extinction in the 1940s by dedicated breeders, have spitz ancestry. Like their corgi cousins, Swedish vallhunds are playful and affectionate family dogs as well as good watchdogs.

DIVERSE HUNGARIAN SHEPHERD DOGS

With unusual coats, a range of sizes, and different personalities, this roundup of Hungarian working dogs really mixes things up! But what they all have in common is a strong work ethic and guarding instincts. A couple of the breeds will do anything to protect their families and property—a super-loyal trait, but one that requires experienced dog handlers and doesn't make these dogs the best playmates. Others adapt well to family life with good training and socialization. They can be distinctive companions.

KUVASZ

The Kuvasz (KOO-vahz) has roots going back to sheep-guarding canines in ancient lands that are now northern Iraq. Their ancestors came to central Europe with sheep breeders 7,000 years ago. Strong and fearless, they're hardwired to protect their loved ones, especially kids. They need very experienced owners who can teach them what is a real threat and what isn't.

FROM:	Hungary
HEIGHT:	26–30 inches (66–75 cm)
WEIGHT:	70–115 pounds (32–52 kg)
COAT:	White; coarse and wavy
GROOMING:	⌇⌇⌇⌇
EXERCISE NEEDS:	●●●●●○
K-9 QUALITIES:	Protective and loyal

KOMONDOR

With their long white dreadlocks—or cords—"koms" definitely stand out from the canine crowd. Possibly brought to central Europe by nomadic Turkic people in the 13th century, the brave and powerful dogs were bred to protect livestock. A komondor (KAH-muhn-dor) is best for owners experienced at handling dogs with strong guarding instincts but, with the right training and socialization, koms may be fine with older kids.

FROM:	Hungary
HEIGHT:	24–31 inches (60–80 cm)
WEIGHT:	79–135 pounds (36–61 kg)
COAT:	White; very long and corded
GROOMING:	⌇⌇⌇⌇
EXERCISE NEEDS:	●●●●●○
K-9 QUALITIES:	Powerful and brave

MUDI

FROM: Hungary

HEIGHT: 15–19 inches (38–47 cm)

WEIGHT: 18–29 pounds (8–13 kg)

COAT: Black, blue, brown, fawn; dense and wavy

GROOMING:

EXERCISE NEEDS:

K-9 QUALITIES: Friendly and adaptable

Don't let their name fool you! Even though it sounds like "moody," these working dogs are actually good-humored and lively pets, making them great for families with kids. They are also handy watchdogs.

PULI

These little mops (whose name is pronounced POO-lee) have a thousand-year history as beloved helpers to Hungarian shepherds. Quick to learn, pulik (plural of puli) get into mischief if bored, but they also can be affectionate family pets.

FROM: Hungary

HEIGHT: 14–17 inches (36–44 cm)

WEIGHT: 23–33 pounds (10–15 kg)

COAT: Black, gray, white, fawn; long and corded

GROOMING:

EXERCISE NEEDS:

K-9 QUALITIES: Intelligent and energetic

PUMI

Koms' corded coats helped them **BLEND IN** with **SHEEP** so they could surprise any wolves that tried to **SNEAK UP** on the flock.

A cross between pulik and terrier-type dogs from Germany and France, pumik trace their roots to the 18th century. Good all-around farm dogs, these intelligent pups also enjoy all aspects of family life, including play.

FROM: Hungary

HEIGHT: 15–19 inches (38–47 cm)

WEIGHT: 18–33 pounds (8–15 kg)

COAT: Black, gray, cream, gold; thick and curly

GROOMING:

EXERCISE NEEDS:

K-9 QUALITIES: High-energy and playful

BORDER COLLIE

You'd think that all the praise heaped on border collies might go to their heads.

They're often called the best herders and the brightest dogs—ever! They excel at agility and obedience competitions, search and rescue, Frisbee catching, and pretty much any dog sport you can name. But at their core, they're steadfast working dogs that are eager to please. Bred on the border of Scotland and England in the late 1800s, they quickly became famous for their shepherding skills. They move sheep along by stalking them in a crouched position and giving them "the eye," an intense stare. Borders' herding instincts are strong and can cause trouble if the dogs aren't properly trained. This breed will herd anything: passing bikes or cars, your cat, your friends—even you! But early and consistent training and socialization will make sure they remain good family members. They also need lots of exercise to satisfy their boundless energy and engaging activities to keep them occupied—or else they'll get bored and into mischief. But if you can meet their needs, they're great companions. Perhaps even some of the best.

FROM:	UK/Scotland and England
HEIGHT:	20–21 inches (50–53 cm)
WEIGHT:	26–44 pounds (12–20 kg)
COAT:	Variety of colors; dense, moderately long
GROOMING:	
EXERCISE NEEDS:	
K-9 QUALITIES:	Intelligent and active

With their smarts and skills, borders and border mixes can **PERFORM AMAZING FEATS,** including skateboarding, tightrope walking, and rolling down manual car windows.

CANINE EINSTEINS

SHETLAND SHEEPDOG

In the rugged Shetland Islands, off the northern tip of Scotland, the sheep are small, the cattle are small, and—you guessed it— the sheepdogs are small. But when it comes to talent, these sheepdogs are supersize! Hardy, smart, and athletic, "shelties" are little powerhouses that can adapt to all sorts of environments. They look like miniature collies (English breeders crossed them with collies (p. 70) in the early 1900s), but they probably started out as mixes of Scandinavian spitz-type dogs, spaniels, and other sheepdogs. Shelties are loyal and loving and good with children—though they may need to be trained not to herd kids by nipping at their ankles. Intelligent and eager to please, shelties love to learn new tricks and compete in dog sports. These popular pets are equal matches to border collies in agility competitions, and they're happy to have jobs to do at home. Their mouths, when open, curve up a bit like they're smiling.

FROM: UK/Scotland
HEIGHT: 14–15 inches (35–38 cm)
WEIGHT: 14–37 pounds (6–17 kg)
COAT: Sable, black and tan, black, blue, with white; thick and long
GROOMING:
EXERCISE NEEDS:
K-9 QUALITIES: Devoted and fun-loving

CANINE EINSTEINS

HERO HOUNDS

Shanna Wilkinson and her little sheltie, Holly, were inseparable— almost like sisters growing up together. They competed in dog sports, including agility and obedience classes. But when Shanna was about to go to college, she started having seizures, sudden attacks that would make her pass out, fall down, and shake uncontrollably. She never knew when they were coming, and she thought she'd have to give up her dreams of college and travel. But Holly didn't let that happen. The sheltie could sense when Shanna was about to have a seizure, and she alerted Shanna so she could get somewhere safe. Shanna trained Holly for two years to become a service dog. She was able to go college and travel with Holly—her best friend and lifeline—by her side.

GUARDIANS OF THE FLOCKS

From the western reaches of southern Europe and into Russia, a variety of tough guardian dogs have worked to protect their flocks.

CATALAN SHEEPDOG

From Catalonia, an area on the eastern coast of Spain, these dogs were bred to guard sheep. They are intelligent, gentle, energetic, and obedient. Catalans love the outdoors but bond easily with families and kids of all ages, and they make good household pets.

FROM: Spain/Catalonia
HEIGHT: 18–22 inches (45–55 cm)
WEIGHT: 45–60 pounds (20–27 kg)
COAT: Fawn, gray, black and tan, sable; rough, medium-length
GROOMING:
EXERCISE NEEDS:
K-9 QUALITIES: Vigilant and fun-loving

MAJORCA SHEPHERD DOG

FROM: Spain/Mallorca
HEIGHT: Up to 29 inches (73 cm)
WEIGHT: Up to 88 pounds (40 kg)
COAT: Black, or black with white markings; short or long
GROOMING:
EXERCISE NEEDS:
K-9 QUALITIES: Independent and protective

Used for centuries to guard sheep and work on farms in the Mediterranean Balearic Islands, these territorial dogs (their name is pronounced may-AWr-kuh) are workers to the core. They're loyal, but because of their strong wills and guarding instincts, they are not the best household companions.

PORTUGUESE SHEEPDOG

Historically, Portuguese sheepdogs, also known as cão da Serra de Aires, herded and watched over a variety of livestock, including cattle, sheep, and pigs. Today, these intelligent animals are becoming popular pets, especially in Europe, and get along well with kids if they grow up together.

FROM: Portugal
HEIGHT: 17–22 inches (42–55 cm)
WEIGHT: 37–60 pounds (17–27 kg)
COAT: Variety of colors; shaggy
GROOMING:
EXERCISE NEEDS:
K-9 QUALITIES: Loyal and hardworking

SOUTH RUSSIAN SHEPHERD DOG

FROM:	Russia
HEIGHT:	24–26 inches (62–65 cm)
WEIGHT:	106–110 pounds (48–50 kg)
COAT:	White, gray, yellow and white, straw; dense and long
GROOMING:	
EXERCISE NEEDS:	
K-9 QUALITIES:	Protective and fierce

These big, powerful dogs were bred to defend their flocks against fierce predators, such as wolves. Vigilant and quick to react, they're best left to experienced dog handlers.

BERGAMASCO

An ancient breed that worked for centuries in Alpine valleys, Bergamascos traditionally watched over flocks of sheep—a job they still do in parts of Europe. As pets, the scruffy pups happily watch over their people, especially kids. Calm and athletic, they're happy to play.

FROM:	Italy
HEIGHT:	21–24 inches (54–62 cm)
WEIGHT:	57–84 pounds (26–38 kg)
COAT:	Gray shades, black; flocked (corded or matted)
GROOMING:	
EXERCISE NEEDS:	
K-9 QUALITIES:	Gentle and independent

MAREMMA SHEEPDOG

Powerful white sheepdogs, Maremmas still protect sheep from wolves in the central plains of Italy. Though they're devoted to their people, they're best owned by experienced dog handlers who know how to control their guarding instincts. They're outdoorsy working dogs, not pets.

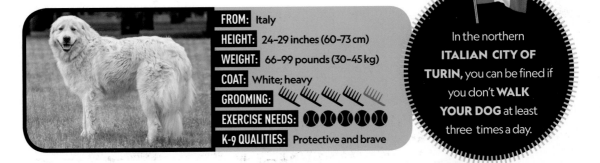

FROM:	Italy
HEIGHT:	24–29 inches (60–73 cm)
WEIGHT:	66–99 pounds (30–45 kg)
COAT:	White; heavy
GROOMING:	
EXERCISE NEEDS:	
K-9 QUALITIES:	Protective and brave

In the northern **ITALIAN CITY OF TURIN,** you can be fined if you don't **WALK YOUR DOG** at least three times a day.

AUSTRALIAN SHEPHERD

"Aussies" actually developed in the American West, where farmers and ranchers needed a versatile dog that could herd sheep and handle other work. They were bred from various herding breeds—including some collie-type dogs from Australia—that had been brought to the United States in the 19th century. Ranch work is complicated and physically demanding, and Aussies have the athleticism and intelligence to handle it—traits that make them excel in dog competitions and in other roles. They're loyal and loving companions that seem to have a "sixth sense," an understanding of what you want or need without being told. With their boundless energy, they're playful and great with kids. But you need to provide Aussies with interesting jobs to do—maybe competing in dog sports, practicing tricks, or learning to pick up your dirty socks from the floor—plus plenty of exercise and training. They instinctively try to herd livestock by nipping at the animals' heels and, if not properly trained, may try to pull that trick on you, your kitty, or passing vehicles. Bored Aussies also will come up with creative ways to entertain themselves—such as remodeling your home or garden, and you probably won't like the results! But if you can devote the time and energy these lively dogs need, you'll have a new best friend.

FROM: U.S.A.

HEIGHT: 18-23 inches (46-58 cm)

WEIGHT: 40-64 pounds (18-29 kg)

COAT: Blue merle, red, red merle, black, with markings; thick, wavy

GROOMING:

EXERCISE NEEDS:

K-9 QUALITIES: Loving and lively

MINIATURE
AMERICAN SHEPHERD

Take all that Aussie goodness and put it in a more portable package and you've got the miniature American shepherd (also known as the North American shepherd). These athletic and loving dogs originally were called miniature Australian shepherds, which tells you a lot about their origins: In California in the 1960s, breeders selectively bred the smallest Aussies they could find to create this breed.

FROM:	U.S.A.
HEIGHT:	13–18 inches (33–46 cm)
WEIGHT:	15–35 pounds (7–16 kg)
COAT:	Blue merle, red, red merle, black, with markings; thick, wavy
GROOMING:	
EXERCISE NEEDS:	
K-9 QUALITIES:	Energetic and loving

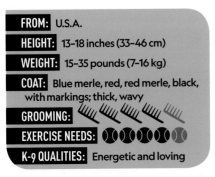

POOCH PROS: VETERINARIANS

Animal doctors, or veterinarians, help keep our pets healthy. Many vets specialize in treating small animals, mainly dogs and cats—but sometimes other critters, such as hamsters, snakes, or birds, too. They provide routine checkups and vaccinations, and they also take care of pets that get hurt or sick. If your pup becomes ill, veterinarians figure out what's wrong by examining your dog and, if needed, taking x-rays or running tests on your pup's blood, urine, or stool in a laboratory. They also treat all kinds of injuries, including cuts and broken bones. Some vets specialize in treating certain types of diseases or performing complicated surgeries. Other vets may treat farm or zoo animals or do research at universities or private companies.

POLISH LOWLAND SHEEPDOG

"PONs," which stands for polski owczarek nizinny, the breed's Polish name, have herded and guarded flocks in the plains of northern Europe for centuries—and still do. But most PONs these days are devoted pets. Good-natured and intelligent, they love their families, including kids, but can be suspicious of strangers.

FROM: Poland
HEIGHT: 17–20 inches (42–50 cm)
WEIGHT: 31–35 pounds (14–16 kg)
COAT: Variety of colors; thick, long, shaggy
GROOMING:
EXERCISE NEEDS:
K-9 QUALITIES: Cheerful and strong-willed

TATRA SHEPHERD DOG

Named for the Tatra Mountains in southern Poland, where they still protect flocks, Tatras are vigilant watchdogs at home. They're gentle with their people but very protective—so probably best for experienced owners used to handling protective pups.

FROM: Poland
HEIGHT: 24–28 inches (60–70 cm)
WEIGHT: 79–130 pounds (36–59 kg)
COAT: White; dense, slightly wavy
GROOMING:
EXERCISE NEEDS:
K-9 QUALITIES: Alert and intelligent

CARPATHIAN SHEPHERD DOG

FROM: Romania
HEIGHT: 23–29 inches (59–73 cm)
WEIGHT: 70–99 pounds (32–45 kg)
COAT: Gray, black, white with patches of color; rough, slightly wavy
GROOMING:
EXERCISE NEEDS:
K-9 QUALITIES: Loyal and devoted

Used for centuries to guard herds in the Carpathian Mountains that run through central and eastern Europe, these hardy dogs still protect flocks and work on farms today. Loyal dogs that form close attachments to their people, early training and socializing help them fit into families.

MIORITIC SHEPHERD DOG

Bred to protect their flocks from wolves, lynxes, and bears, mioritics (me-uh-REE-tic) are courageous canines. They can make good family pets if socialized early and well trained on a regular basis.

FROM: Romania
HEIGHT: 25–29 inches (65–75 cm)
WEIGHT: 77–154 pounds (35–70 kg)
COAT: Black and white, gray, white; thick, wavy
GROOMING:
EXERCISE NEEDS:
K-9 QUALITIES: Protective and loyal

Mioritic shepherd dogs, with their legendary **STRENGTH** and **BRAVERY,** were used in the armies of medieval kings.

CZECHOSLOVAKIAN VLCAK

Intentionally bred by crossing German shepherd dogs (p. 62) with wolves, these dogs, also known as Czechoslovakian wolfdogs, have served in the Czechoslovakian army and, more recently, as search-and-rescue dogs. Quick and fearless, these wolfdogs—which howl!—are also devoted to their families and make good playmates. (Their name is pronounced vil-chaak).

FROM: Czech Republic
HEIGHT: 24–26 inches (60–65 cm)
WEIGHT: 44–57 pounds (20–26 kg)
COAT: Gray; straight, thick
GROOMING:
EXERCISE NEEDS:
K-9 QUALITIES: Fearless and devoted

SLOVENSKY CUVAC

FROM: Slovakia
HEIGHT: 23–28 inches (59–70 cm)
WEIGHT: 68–97 pounds (31–44 kg)
COAT: White; slightly wavy
GROOMING:
EXERCISE NEEDS:
K-9 QUALITIES: Intelligent and protective

Originating from arctic wolves and originally developed to protect herds in the mountains, cuvac (chew-VOTCH) dogs more recently have been bred to be good pets. With proper training, these watchful and devoted guard dogs can be loving companions that enjoy living with large families.

CANINE IQ

Even if dogs are not the smartest animals on the planet—a ranking that's much debated anyway—many believe they have the best "people smarts" around.

HOW SMART ARE THEY?

As they evolved alongside us, dogs developed an uncanny ability to "read" humans: our gazes, our body movements, our moods, and even our health. For example, scientists have discovered that the right side of the human face reveals our emotions. Without even knowing it, people instinctively look at the right side of someone's face for cues about how they're feeling. Amazingly, it turns out, so do dogs! Dogs also learn to understand our gestures and words and to react appropriately. They also have memory skills strong enough to learn hundreds, even a thousand words. They understand that objects exist even if they can't see them—that's tougher than it sounds! Dogs can learn how to do things simply by watching, and if they can't figure out how to solve a difficult task, they'll turn to their people for help. Their closest relatives, wolves, would never think of doing that!

CHASER, THE "SMARTEST DOG IN THE WORLD"

It takes more than learning how to sit and shake hands to be crowned the world's smartest dog. Chaser, a border collie, knows the name of a thousand different things—mainly toys—and she can tell all of them apart. She also knows verbs—that "nosing" a Frisbee is different than "fetching" it. And if you ask her to take a ball to her toy doll, she'll do just that. How'd she learn so much? Lucky for Chaser, her person, John Pilley, knows a thing or two about how brains work and how brains learn. He's a retired psychology professor, and he patiently taught Chaser everything she knows. Plus, Chaser's a border collie, widely believed to be the smartest dog breed. But Pilley believes Chaser is not that much more exceptional than other dogs and that all dogs can learn a lot more than we give them credit for. He says it's important to nurture their natural instincts and form strong relationships with them. Start teaching them simple actions, like sit or lie down, then teach only one object at a time, repeating its name while they play with it. Practice makes perfect!

BOUVIER DES FLANDRES

With their walrus-like mustaches and long, droopy eyebrows, Bouviers are distinctive-looking dogs. Developed as farm dogs (*bouvier* means "bovine [cow] herder"), they're still great at herding livestock and protecting the farm. But they also take on other roles: police K-9, service dog, and, best of all, family pet. They love people and are good companions for bigger kids. But they still love having jobs to do. (Their name is pronounced boo-vee-ay duh FLAHN-durz).

Bouviers are a lot of things, but "tidy" isn't one of them. **ONE OF THEIR NICKNAMES IS "DIRTY BEARD."** And, yes, that means you can expect them to drag their food and water through the house.

FROM:	Belgium, France
HEIGHT:	23–27 inches (59–68 cm)
WEIGHT:	60–88 pounds (27–40 kg)
COAT:	Variety of colors; very thick, rough
GROOMING:	
EXERCISE NEEDS:	
K-9 QUALITIES:	Loyal and protective

BOUVIER DES ARDENNES

These energetic, scruffy dogs are willing workers, bred to drive cattle, but they happily adjust to home life with a family. Comfortable in a variety of situations, Bouvier des Ardennes are curious, playful, and sociable and make great pets, though are possibly too rowdy for little kids.

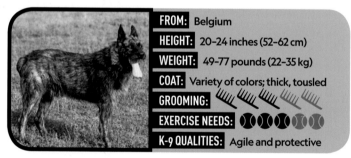

FROM:	Belgium
HEIGHT:	20–24 inches (52–62 cm)
WEIGHT:	49–77 pounds (22–35 kg)
COAT:	Variety of colors; thick, tousled
GROOMING:	
EXERCISE NEEDS:	
K-9 QUALITIES:	Agile and protective

SCHAPENDOES

FROM:	Netherlands
HEIGHT:	16–20 inches (40–50 cm)
WEIGHT:	26–44 pounds (12–20 kg)
COAT:	Variety of colors; full, wavy
GROOMING:	
EXERCISE NEEDS:	
K-9 QUALITIES:	Friendly and adaptable

These shaggy herding dogs—related to breeds from Poland and Hungary—are speedsters that can leap obstacles with ease and love to tackle any job you give them. Athletic and sturdy, schapendoes (ska-PEN-doz) make great pets for active families. They're also known as Dutch sheepdogs.

DUTCH SHEPHERD DOG

FROM: Netherlands

HEIGHT: 20–24 inches (51–62 cm)

WEIGHT: 65–67 pounds (29–30 kg)

COAT: Multiple brindle shades (gray, blue, gold, silver); short or long

GROOMING:

EXERCISE NEEDS:

K-9 QUALITIES: Loyal and affectionate

Related to their German and Belgian cousins, these all-purpose workers are loyal companions. Eager to please and obedient, Dutch shepherds are easy to train and have been used for police work, for security, and as guide dogs. They also can be great family dogs and watchful companions for kids.

SAARLOOS WOLFDOG

Saarloos wolfdogs are the result of crossbreeding a German shepherd dog (p. 62) and a wolf. The goal was to create a hardy working dog with more of the wolf's natural traits, but the Saarloos (pronounced shar-lows) wolfdogs—like wolves—were too shy around strangers and avoided unknown situations. They turned out to be better pets.

FROM: Netherlands

HEIGHT: 24–30 inches (60–75 cm)

WEIGHT: 77–88 pounds (35–40 kg)

COAT: Gray, brown, cream; thick

GROOMING:

EXERCISE NEEDS:

K-9 QUALITIES: Loyal but independent and strong-willed

WHITE SWISS SHEPHERD DOG

White Swiss shepherd dogs are intelligent and obedient, and they excel in a variety of roles: search and rescue, tracking, and all kinds of sports. Social, playful, and gentle, they make great family pets—like white German shepherds, only a bit more laid-back.

FROM: Switzerland

HEIGHT: 21–26 inches (53–66 cm)

WEIGHT: 55–88 pounds (25–40 kg)

COAT: White; thick

GROOMING:

EXERCISE NEEDS:

K-9 QUALITIES: Intelligent and gentle

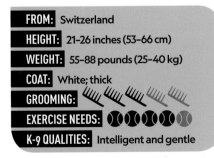

MOUNTAIN DOGS & MASTIFFS

Mountain dogs are hardy working dogs that were developed as guardian sheepdogs—big and powerful enough to protect their flocks from predators or to tackle farm jobs requiring some heft— but are generally a bit less agile and a bit brawnier than the sheepdogs you've already met. These guardians extend their protective nature to people, and some of the breeds best known for rescuing people are mountain dogs.

Mastiff-type dogs—solidly built dogs with muscular necks, broad muzzles, and large lips— are different kinds of guardians. Often referred to as Molossian dogs or Molossers, these canine hulks resemble the enormous dogs seen in art and artifacts from the ancient world. Most of these breeds were developed to be working dogs, but some were bred to be warriors and fighting dogs. Though many of these breeds are massive, this grouping also includes smaller muscular dogs with broad heads and short muzzles. These days, good breeders work to raise lovers, not fighters. With proper training and socializing, most of these dogs can be great pets.

If you like puppies, Bernese mountain dogs might be for you. The dogs **MATURE SLOWLY,** keeping their **PUPPYLIKE ENERGY** (and mischief!) for years.

BERNESE
MOUNTAIN DOG

These strong, all-around farm dogs hail from the farming regions of the Swiss area of Bern.

With an ancestry that may go back 2,000 years to mastiff-type dogs that came with the Roman armies that conquered the region, these dogs traditionally took on a variety of jobs. They drove cattle to pasture or to market, served as watchdogs on farms, and even pulled small carts. Sometimes a pair of "Berners" would be hooked up to a milk cart and they worked as a team to pull it! During the industrial revolution of the late 1800s, Berners lost some of their traditional jobs to machines and almost died out as a breed. But in the early 1900s, breeders worked to bring them back, this time as pets—another role that's perfect for them. Berners love their families and enjoy hanging at home. They're affectionate toward kids (but their size may intimidate younger kids). Easy to train, Berners enjoy a range of activities, including obedience, tracking, and drafting (pulling a cart or wagon). They also love hiking—they can carry their own water and maybe yours, too! These mellow pooches also make great therapy dogs. They're protective and make great watchdogs, and their popularity as pets is well deserved.

HERO HOUNDS

Nico, a three-year-old Bernese mountain dog, was walking with his owner on a California, U.S.A., beach when he saw a man and a woman struggling in the water. They had been boogie-boarding but got caught in a riptide, a strong ocean current that was pulling them ever farther from the shore. They were exhausted and terrified. Nico raced into the water and swam out to them. Nico's astonished owner, Dan Clarke, yelled to the woman to grab the big dog "anywhere you can." She wrapped one arm around Nico and kept the other on her board to help her float. Nico battled the current and got her safely to shore. Then he plunged back into the water and rescued her husband, too. The couple were amazed and asked if Nico was a trained lifesaving dog. But Nico's owner was just as surprised as they were: Nico had no special training and no experience like that. It was pure instinct. Nico knew they were in trouble, and he knew he could help.

Nico

GREAT PYRENEES

Once known as the royal dog of France, Great Pyrenees' traditional role was guarding flocks of sheep in the Pyrenees Mountains of France and Spain. Their white coats allowed them to blend in with the sheep, so they could catch predators by surprise. Despite their watchful, protective nature, "Pyrs" are mellow pets and gentle with kids. They enjoy outdoor activities, such as drafting (pulling carts), but they don't require tons of exercise.

FROM:	France
HEIGHT:	26–28 inches (65–70 cm)
WEIGHT:	88–110 pounds (40–50 kg)
COAT:	White, possibly with tan patches; dense, wavy
GROOMING:	
EXERCISE NEEDS:	
K-9 QUALITIES:	Loving, smart and strong-willed

Great Pyrenees are naturally **NOCTURNAL**, like owls or bats! That's because they had to **PROTECT THEIR FLOCKS** at night while the shepherds slept. And, yes, that means they may bark at night.

GREATER SWISS MOUNTAIN DOG

The largest of Switzerland's farm dog breeds, "Swissys" traditionally guarded and herded cattle and sometimes paired up to haul carts loaded with milk and cheeses. Saved from extinction in the early 20th century, these gentle giants are still rare but have a devoted following. They're good watchdogs and, with appropriate training and socializing, they are calm and devoted family pets that adapt easily to a variety of lifestyles.

FROM:	Switzerland
HEIGHT:	24–28 inches (60–72 cm)
WEIGHT:	80–130 pounds (36–59 kg)
COAT:	Tricolor; short
GROOMING:	
EXERCISE NEEDS:	
K-9 QUALITIES:	Easygoing and loyal

ENTLEBUCHER MOUNTAIN DOG

FROM: Switzerland
HEIGHT: 17–20 inches (42–50 cm)
WEIGHT: 47–62 pounds (21–28 kg)
COAT: Tricolor; short
GROOMING:
EXERCISE NEEDS:
K-9 QUALITIES: High-spirited and loving

"Entles" (the full word is pronounced ENT-leh-boo-cur) are the smallest of the Swiss mountain dogs, but they're still good-size, powerful dogs. They may knock you over with their enthusiastic greetings. They need lots of exercise and jobs to do, whether that's watching the kids or training for agility.

APPENZELLER SENNENHUNDE

Larger than Entles, these big pups, also called Appenzeller mountain dogs, used to be considered the same breed, and have all the lovable enthusiasm of their smaller cousins. Adaptable family pets, Appenzellers fit in even in urban life but need exercise and jobs—learning tricks or helping walk you to the school bus—to keep them busy.

FROM: Switzerland
HEIGHT: 20–22 inches (50–56 cm)
WEIGHT: 49–71 pounds (22–32 kg)
COAT: Tricolor; short
GROOMING:
EXERCISE NEEDS:
K-9 QUALITIES: Versatile and affectionate

HOVAWART

FROM: Germany
HEIGHT: 23–28 inches (58–70 cm)
WEIGHT: 62–99 pounds (28–45 kg)
COAT: Black, blond, black and gold; dense, medium-length
GROOMING:
EXERCISE NEEDS:
K-9 QUALITIES: Strong-willed but loyal and playful

The residents of **RABBIT HASH,** Kentucky, U.S.A., value loyalty—and, evidently, a keen sense of smell—in a mayor. They've **ELECTED DOGS** as their **MAYORS** ever since 1998!

VOTE

Once the defender of German castles, hovawarts trace their ancestry back to farm dogs in the 13th century. Obedient and loyal to their families, they're still good watchdogs but also make fun pets. They're playful and, when properly socialized, can be great with kids.

CANE CORSO

Bred to hunt wild boars and guard property, cane corso (KAH-nay KOR-so) dogs today are mainly guard dogs and trackers. They're large and powerful, and they need owners experienced at training dogs with strong guarding instincts. They're also loyal and enjoy hanging out with their families, but they're not really lovey-dovey pets. Their protective instincts kick in around strangers and other animals, and they take their guarding responsibilities seriously. They are best suited for experienced handlers and are not really an appropriate pet for children.

FROM: Italy

HEIGHT: 24–27 inches (60–68 cm)

WEIGHT: 88–110 pounds (40–50 kg)

COAT: Black, gray, red, brindle; short, glossy

GROOMING:

EXERCISE NEEDS:

K-9 QUALITIES: Powerful and headstrong

Mamma mia! A 145-pound (66-kg) cane corso named **SWEETPEA** gave birth to **20 HEALTHY PUPPIES** in 2009. Litters usually range from three to seven puppies.

YUGOSLAVIAN
SHEPHERD DOG

Believed to be one of the oldest breeds in southeastern Europe, with roots dating back 2,000 years, Yugoslavian shepherd dogs, also known as Šarplaninac dogs, historically guarded livestock and property in the mountainous region of their homelands. Today, they've moved into other regions, but their role hasn't changed: These brave canines are still outdoor working dogs and guards. They like their owners, but they're not really pets.

FROM: Macedonia
HEIGHT: 20–24 inches (51–61 cm)
WEIGHT: 66–99 pounds (30–45 kg)
COAT: White, tan, gray, black, sable; dense, medium-length

GROOMING:
EXERCISE NEEDS:
K-9 QUALITIES: Independent and protective

AIDI

First identified in the Sahara region and in the Atlas Mountains of Morocco, these dogs (their name is pronounced ah-ee-die) have a "sixth sense" when it comes to detecting threats. Nomadic tribes used to post the most alert and aggressive of these dogs on the outside of their camps at night for protection from rival tribes. Today, these dogs can be docile and affectionate, but their guarding instincts might not make them the best indoor pets.

FROM: North Africa
HEIGHT: 21–24 inches (53–61 cm)
WEIGHT: 51–55 pounds (23–25 kg)
COAT: White, fawn, brown, black, with markings; thick, medium-length

GROOMING:
EXERCISE NEEDS:
K-9 QUALITIES: Fearless and faithful

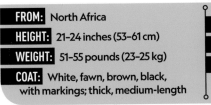

LEONBERGER

During the Victorian-era dog craze of the mid-19th century, Leonbergers—developed by crossbreeding St. Bernards (p. 99) and Newfoundlands (p. 98)—became all the rage with celebrities and the wealthy classes. Now "Leos" are gentle, loving members of any family, though the friendly giants may be too big for young kids.

FROM: Germany
HEIGHT: 28–31 inches (72–80 cm)
WEIGHT: 99–170 pounds (45–77 kg)
COAT: Gold, sandy, red; thick, fairly long
GROOMING:
EXERCISE NEEDS:
K-9 QUALITIES: Sweet and loyal

CASTRO LABOREIRO DOG

FROM: Portugal
HEIGHT: 22–25 inches (55–64 cm)
WEIGHT: 55–88 pounds (25–40 kg)
COAT: Brindle, gray; thick, short
GROOMING:
EXERCISE NEEDS:
K-9 QUALITIES: Brave and vigilant

Named for a village in a mountainous region of northern Portugal, these powerful livestock guardians have a distinctive alarm bark that starts low and ends high. They bond with family members but can be hostile toward others. They're best with experienced handlers or as working dogs.

ESTRELA MOUNTAIN DOG

Bred to protect flocks against wolves in Portugal's Estrela Mountains, Estrelas are loyal and affectionate to their owners. With strong protective instincts, they need ongoing training and socializing to fit into family life.

FROM: Portugal
HEIGHT: 24–28 inches (62–72 cm)
WEIGHT: 77–132 pounds (35–60 kg)
COAT: Fawn, gray, black brindle; thick, slightly wavy, long or short
GROOMING:
EXERCISE NEEDS:
K-9 QUALITIES: Strong-willed but loyal

PORTUGUESE WATCHDOG

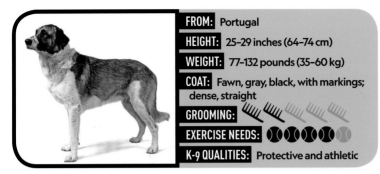

FROM: Portugal

HEIGHT: 25–29 inches (64–74 cm)

WEIGHT: 77–132 pounds (35–60 kg)

COAT: Fawn, gray, black, with markings; dense, straight

GROOMING:

EXERCISE NEEDS:

K-9 QUALITIES: Protective and athletic

Considered one of the best watch-dogs on southwestern Europe's Iberian Peninsula, these brave dogs, also known as rafeiro do Alentejo dogs, are probably descended from powerful mastiffs introduced into the region by nomadic herders. Suspicious of strangers, these dogs are best for experienced handlers.

PYRENEAN MASTIFF

The ancestors of these mastiff-type dogs may have been brought to southern Europe more than 3,000 years ago by Phoenician traders. Brave enough to defend flocks against wolves and bears, they still make excellent guard dogs at home. Gentle and friendly with their families, they can be good companions for older kids, but they need good training and socialization because of their protective instincts.

TOWERING HEIGHTS

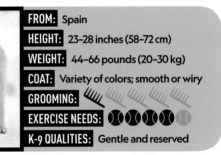

FROM: Spain

HEIGHT: 23–28 inches (58–72 cm)

WEIGHT: 44–66 pounds (20–30 kg)

COAT: Variety of colors; smooth or wiry

GROOMING:

EXERCISE NEEDS:

K-9 QUALITIES: Gentle and reserved

SPANISH MASTIFF

FROM: Spain

HEIGHT: 28–31 inches (72–80 cm)

WEIGHT: 115–221 pounds (52–100 kg)

COAT: Variety of colors; thick, medium-length

GROOMING:

EXERCISE NEEDS:

K-9 QUALITIES: Calm and affectionate and strong-willed

With ancestry stretching back more than 2,000 years, Spanish mastiffs have been used to protect and drive livestock. Gentle with their families but possibly aggressive toward strangers and animals, they need expe-rienced owners and consistent training and socialization.

HEAVYWEIGHTS

NEWFOUNDLAND

With hearts seemingly as big as their bodies, "Newfies" are wonderful—but a bit slobbery!—family dogs that love kids. Their exact origins are uncertain. Their ancestors were possibly a mix of indigenous dogs, Nordic breeds, or Great Pyrenees (p. 92) brought to North America by indigenous Basque people from Spain and France. What's clear is that these gentle giants were ideally suited for work on the eastern Canadian island that gave them their name. As comfortable in the water as on the land, Newfies have warm, water-resistant coats and webbed feet. They pulled carts on land, helped fishermen haul in heavy nets, swam lifelines out to victims of shipwrecks, and pulled kids out of deep water. Newfies are famous for their water rescues and make excellent lifeguards. But, most of all, they make great pets. In some countries, a white-and-black variant of the breed is known as a Landseer—named after a 19th-century British artist who loved to paint them.

FROM: Canada
HEIGHT: 26–28 inches (66–71 cm)
WEIGHT: 110–152 pounds (50–69 kg)
COAT: Black or dark brown, with or without white patches; dense, medium-length

GROOMING:
EXERCISE NEEDS:
K-9 QUALITIES: Sweet and devoted

HERO HOUNDS

It's not hard to find stories about Newfies saving lives, but few are as dramatic as the story of Rigel. He belonged to the first officer of the *Titanic*, the infamous ocean liner that struck an iceberg and sank in 1912. As the ship went down, Rigel was plunged into the icy water. When he couldn't find his companion, Rigel swam next to a lifeboat, which slowly drifted away from the others. The ship *Carpathia*, which arrived hours later to rescue survivors, didn't see the lone lifeboat and was on a collision course toward it. The people inside, overcome by the cold, were too weak to shout. But Rigel, still swimming next to the lifeboat, barked loudly, stopping the *Carpathia*. The crew rescued the lifeboat's passengers and the dog who saved them. Though the *Titanic*'s first officer, Rigel's companion, had gone down with his ship, one of the *Carpathia*'s crew adopted the Newfoundland. Rigel's story was a heroic tale coming out of the tragedy, though some people say it was made up. But even if it didn't really happen, it shows how much people wanted to hear something uplifting after the disaster—and how strongly they believed a dog could be a hero.

SAINT BERNARD

These lovable giants may be the world's most famous dogs. Originally working in Alpine valley farms and dairies, where they'd pull carts and guard livestock, Saints were discovered to be excellent pathfinders in the snow. Bred and kept by monks at the Great St. Bernard Hospice, located along one of the highest mountain passes in the Swiss Alps, the dogs regularly rescued travelers who'd lost their way in the wintry conditions. Over the years, they saved 2,000 lives! Though St. Bernards still live at the hospice, they're now companions instead of rescuers—a perfect role for them. Calm and gentle, Saints love to stick close to their families. They're great with kids (though they could easily knock over toddlers!) and enjoy dog sports, such as obedience, drafting (pulling a cart), and weight pulling.

FROM:	Switzerland
HEIGHT:	28–30 inches (71–76 cm)
WEIGHT:	130–180 pounds (59–81 kg)
COAT:	Orange and white, brindle; smooth or rough
GROOMING:	
EXERCISE NEEDS:	
K-9 QUALITIES:	Gentle and loving

HEAVYWEIGHTS

The helpful spirit of Newfies and St. Bernards was captured in **NANA,** the canine caretaker of the Darling children in **PETER PAN.** In the Walt Disney animated movie, Nana is a St. Bernard, but in the original play, author J. M. Barrie described Nana as a **NEWFIE**—though he wrote that on stage, "she will probably be played by a boy, if one clever enough can be found."

HERO HOUNDS

The most famous of the rescue dogs at the Great St. Bernard Hospice in the Swiss Alps was Barry—or, if you want to be formal, Barry der Menschenretter (Barry the People Rescuer). The high Alpine pass near the hospice was so dangerous that some people called it the "White Death." But it didn't stop Barry. Between 1800 and 1812, he helped find and rescue more than 40 travelers who'd become stranded.

GUARDIANS TO THE CORE

These impressive breeds from Europe and Asia have guarded flocks for centuries. Brave and watchful, their protective natures run deep. Many of these breeds still work as watchdogs—a role they fill expertly. A few have adapted to embrace family life, but most need experienced dog owners willing to provide them with early and ongoing training and socialization.

KARST SHEPHERD DOG

The oldest breed from Slovenia, Karst shepherd dogs have herded and guarded livestock for centuries in Slovenia and are considered a national treasure. Intelligent and loyal, Karsts are devoted and can make good pets if raised in their families from a young age.

FROM: Slovenia
HEIGHT: 21–25 inches (54–63 cm)
WEIGHT: 55–93 pounds (25–42 kg)
COAT: Gray shades with dark streaks; long, thick
GROOMING:
EXERCISE NEEDS:
K-9 QUALITIES: Obedient and reliable

CAUCASIAN SHEPHERD DOG

FROM: Russia
HEIGHT: 26–30 inches (67–75 cm)
WEIGHT: 99–154 pounds (45–70 kg)
COAT: Variety of colors; dense, thick, long or short
GROOMING:
EXERCISE NEEDS:
K-9 QUALITIES: Powerful and protective

Caucasian shepherd dogs are either the **MOUNTAIN TYPE** (with a long coat and a heavy body mass) or the **STEPPE TYPE** (with a shorter coat and lighter body mass).

Courageous and dedicated watchdogs that traditionally guarded livestock, Caucasian shepherd dogs have strong territorial instincts and can act quickly when they feel that their families or property are being threatened. They need owners who have experience raising dogs with strong guarding instincts.

CENTRAL ASIAN SHEPHERD DOG

FROM:	Central Asia
HEIGHT:	26–31 inches (65–78 cm)
WEIGHT:	88–174 pounds (40–79 kg)
COAT:	Variety of colors; dense, short or long
GROOMING:	
EXERCISE NEEDS:	
K-9 QUALITIES:	Fearless and independent

These massive dogs are said to have developed over 4,000 years ago from the ancient dogs in Tibet related to various shepherd breeds and Tibetan mastiffs (below). Used for hundreds of years to protect livestock and property, these powerful dogs are obedient working dogs but not ideal pets.

TIBETAN KYI APSO

These rare, bearded dogs (their name is pronounced kee AHP-soh) traditionally guarded livestock and homes. Alert and quick, they also made effective hunters. These scruffy pups are playful and affectionate with their people, but they need good training and socializing so they don't become overly protective.

FROM:	Tibet, China
HEIGHT:	22–28 inches (56–71 cm)
WEIGHT:	68–84 pounds (31–38 kg)
COAT:	Variety of colors; dense, wiry
GROOMING:	
EXERCISE NEEDS:	
K-9 QUALITIES:	Agile and intelligent

TIBETAN MASTIFF

Tibetan mastiffs historically guarded the livestock of nomadic shepherds in the Himalaya. A century of selective breeding in western Europe and North America has made them less aggressive, but they're still watchful and protective of their families. They're better companions for experienced adults.

FROM:	Tibet, China
HEIGHT:	24–30 inches (61–76 cm)
WEIGHT:	75–160 pounds (34–73 kg)
COAT:	Black or gray, with markings, or gold; dense, straight
GROOMING:	
EXERCISE NEEDS:	
K-9 QUALITIES:	Independent and loyal

Talk about a **PRICEY PUP!** A Chinese property developer reportedly paid **$1.9 MILLION** to buy a golden-haired Tibetan mastiff puppy.

SHOW-OFFS

Your dog doesn't have to be on TV to be a star! Canine competitions give dogs the opportunity to show off their talents—and your training skills. They're a great way to keep dogs happy and healthy and to strengthen their bonds with you.

DISC DOGS

Some dogs live to catch flying discs! If yours is one of them, a variety of disc-catching competitions may be the ticket. Some judge on distance, while others go for style.

RALLY

Think your dog is really well trained? Rally might be the competition for you. A dog and handler move through a course of stations where they have to perform skills, such as sitting or jumping a hurdle.

CONFORMATION

When someone says "dog show," they're usually talking about competitions judging dogs' conformation—how they're built and how they move—and how closely that matches the ideal build and movement for their breed.

FLYBALL

For the pups that like to hang with their buddies, flyball is a relay race where teams of dogs sprint over hurdles to a box that releases a tennis ball for them to bring back.

NOSE WORK

Nose-work competitions give pooches the opportunity to show off their super sniffers. The dogs have to find smelly things hidden in different places. Any dog can compete—not just hounds.

AGILITY

Canine athleticism meets obstacles. In agility competitions, dogs run a course in which they jump hurdles, race through tunnels, scamper up and down teeter-totters, and weave through poles.

FREESTYLE

If you want to show off your canine's creative side, how about dancing with your dog? Freestyle competitions are choreographed performances by a dog-and-handler team. Twists and turns, walking backward, dancing, jumping—anything goes!

WATCHFUL DOGS FROM TURKEY

Protective and loyal, these pups are brave enough to stand up to the fiercest of predators. They're true guardians at heart—so not the best prospects for pets, especially in homes with young kids. To live in a home, they need experienced owners, early and ongoing socializing and training, and meaningful jobs to perform.

ANATOLIAN SHEPHERD DOG

These rugged and powerful livestock guardians are all work and no play—and they like it that way. They're calm with their people and always up for a romp, but their guarding instincts need skillful handling.

FROM: Turkey
HEIGHT: 27–32 inches (69–81 cm)
WEIGHT: 90–149 pounds (41–68 kg)
COAT: Variety of colors; dense, medium to long
GROOMING:
EXERCISE NEEDS:
K-9 QUALITIES: Independent and watchful

TOWERING HEIGHTS

AKBASH SHEPHERD DOG

FROM: Turkey
HEIGHT: 27–34 inches (69–86 cm)
WEIGHT: 75–140 pounds (34–64 kg)
COAT: White, cream; coarse, medium or long
GROOMING:
EXERCISE NEEDS:
K-9 QUALITIES: Protective and quiet

To protect their flocks, these all-white dogs camouflage themselves among the sheep so they can take predators by surprise. They're totally dedicated to their charges—and that can include people, too—but more as protectors than pets.

TOWERING HEIGHTS

KANGAL SHEPHERD DOG

A national treasure in Turkey, Kangals have protected flocks of sheep from wolves, jackals, and bears for centuries. These gentle dogs work by standing guard, using their massive size to frighten away predators instead of fighting them. They're not very playful, but they make good family watchdogs—though they're too big to be around young kids.

FROM: Turkey
HEIGHT: 28–32 inches (71–81 cm)
WEIGHT: 90–145 pounds (41–66 kg)
COAT: Cream, tan, gray, sable, with black "mask"; dense, short
GROOMING:
EXERCISE NEEDS:
K-9 QUALITIES: Loyal and calm

CONFIDENT DOGS FROM ASIA

These two breeds are different in many ways—one's a wrinkled guardian and hunter from China, the other is a short-haired fighter from Japan—but they're both self-confident and tough canines.

TOSA

The largest of the Japanese breeds, Tosas are known as "canine sumo wrestlers." These courageous dogs were bred on the island of Shikoku to be fighting dogs. Tosas aren't the best choice for families with young children: They can mistake kids' roughhousing to be fighting and may step in to end the "fight."

HEAVYWEIGHTS

FROM: Japan
HEIGHT: 22–24 inches (55–61 cm)
WEIGHT: 82–198 pounds (37–90 kg)
COAT: Red, gold, brown, black, brindle; short
GROOMING:
EXERCISE NEEDS:
K-9 QUALITIES: Fearless and powerful

CHINESE SHAR-PEI

Best known for their wrinkled skin, shar-peis (pronounced shar-PAY) originally were used mainly for guarding livestock and property, herding flocks, and hunting game. The name itself translates to "sand skin" in Cantonese. Generally friendly, these ancient dogs bond most strongly with one person but need thorough socialization to be good family dogs.

In **ANCIENT CHINA,** the shar-pei's wrinkly skin and purplish tongue were thought to frighten away evil spirits.

FROM: China
HEIGHT: 18–20 inches (46–51 cm)
WEIGHT: 40–55 pounds (18–25 kg)
COAT: Variety of colors; short, wrinkly
GROOMING:
EXERCISE NEEDS:
K-9 QUALITIES: Intelligent but a bit stubborn

GREAT DANE

Despite their names, these towering beauties didn't originate in Denmark. Their original name, Deutch Dogge (German mastiff), was changed in the late 19th century due to European tensions with Germany. German hunters bred the dogs to hunt ferocious wild boars; later, the dogs commonly guarded large estates. But that's all in the past. Today, these easygoing dogs prefer to hang out at home with their people and, despite their size, are as happy in apartments as in large manors. They're affectionate family dogs that love kids—but a wag of their powerful tails can send a toddler tumbling, and you can imagine what happens if they're allowed to jump up on people! Danes' backgrounds aren't certain, but they probably got their height from Irish wolfhounds (p. 122). Their sleek bodies likely came from greyhounds (p. 123) and their heft from mastiffs (p. 115). Danes' bodies aren't the only part of them that's huge: so are their hearts.

FROM:	Germany
HEIGHT:	28–32 inches (71–81 cm)
WEIGHT:	110–190 pounds (50–86 kg)
COAT:	Fawn, blue, black, brindle, harlequin (white with black patches); short, smooth
GROOMING:	
EXERCISE NEEDS:	
K-9 QUALITIES:	Gentle and devoted pets

TOWERING HEIGHTS

HEAVYWEIGHTS

Not many dogs are taller than most professional **BASKETBALL PLAYERS,** but Freddy, a Great Dane that lives in England, stands 7 feet 6 inches (2.29 m) on his hind legs. He can drink straight from the **KITCHEN FAUCET** and snacks on roast chicken—an entire **CHICKEN** at a time!

ROTTWEILER

These large, powerful dogs, descendants of Roman herding and guard dogs, historically drove cattle, pulled carts, and protected property. "Rotties" are thinking dogs, bred to use independent judgment when their families or territories come under threat. They have strong protective instincts, but whether they become gentle family dogs—or the opposite—depends on how their owners raise them. Rotties are not naturally bad-tempered, and proper socializing and training will make them good pets. They do best when they have jobs, and they excel as service, herding, and police dogs. Even gentle Rotties, however, should be watched around little kids and older folks. They were bred to move cattle by bumping into them. You don't want them to body-slam Granny!

FROM:	Germany
HEIGHT:	23–27 inches (58–69 cm)
WEIGHT:	84–130 pounds (38–59 kg)
COAT:	Black and tan; short, smooth
GROOMING:	
EXERCISE NEEDS:	
K-9 QUALITIES:	Muscular and loyal

HERO HOUNDS

In 1991, Kathie Vaughn was driving a used van when it began to fishtail and fill with black smoke. She stopped and opened the van's door, shoved out her Rottweiler, Eve, then swung most of her wheelchair onto the street. In the thick black smoke, Kathie—who was paralyzed from the waist down—couldn't find its wheels. She was stuck—and she knew the van could explode at any minute! Suddenly, Kathie felt something grab her ankle. It was Eve! The Rottie pulled Kathie away from the van, just before it burst into flames, and then into a nearby ditch. But they weren't safe yet. The flames were approaching the van's gas tank, which would make a big explosion. Eve bent down so Kathie could grab her collar, then the dog pulled her 20 feet (6 m) to safety.

FEARLESS GUARDIANS FROM AROUND THE GLOBE

In many countries, strong, fearless dog breeds developed to tackle jobs that required extreme courage, such as hunting ferocious game or protecting livestock from wolves or bears. While most of these breeds continue to be excellent working dogs, they can also be calm, good-tempered, and friendly with their people. But with their strong protective and hunting instincts, they need experienced dog owners willing to put in the effort to thoroughly train and socialize them.

FILA BRASILEIRO

FROM:	Brazil
HEIGHT:	24–30 inches (60–75 cm)
WEIGHT:	90–100 pounds (41–45 kg)
COAT:	Variety of colors; short
GROOMING:	
EXERCISE NEEDS:	
K-9 QUALITIES:	Courageous and protective

Bred to guard ranches and protect livestock, these beautiful, fearless dogs (whose name is pronounced FEEL-ah brah-zee-YAIR-oh) can be affectionate with their families. But they may not be ideal pets. With strong guardian instincts, they may misinterpret rough play as a threat and try to stop it.

URUGUAYAN CIMARRON

The mascots of the Uruguayan army, these fearless dogs (whose name is pronounced ur-i-GWY-en si-mah-RON) are descended from dogs brought by Spanish and Portuguese colonists. They're great guard dogs but not the best choice for a pet.

FROM:	Uruguay
HEIGHT:	22–24 inches (55–61 cm)
WEIGHT:	73–99 pounds (33–45 kg)
COAT:	Fawn, brindle; short
GROOMING:	
EXERCISE NEEDS:	
K-9 QUALITIES:	Strong and agile

DOGO ARGENTINO

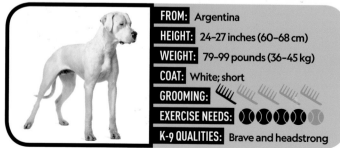

FROM:	Argentina
HEIGHT:	24–27 inches (60–68 cm)
WEIGHT:	79–99 pounds (36–45 kg)
COAT:	White; short
GROOMING:	
EXERCISE NEEDS:	
K-9 QUALITIES:	Brave and headstrong

Bred in the 1920s to hunt big game, these powerful dogs (their name is pronounced doh-goh ar-hen-TEE-no) can be gentle but overprotective. They need expert training and socializing to understand what is a real threat—and what isn't.

BOERBOEL

FROM: South Africa

HEIGHT: 22–27 inches (55–69 cm)

WEIGHT: 165–200 pounds (75–91 kg)

COAT: Variety of colors; short

GROOMING:

EXERCISE NEEDS:

K-9 QUALITIES: Devoted and calm

HEAVYWEIGHTS

These large dogs, developed from mastiff type dogs in the 17th century, were bred to guard property. In the hands of experienced owners who know how to train and socialize them, they can be affectionate family dogs, good with older kids. (Their name is pronounced bur-bul).

BROHOLMER

Developed centuries ago as a hunting dog, these large dogs later guarded farms. Good-tempered and playful, they can make good family pets.

FROM: Denmark

HEIGHT: 28–30 inches (70–75 cm)

WEIGHT: 88–154 pounds (40–70 kg)

COAT: Golden red, black; short

GROOMING:

EXERCISE NEEDS:

K-9 QUALITIES: Watchful and friendly

Dogs really do **WATCH TV!** They recognize the pictures, but it's usually **CERTAIN SOUNDS** that get them to tune into what's on the screen.

BOXER

 Ah, the beloved boxer! These fun-loving dogs are super popular, and with good reason.

Bright, energetic, and a bit mischievous, boxers are always up for a romp. Unless, of course, they're in the mood to cuddle up next to you on the sofa for a good snooze. They're great with kids—tolerant and playful—and they stay that way from puppyhood to old age. They need to get out every day to burn off some of their energy. If they don't, they'll find ways to entertain themselves, maybe "redecorating" your home—and you probably won't like their choices! It's better to channel boxers' energy into play or dog competitions, such as agility, obedience, and flyball (see p. 103).

Boxers are smart, but their intelligence doesn't translate into a willingness to do everything you say. They can be a handful to train, probably because they get bored with repetitious commands. But patience and persistence pay off. Boxers can take on all sorts of roles. They were among the first breeds trained as police dogs in Germany. Today, boxers perform search-and-rescue and guard work and are recruited for police and military service.

Boxers were working dogs, developed in the late 19th century in Germany to have strength and endurance. Like other bull breeds, boxers can trace their ancestry back to warrior dogs from around 2500 B.C. Since the late 1800s, they've been selectively bred to be gentle, happy, and fun-loving pets. Boxers bond with their people, and they want to keep them safe.

POOCH PROS: DOG WALKERS AND SITTERS

Do you enjoy getting outside for some exercise? So do dogs, of course! Plus, they need to go outside so they can "go" (you know, in that way). But sometimes their owners can't take them out because they're at school or at work for long stretches of the day. When that happens, they hire dog walkers to take their pets for a walk or run. Sometimes they even hire dog sitters to stay at their homes and take care of their pets while they're out of town. You don't need formal training to become a dog walker or sitter. Loving dogs and being outside are job requirements, but they aren't the only keys to success. You have to be responsible, taking your four-legged clients out when you said you would—no matter what the weather. You also need a good understanding of dog behavior and body language so you can keep dogs safe around other people and other dogs. If you can check all those boxes, dog walking is a great way to spend time with pups. And it's a job you can have even when you're a kid!

FROM: Germany

HEIGHT: 21–25 inches (53–63 cm)

WEIGHT: 55–71 pounds (25–32 kg)

COAT: Fawn, brindle, with white markings; short, smooth

GROOMING:

EXERCISE NEEDS:

K-9 QUALITIES: Playful and loyal

What's in a name? Some people think "boxer" refers to the **BOXING-LIKE** moves the dogs make with their **FRONT LEGS** when they play.

BULLDOG

These good-natured, amusing dogs are ready to soak up love and happily slobber all over you in return. They adore kids and laid-back lifestyles. Like all dogs, they need exercise. But take a decent walk, and they're ready to plop down next to you for a nap, probably snoring the whole time. These lovable, popular pets have changed a lot from the days when their ferocious ancestors were used in the cruel sport of bullbaiting (the practice of training dogs to attack a tethered bull), which gave the breed its name but was banned in England in 1835. Starting in the dog craze of the late 1800s, breeders selectively bred bulldogs into today's squat, heavily muscled dogs with massive heads, turned-up noses, and slobbery jowls. Though they don't look much like their ancestors, they kept quite a bit of their courage and tenacity. Today, bulldogs are cool canines—literally, they need to be kept cool! Their build can't tolerate heat or excessive exercise, so they need to live in air-conditioned comfort. But that keeps them close to their families, which is where these affectionate dogs want to be.

FROM:	UK/England
HEIGHT:	15–16 inches (38–40 cm)
WEIGHT:	51–55 pounds (23–25 kg)
COAT:	Variety of colors; short, smooth
GROOMING:	
EXERCISE NEEDS:	
K-9 QUALITIES:	Adoring and adorable

OLDE ENGLISH BULLDOGGE

FROM:	U.S.A.
HEIGHT:	16–20 inches (41–51 cm)
WEIGHT:	50–80 pounds (23–36 kg)
COAT:	Variety of colors; short, glossy
GROOMING:	
EXERCISE NEEDS:	
K-9 QUALITIES:	Friendly and strong

If you traveled back to the 19th century to see bulldogs, they'd look like these. But this breed is actually new! Olde English bulldogges were developed in the 1970s to re-create the originals. A bit more athletic than bulldogs (p. 112), they share the same courageous and loving nature and are great family pets.

AMERICAN BULLDOG

Bred from dogs that came to America with early English settlers, American bulldogs are taller and more energetic than their English cousins. They're loyal, affectionate, and entertaining pets, and they do best with good socializing and training to keep them on their best behavior.

FROM:	U.S.A.
HEIGHT:	20–27 inches (51–69 cm)
WEIGHT:	60–125 pounds (27–57 kg)
COAT:	Variety of colors; short, smooth
GROOMING:	
EXERCISE NEEDS:	
K-9 QUALITIES:	Loving and protective

ALAPAHA BLUE BLOOD BULLDOG

FROM:	U.S.A.
HEIGHT:	18–24 inches (46–61 cm)
WEIGHT:	55–90 pounds (25–41 kg)
COAT:	White with colored patches; short
GROOMING:	
EXERCISE NEEDS:	
K-9 QUALITIES:	Protective and affectionate

Historically used to guard plantations in the southern state of Georgia, U.S.A., Alapaha blues retain their protective instincts but are easily trained. In the homes of experienced owners, they're loyal pets that can be active playmates for kids.

Breeder Papa Buck Lane named Alapaha blues after the **ALAPAHA RIVER** in Georgia, U.S.A., and his belief that his beloved dogs were noble. (**"BLUE BLOOD"** refers to noble birth or status.)

BULLMASTIFF

The bullmastiff's name gives away the breed's origins. English gamekeepers in the 1800s crossed mastiffs and bulldogs to help protect large estates from poachers who'd sneak in at night to capture game. This fearless, intelligent, and quick breed, known as the "gamekeeper's night dog," would quietly sneak up on poachers and knock them down, holding them until the gamekeeper arrived the next morning. Even back then, bullmastiffs combined their strength with affection for their people—traits that make them great pets today. They're loyal and devoted to their families, especially kids—though their size makes them better suited for bigger kids. They're less loving toward other pets or neighborhood dogs, so bullmastiffs might not "play nicely" at a dog park. They're also protective of their families, willing to do anything to keep their people safe. Sweet, a bit slobbery, and spirited, they're loyal and loving pets.

FROM:	UK
HEIGHT:	24–27 inches (61–69 cm)
WEIGHT:	90–130 pounds (41–59 kg)
COAT:	Fawn, red, brindle, with black muzzle; short, flat
GROOMING:	
EXERCISE NEEDS:	
K-9 QUALITIES:	Strong-willed but devoted

MASTIFF

"Massives" might be a better name for these enormous dogs, which can easily outweigh many adults. Yes, mastiffs are the largest dog breed by weight—but they're truly gentle giants. They have a noble lineage, tracing their origins back thousands of years, probably to Asia. Loyal guardians throughout the world, mastiff-type dogs were depicted in art in Egyptian monuments from 3000 B.C. Despite a history of working as warriors and guards, mastiffs today are peaceful and affectionate family pets. They're gentle with kids and kitties alike, but their size might be too imposing for young tots. They're not the easiest dogs to keep. They're powerful, a bit stubborn and slobbery, and they eat a lot. But they're loving dogs who'd be happy to snuggle up with you on the couch—if only they'd fit! They're not aggressive, but they'll protect their families. If their big, scary barks don't frighten off troublemakers, their size surely will. With their families, their devotion is super size, just like their bodies.

FROM:	UK
HEIGHT:	28–30 inches (70–77 cm)
WEIGHT:	175–230 pounds (79–104 kg)
COAT:	Fawn, apricot, brindle, with black muzzle; short
GROOMING:	
EXERCISE NEEDS:	
K-9 QUALITIES:	Devoted but a bit stubborn

HEAVYWEIGHTS

A mastiff was one of the passengers on board the **MAYFLOWER**, the famous ship that ferried the **PILGRIMS** from England to North America in 1620. Records show that the dog was brought, along with an English springer spaniel, to guard the **NEW COLONY.**

DOGUE DE BORDEAUX

With roots in France going back at least 600 years, these "DDBs"—relatives of multiple mastiff breeds—guarded estates and hunted big game with the aristocracy. After the French Revolution, from 1789 to 1799, they found new work as farm dogs and butchers' dogs. Strong and stubborn, DDBs (their name is pronounced dohg duh bor-DOH) need experienced owners to consistently train and socialize them. It's worth the effort; they can make loving family pets. But they do need to hang out in air-conditioned comfort.

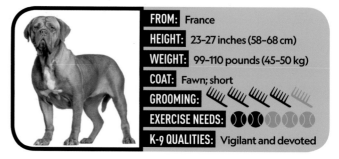

FROM:	France
HEIGHT:	23–27 inches (58–68 cm)
WEIGHT:	99–110 pounds (45–50 kg)
COAT:	Fawn; short
GROOMING:	
EXERCISE NEEDS:	
K-9 QUALITIES:	Vigilant and devoted

NEAPOLITAN MASTIFF

FROM:	Italy
HEIGHT:	24–30 inches (60–75 cm)
WEIGHT:	110–154 pounds (50–70 kg)
COAT:	Variety of colors; short
GROOMING:	
EXERCISE NEEDS:	
K-9 QUALITIES:	Protective and loyal

Few dogs are as imposing as "Neos." With their massive size and intimidating expression, it's no surprise that these mastiffs work as guards, police K-9s, and military dogs. The roles suit them. With roots going back to Roman warrior dogs, Neos have strong protective instincts. In experienced hands, they make loyal companions for grown-ups and older kids. They bond closely to their people—and drool all over them.

⭐ PUP STARS

In the Harry Potter movies, Neapolitan mastiffs played the massive but sweet dog Fang, sidekick to the equally massive but sweet character Rubeus Hagrid. In the books, Fang is described as a boarhound—a term that usually refers to Great Danes—but the Neos got the movie roles. Over the series of movies, seven Neos—Hugo, Bully, Bella, Vito, Luigi, Monkey, and Uno—played Fang.

SAINT MIGUEL CATTLE DOG

FROM:	Portugal/Azores
HEIGHT:	19–24 inches (48–60 cm)
WEIGHT:	44–77 pounds (20–35 kg)
COAT:	Brindle (fawn or gray); short, smooth
GROOMING:	
EXERCISE NEEDS:	
K-9 QUALITIES:	Protective and calm

Quiet and loyal with trusted owners, these intelligent dogs, also known as Azores cattle dogs, herd and guard cattle. They do best as outdoor working dogs, not family pets.

PERRO DE PRESA CANARIO

Bred in the 19th century from bulldog, mastiff, and native breeds, these dogs, also known as by the name dogo Canario, were originally fighting dogs but are natural guardians today. They're a challenge to control and aren't the best choice for pets.

FROM:	Spain/Canary Islands
HEIGHT:	22–26 inches (56–66 cm)
WEIGHT:	88–143 pounds (40–65 kg)
COAT:	Fawn, black, brindle: rough, short
GROOMING:	
EXERCISE NEEDS:	
K-9 QUALITIES:	Strong-willed but loyal

CA DE BOU

FROM:	Spain/Mallorca
HEIGHT:	20–23 inches (52–58 cm)
WEIGHT:	66–84 pounds (30–38 kg)
COAT:	Fawn, black, brindle; short
GROOMING:	
EXERCISE NEEDS:	
K-9 QUALITIES:	Calm and obedient

Dogs like to chill to **CLASSICAL MUSIC.** When researchers played it for dogs in kennels, they **SLEPT** better and **DIDN'T BARK** as much as without it.

Excellent watchdogs, these mastiffs have the courage of their bullbaiting ancestors but aren't the best choice for casual pet owners because of their strength and aggressive instincts. They're also known as Mallorca mastiffs.

SIGHT
HOUNDS

A better name for sight hounds might be "speed hounds." These streamlined dogs are built for running. Their backs are strong and flexible so they can stretch out in cheetah-like strides as their powerful hind legs thrust them forward. At full speed, they carry their slim heads low, making them even more aerodynamic. And they leap through the air, their bodies leaving the ground as they gallop along— which they can do for a remarkably long time. Sight hounds have deep chests, giving plenty of room for their lungs to work and their unusually large hearts to pump oxygen-rich blood to their muscles. No wonder that these speedsters originally were bred to be hunting dogs, running down prey and cornering fast. And, yes, that's where their great eyesight comes in. They use it to follow their prey. Selective breeding over centuries created these dogs, which were favorite hunting dogs of wealthy classes, including sheikhs in the Middle East, ancient Egyptian pharaohs, and Russian tsars. But you don't have to be royalty to own one of these regal dogs today. Some sight hounds, such as greyhounds, are racing dogs, but most are great family pets. Just be sure to keep them on a leash. If they take off after a rabbit, you won't be able to catch them!

BORZOI

Don't let the borzoi's elegant looks fool you. These regal dogs, favorites of the Russian aristocracy from 1650 through the late 1800s, didn't sit around being pampered. They were fearless hunters, capable of taking down a full-grown wolf—and, indeed, they used to be called Russian wolfhounds. Their exact ancestry is uncertain, but some experts believe borzois were developed from Russian bearhounds, coursing hounds, and tall sheepdogs. Others think they're a mix of heavy-coated Russian dogs and Arabian greyhounds. Whatever their origins, they're clearly regal dogs—which put them in danger when revolutions in the early 1900s forced the Russian aristocracy out of power. Luckily, the breed survived around the world, because these speedsters make terrific pets and are great with kids.

FROM:	Russia
HEIGHT:	27–29 inches (69–74 cm)
WEIGHT:	60–105 pounds (27–48 kg)
COAT:	Variety of colors; long, silky
GROOMING:	
EXERCISE NEEDS:	
K-9 QUALITIES:	Gentle and a bit stubborn

SUPREME SPEEDSTERS

Like many sight hounds, **BORZOIS LOVE TO RUN,** and they excel at dog sports, such as lure coursing (chasing fake prey).

AFGHAN HOUND

If any dog were going to beat the borzoi for the "most elegant dog" award, it would be the Afghan hound. With their long, silky hair, these gorgeous dogs are among the most dignified-looking canines. Deep inside, however, they're hunters. Some experts believe Afghan hounds trace their ancestry back centuries to dogs brought by traders to Afghanistan, where tribal chiefs used them to hunt fast-running game. Today, they're calm pets that bond deeply with their families. When raised with kids, they're gentle—but they're not likely to romp around with you!

SUPREME SPEEDSTERS

FROM:	Afghanistan
HEIGHT:	25–29 inches (64–74 cm)
WEIGHT:	50–60 pounds (21–29 kg)
COAT:	Variety of colors; long, silky

GROOMING:
EXERCISE NEEDS:
K-9 QUALITIES: Elegant but mischievous

SALUKI

Elegant salukis are among the world's oldest dog breeds, with ancestry going back to 300 B.C. Genetic evidence shows they're among a small group most closely related to dogs' wolf ancestors, and archaeologists have found mummified Salukis with Sumerian pharaohs in the area that is now southern Iraq. Revered in the Middle East, these dogs were bred to run down hares and gazelles in the harsh, desert terrain. They hunted alongside nomadic companions, who also used falcons. Developed into sprinters, they need to run—but they also love to lounge on the sofa. They're gentle, but not especially playful, pets.

SUPREME SPEEDSTERS

FROM:	Persia (present-day Iran)
HEIGHT:	23–28 inches (58–71 cm)
WEIGHT:	35–65 pounds (16–29 kg)
COAT:	Variety of colors; smooth and silky, feathered

GROOMING:
EXERCISE NEEDS:
K-9 QUALITIES: Independent and calm

IRISH WOLFHOUND

Go big or go home. That could be Irish wolfhounds' motto—except these dogs are both big and serious homebodies! The world's tallest dogs, when they're on their hind legs, they can stretch taller than a lot of adults. But despite their fearsome name and history of hunting wolves in Ireland and Great Britain, they're gentle giants that are all too happy taking over your furniture or swiping dinner off the counter as they walk by.

FROM:	Ireland
HEIGHT:	28–34 inches (71–86 cm)
WEIGHT:	105–150 pounds (48–68 kg)
COAT:	Variety of colors; rough, harsh, wiry
GROOMING:	
EXERCISE NEEDS:	
K-9 QUALITIES:	Loving and mellow

TOWERING HEIGHTS

SCOTTISH DEERHOUND

Scottish deerhounds are shaggier versions of their Celtic cousins, the Irish wolfhounds. Known as far back as the 16th century, they helped the aristocracy hunt deer. Though they're not the most playful, they do enjoy a good run—and then snoozing next to you on the sofa.

FROM:	UK/Scotland
HEIGHT:	28–32 inches (71–81 cm)
WEIGHT:	70–130 pounds (32–59 kg)
COAT:	Blue-gray, red shades, black brindle; thick, harsh, wiry
GROOMING:	
EXERCISE NEEDS:	
K-9 QUALITIES:	Affectionate and sweet

TOWERING HEIGHTS

WHIPPET

FROM: UK
HEIGHT: 17–20 inches (43–51 cm)
WEIGHT: 20–40 pounds (11–18 kg)
COAT: Variety of colors; short, fine
GROOMING:
EXERCISE NEEDS:
K-9 QUALITIES: Beautiful and calm

Developed in the late 18th century from small greyhounds and terriers, whippets were bred to chase down rabbits and vermin, such as rats. Their name derives from a 17th century English word meaning "move briskly." Today, these speedsters—that still enjoy running—are adoring pets who also enjoy a good snuggle.

GREYHOUND

These tall and sleek dogs can hit speeds of 45 miles per hour (72 km/h) and enjoy a good run, but they're perfectly happy lounging around the home. In fact, they're nicknamed the "40-mph couch potato"! Widely thought to trace their origins to the ancient dogs depicted in Egyptian tombs around 4000 B.C., Greyhounds, as we know them today, were actually bred by ancient Celts in eastern Europe or Eurasia around that time.

FROM: UK/England
HEIGHT: 27–30 inches (69–76 cm)
WEIGHT: 60–66 pounds (27–30 kg)
COAT: Variety of colors; short, smooth
GROOMING:
EXERCISE NEEDS:
K-9 QUALITIES: Loving and adaptable

Greyhounds don't just cover ground fast. Some seem to **FLY THROUGH THE AIR!** A greyhound named **CINDERELLA MAY** cleared a jump that was 5 feet 8 inches (172.7 cm) high.

SUPREME SPEEDSTERS

ITALIAN GREYHOUND

These miniature greyhounds have all the heart of their larger relatives—but, like some other toy dogs, are too fragile for rambunctious play. Energetic Italian greyhounds love a good run, but they also love being pampered. So, yes, go ahead and put a sweater on them in the winter. They'll appreciate it.

FROM: Greece, Turkey
HEIGHT: 13–15 inches (33–38 cm)
WEIGHT: 8–10 pounds (4–5 kg)
COAT: Variety of colors; short, soft
GROOMING:
EXERCISE NEEDS:
K-9 QUALITIES: Playful and sweet

WORLD SPEEDSTERS

It's no surprise that people all over the world have developed varieties of swift sight hounds. With their athletic skills and charms, these hounds have been excellent hunting companions throughout the ages. In different regions, these dogs have adapted to different climates and terrain, with some racing across the hot sands and others through forests and plains. Today, most make great pets.

HUNGARIAN GREYHOUND

With ancestors brought to Hungary more than 1,000 years ago, these rugged dogs aren't actually descendants of greyhounds (p. 123) but instead came from a unique mix of scent and sight hounds. A bit more protective than other sight hounds, they're still calm and gentle pets that get along great with kids.

FROM: Hungary
HEIGHT: 24–28 inches (62–70 cm)
WEIGHT: 55–88 pounds (25–40 kg)
COAT: Variety of colors; short, smooth
GROOMING:
EXERCISE NEEDS:
K-9 QUALITIES: Loyal and protective

AZAWAKH

FROM: Mali
HEIGHT: 24–29 inches (60–74 cm)
WEIGHT: 33–55 pounds (15–25 kg)
COAT: Fawn; short
GROOMING:
EXERCISE NEEDS:
K-9 QUALITIES: Loyal and protective

These long-legged speedsters developed in the African Sahara, where they were hunters, guardians, and companions to nomadic desert tribes. Loving toward their families, Azawakhs are the most protective of the sight hounds.

SLOUGHI

These quiet athletes are prized in North Africa, where they were hunting companions to the nomadic Berber people. They're affectionate and loyal dogs that enjoy living at home with their favorite people.

FROM: North Africa
HEIGHT: 24–28 inches (61–72 cm)
WEIGHT: 44–60 pounds (20–27 kg)
COAT: Sandy; short, tough, fine
GROOMING:
EXERCISE NEEDS:
K-9 QUALITIES: Clever and affectionate

POLISH GREYHOUND

FROM:	Poland
HEIGHT:	27–31 inches (68–80 cm)
WEIGHT:	60–80 pounds (27–36 kg)
COAT:	Variety of colors; short
GROOMING:	
EXERCISE NEEDS:	
K-9 QUALITIES:	Strong and protective

The powerful Polish greyhound loves to run. Possibly a mix of greyhound (p. 123) and borzoi (p. 120), these dogs were bred to hunt large birds and wolves. They're loving with their people but more protective and territorial than other sight hounds, so they are better with experienced owners.

SPANISH GREYHOUND

Originally royal hunting dogs, Spanish greyhounds became popular racing and coursing (prey-chasing) dogs. They're descended from dogs brought by Celts to the Iberian Peninsula (the area of Spain and Portugal) around 500 B.C. These rare pups are laid-back pets but not the most playful.

FROM:	Spain
HEIGHT:	23–28 inches (58–72 cm)
WEIGHT:	44–66 pounds (20–30 kg)
COAT:	Variety of colors; smooth or wiry
GROOMING:	
EXERCISE NEEDS:	
K-9 QUALITIES:	Gentle and reserved

RAMPUR GREYHOUND

Fast and powerful, Rampur greyhounds were kept by Indian princes to hunt big game, such as deer, jackals, and wild boars. They probably were developed by crossing greyhounds (p. 123) with native Indian dog breeds. Gentle around their owners' kids, they tend to be one-person dogs and are kept more often as hunting companions than as pets.

In Homer's ancient Greek epic **THE ODYSSEY,** when the hero Odysseus returns home after 10 years, only his faithful greyhound, **ARGUS,** recognizes him.

FROM:	India
HEIGHT:	22–30 inches (56–75 cm)
WEIGHT:	59–66 pounds (27–30 kg)
COAT:	Variety of colors; short
GROOMING:	
EXERCISE NEEDS:	
K-9 QUALITIES:	Powerful and protective

SCENT
HOUNDS

Sight hounds follow prey with their eyes, so scent hounds use ... you guessed it ... their noses! All dogs have a great sense of smell, but scent hounds stand out from the pack. Their super schnozes, packed with smell-detecting sensors, give them an amazing ability to track prey—even if the trail crosses rivers or is several days old. Scent hounds' mouths and ears may help them smell, too! Their long, floppy ears fan smells up to their noses, and their droopy lips hold scent molecules near their sniffers.

Scent hounds aren't as speedy as sight hounds, but they've got great endurance. They trace their origins back to the ancient Greek mastiff-type warrior dogs. Dog historians believe that, thousands of years ago, the Celtic people used mastiff-type dogs with the best senses of smell to help them hunt. They selectively bred the best trackers, creating mastiff-size scent hounds. Over the centuries, some of these scent hounds may have been crossed with sleeker sight hounds, producing lighter, friendlier dogs with better speed and stamina. About a thousand years ago, monks at St. Hubert's monastery in Belgium began to selectively breed scent hounds to create specific good-natured breeds to hunt in packs. As the dogs chased game, they barked so hunters could follow. Since then, scent hounds have become super specialized. Breeders selectively developed them to match the terrain, climate, and game of specific places. The result? Many scent hounds in all shapes and sizes.

THE TALENTED SWISS HOUNDS

A mosaic dating back to when Romans controlled Swiss territory—nearly 2,000 years ago—shows packs of scent hounds that look a lot like today's Swiss hounds, also known as laufhunds. It's not surprising. The Swiss hounds' ancestors are among the world's oldest scent hounds. From the 1400s through the 1700s, Swiss dogs gained a reputation as some of the best tracking dogs in Europe. By the late 1800s, five distinct varieties of Swiss hound were recognized, each developed in a separate Swiss region. They vary by color, but all Swiss hounds are excellent trackers. They're also fond of their families and like to lick, cuddle, and play. Not many are kept as pets, but they fit in well with families if they receive good training and socialization.

FROM: Switzerland
HEIGHT: 18–23 inches (45–59 cm)
WEIGHT: 33–44 pounds (15–20 kg)
COAT: Colors vary by type; short

GROOMING:
EXERCISE NEEDS:
K-9 QUALITIES: Friendly and obedient

BERNESE HOUNDS

Bernese hounds originally come from a French- and German-speaking region in west-central Switzerland.

LUCERNE HOUNDS

Lucerne hounds hail from a German-speaking central Swiss region in the foothills of the Swiss Alps.

ST. HUBERT JURA HOUNDS

St. Hubert Jura hounds share a common history with Bruno Jura hounds but tend to be a bit larger and have smoother coats.

BRUNO JURA HOUNDS

Bruno Jura hounds developed in the northwestern Swiss Jura Mountains region, which borders France.

SCHWYZ HOUNDS

Schwyz hounds were first raised in central Switzerland in a German-speaking region nestled between the Alps and large lakes.

For thousands of years, **HUNTERS** have brought their hounds and horses to **CHURCH.** It's been an annual tradition since the eighth century, when St. Hubert of Liége, the **CHRISTIAN PATRON SAINT** of hunters, blessed the dogs before a hunt.

FANTASTIC FRENCH PACK HOUNDS

Bred from a variety of hounds in the 19th and early 20th centuries, these breeds were developed to hunt in large packs, typically following hunters on horseback. They're loyal and affectionate to their people and are often in outdoor kennels that house packs of 20 to 100 hounds—though they're happy to have you come and visit!

FRENCH TRICOLOR HOUND

The youngest breed of French hounds—developed in the mid-1900s—these athletic pups quickly became the most popular pack hounds in France because of their energy and dedication to hunting.

FROM:	France
HEIGHT:	24–28 inches (60–72 cm)
WEIGHT:	60–77 pounds (27–35 kg)
COAT:	Tricolor; short, fine
GROOMING:	
EXERCISE NEEDS:	
K-9 QUALITIES:	Energetic and intelligent

FRENCH WHITE AND BLACK HOUND

FROM:	France
HEIGHT:	24–28 inches (62–72 cm)
WEIGHT:	57–66 pounds (26–30 kg)
COAT:	White and black with blue speckling; short, dense
GROOMING:	
EXERCISE NEEDS:	
K-9 QUALITIES:	Fast and friendly

These hounds never give up! Descended from foxhounds, they're big and powerful and seem to have endless endurance. It's easy to see why they're growing in popularity in France.

FRENCH WHITE AND ORANGE HOUND

One of the newest French hounds, these outgoing dogs are fairly rare, but they have great personalities. A bit more easygoing than other pack dogs, they may adapt to life as pets if raised in a home from puppyhood—especially if there are other dogs in the house.

FROM:	France
HEIGHT:	24–28 inches (62–70 cm)
WEIGHT:	60–70 pounds (27–32 kg)
COAT:	White and orange; short, fine
GROOMING:	
EXERCISE NEEDS:	
K-9 QUALITIES:	Friendly and energetic

GREAT ANGLO-FRENCH
TRICOLOR HOUND

FROM: France

HEIGHT: 24–28 inches (60–70 cm)

WEIGHT: 66–77 pounds (30–35 kg)

COAT: Tricolor; short, coarse

GROOMING:

EXERCISE NEEDS:

K-9 QUALITIES: Powerful and skilled

Strong and compact, these French hounds are the most closely related to their English cousins, the English foxhounds (p. 133)—and that's probably where they get their stamina. They are friendly but happiest when hunting.

GREAT ANGLO-FRENCH
WHITE AND ORANGE HOUND

Bred in the early 1800s, these hounds live to hunt, and they have the stamina to keep at it. Though they're good-natured, they don't settle well into a typical home life with a family. They love to run with their packs.

FROM: France

HEIGHT: 24–28 inches (60–70 cm)

WEIGHT: 76–78 pounds (34–35 kg)

COAT: White and orange; short, thin, sleek

GROOMING:

EXERCISE NEEDS:

K-9 QUALITIES: Energetic and friendly

GREAT ANGLO-FRENCH
WHITE AND BLACK HOUND

Rarely kept as pets, these big, energetic dogs have been hunting big game since the 1800s. They're active and sweet, but they still prefer their canine packs to domestic life.

FROM: France

HEIGHT: 24–28 inches (62–72 cm)

WEIGHT: 66–77 pounds (30–35 kg)

COAT: White and black; short

GROOMING:

EXERCISE NEEDS:

K-9 QUALITIES: Loyal and athletic

The "great" in these breeds' names means they were bred to take down great **BIG ANIMALS**—not that the dogs themselves are great in size. But they're definitely great **PACK DOGS!**

BILLY

These rare pack dogs—valued for their speed on the hunt—are so easygoing and friendly that they also make gentle, kid-loving pets. But you better be ready to play—they have boundless energy! The breed's name may seem unusual (for dogs), but it refers to the Château de Billy, a castle in central France where they were bred in the late 1800s.

FROM: France
HEIGHT: 21–28 inches (53–70 cm)
WEIGHT: 55–73 pounds (25–33 kg)
COAT: White with mottling; short, harsh
GROOMING:
EXERCISE NEEDS:
K–9 QUALITIES: Brave and outgoing

GASÇON-SAINTONGEOIS

These rare but skillful deer hunters (whose name is pronounced gas-CON san-tong-wah) are also calm and affectionate. They make some of the best family dogs of the hunting breeds.

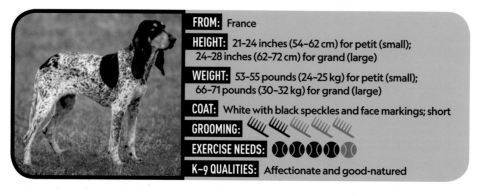

FROM: France
HEIGHT: 21–24 inches (54–62 cm) for petit (small); 24–28 inches (62–72 cm) for grand (large)
WEIGHT: 53–55 pounds (24–25 kg) for petit (small); 66–71 pounds (30–32 kg) for grand (large)
COAT: White with black speckles and face markings; short
GROOMING:
EXERCISE NEEDS:
K–9 QUALITIES: Affectionate and good-natured

GRAND GRIFFON VENDÉEN

The oldest and largest of the griffon Vendéen breeds, with roots going back to the 16th century, these good-natured dogs are skilled hunters and friendly family companions for experienced dog owners. (Their name is pronounced gron gree-FOHN vehn-DAY-uhn).

FROM: France
HEIGHT: 24–27 inches (60–68 cm)
WEIGHT: 66–77 pounds (30–35 kg)
COAT: Fawn, white and orange, black and white, black and tan, tricolor; coarse, bushy
GROOMING:
EXERCISE NEEDS:
K–9 QUALITIES: Intelligent and independent

GRAND BLEU DE GASCOGNE

With ancestry as old as any hunting dog, these large pups are excellent trackers that can sniff out even the faintest trail. They're completely focused on hunting and are happiest as pack dogs. With lots of training, they may be raised as pets in homes (with large yards).

FROM: France
HEIGHT: 24–28 inches (60–70 cm)
WEIGHT: 73–88 pounds (33–40 kg)
COAT: Blue with black patches and tan markings; short, thick
GROOMING:
EXERCISE NEEDS:
K-9 QUALITIES: Athletic and friendly

The Marquis de Lafayette, a French **ARISTOCRAT** and military officer who fought in the American Revolution, gave a pack of seven grand bleu de Gascogne hounds to **GEORGE WASHINGTON.** Washington said the dogs' deep howls reminded him of **BELLS.**

ENGLISH FOXHOUND

Popular in the 1700s and 1800s, these skillful hunting dogs historically were pack dogs. But these days, they also love living with active families, where they can play with kids (and, possibly, bark a lot to tell everyone how much fun they're having). Many hunting dog breeds have English foxhound ancestry.

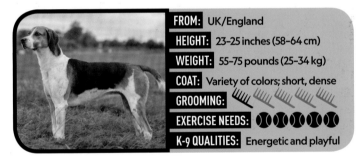

FROM: UK/England
HEIGHT: 23–25 inches (58–64 cm)
WEIGHT: 55–75 pounds (25–34 kg)
COAT: Variety of colors; short, dense
GROOMING:
EXERCISE NEEDS:
K-9 QUALITIES: Energetic and playful

OTTERHOUND

FROM: UK/England
HEIGHT: 24–27 inches (61–69 cm)
WEIGHT: 66–115 pounds (30–52 kg)
COAT: Variety of colors; rough, shaggy
GROOMING:
EXERCISE NEEDS:
K-9 QUALITIES: Affectionate and energetic

These rare dogs, which really did hunt otters until the sport was banned, are big, mischievous, and messy. But they're also good-natured, playful, and friendly pets. They need a lot of exercise so they don't get into too much mischief.

BLOODHOUND

With their amazing sense of smell, bloodhounds can pick up a scent that's several days old and follow the trail long distances over any terrain and in any weather.

When they put their noses to the ground, their wrinkly skin and droopy ears flop forward, forming a cup around their nostrils, which may help trap scent particles. With up to 300 million scent receptors in their noses—60 times the amount humans have—bloodhounds are at least a thousand times better than people at distinguishing scents. Their long necks and muscular shoulders allow them to keep their noses on a trail for miles. Prized by search-and-rescue teams and police, bloodhounds' findings are accepted as evidence in courts of law. Yes, they're that good!

Just why they're named bloodhounds is a matter of debate. It may, indeed, be because of their amazing ability to follow a "blood scent," meaning living creatures (bleeding or not). But it also may refer to these dogs' long history of having their bloodlines recorded. Bloodhounds trace their heritage to the first scent hounds developed by the monks at St. Hubert's monastery in Belgium—and they're still sometimes called St. Hubert hounds. William the Conqueror, king of England from 1066 to 1087, brought some of those hounds to Britain, and they became the ancestors of today's bloodhounds.

Bloodhounds may be great police K-9 dogs, but it's only because of their tracking abilities. They're way too sweet to be good guards! It's that gentle, friendly nature that makes them excellent family pets—if you can handle a large, clumsy, drooling dog. Adult bloodhounds are calm and trustworthy arounds kids, whom they love, but they're not particularly playful. Though they live inside, they also need secure yards for exercise. If bored, they'll get into mischief—and, trust us, you don't want that!

HERO HOUNDS

It was 1909, and ace police detective Nick Carter was investigating a suspicious barn fire in Kentucky, U.S.A. Police suspected foul play, but the barn had burned to the ground four days earlier, making evidence hard to find. That didn't stop Nick Carter. He circled around the charred ruins. Then, suddenly, he lifted his tail and took off. Nick Carter was no ordinary officer; he was a police bloodhound! Named after a fictional detective in popular crime novels, the determined detective followed a trail for a mile (1.6 km) to a farmhouse, where the arsonist was hiding. Nick Carter got his man! It was one of more than 650 finds the bloodhound made. Nick Carter's tracking ability was so legendary that crowds would gather to watch him work. Over his career, he sent 126 criminals to jail.

Bloodhounds have been known to **FOLLOW TRAILS** for more than 130 miles (209 km).

FROM: UK, Belgium

HEIGHT: 23–27 inches (58–69 cm)

WEIGHT: 79–110 pounds (36–50 kg)

COAT: Black on tan, liver and tan; smooth, short

GROOMING:

EXERCISE NEEDS:

K-9 QUALITIES: Sweet but slightly stubborn

TENACIOUS NORTH AMERICAN COONHOUNDS

Despite their specialized name, coonhounds are versatile hunters. Better yet, most are great pets that adore kids. Though they're sweet, loyal dogs, they can be noisy. Proper socialization and training can keep the barking down and help them get along with—instead of hunt—your kitty. These canines should also be given jobs, such as training for dog competitions, to keep them happy.

BLACK AND TAN COONHOUND

Famous for their "cold noses"— their skill at following old trails with barely any scent left—these adaptable hounds are mainly kept as hunting companions. But they're just as happy tracking you around your house.

FROM:	U.S.A.
HEIGHT:	23–27 inches (58–69 cm)
WEIGHT:	51–75 pounds (23–34 kg)
COAT:	Black with tan markings; short, shiny
GROOMING:	
EXERCISE NEEDS:	
K-9 QUALITIES:	Friendly and happy

REDBONE COONHOUND

FROM:	U.S.A.
HEIGHT:	21–27 inches (53–69 cm)
WEIGHT:	46–71 pounds (21–32 kg)
COAT:	Red; short, smooth, glossy
GROOMING:	
EXERCISE NEEDS:	
K-9 QUALITIES:	Easygoing and versatile

Bred in the American South, especially Georgia and Tennessee, and named after Peter Redbone, an early Tennessee breeder, these fast, agile hounds can follow hot or cold trails through swamplands or over hilly, rocky terrain. They're loyal and loving family pets that like to show off their skills in dog sports.

BLUETICK COONHOUND

Developed in the 1700s from English foxhounds and grand bleu de Gascogne dogs, these hounds make playful pets, but they need jobs to do, such as training for dog competitions. The name "bluetick" comes from their distinctive markings.

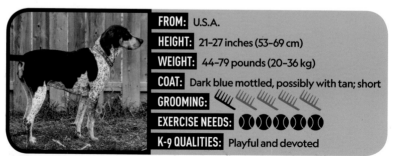

FROM:	U.S.A.
HEIGHT:	21–27 inches (53–69 cm)
WEIGHT:	44–79 pounds (20–36 kg)
COAT:	Dark blue mottled, possibly with tan; short
GROOMING:	
EXERCISE NEEDS:	
K-9 QUALITIES:	Playful and devoted

TREEING WALKER COONHOUND

FROM:	U.S.A.
HEIGHT:	20–27 inches (51–68 cm)
WEIGHT:	51–71 pounds (23–32 kg)
COAT:	Tricolor, white, black, with markings; short, smooth
GROOMING:	
EXERCISE NEEDS:	
K-9 QUALITIES:	Loving and high-energy

Descended from the earliest American (p. 138) and English foxhounds (p. 133) brought to America, these popular dogs are named for their ability to chase animals up trees and for the Walker family, who developed them. They love people and can be great pets and playmates for kids.

AMERICAN ENGLISH COONHOUND

These tireless and speedy hounds were developed from the English foxhounds (p. 133) and other scent hounds brought by European colonists so they could follow hot or cold trails over rough terrain. Fond of barking and howling, these strong-willed hounds need patient training, but they can be loyal pets.

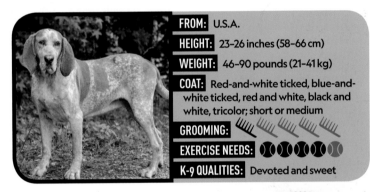

FROM:	U.S.A.
HEIGHT:	23–26 inches (58–66 cm)
WEIGHT:	46–90 pounds (21–41 kg)
COAT:	Red-and-white ticked, blue-and-white ticked, red and white, black and white, tricolor; short or medium
GROOMING:	
EXERCISE NEEDS:	
K-9 QUALITIES:	Devoted and sweet

PLOTT

Developed in the 1750s in the Great Smoky Mountains by the Plott family, these versatile hounds—whose ancestry includes boar-hunting Hanoverian scent hounds (p. 167)—are as happy being part of family life as they are hunting.

FROM:	U.S.A.
HEIGHT:	20–25 inches (51–64 cm)
WEIGHT:	40–60 pounds (18–27 kg)
COAT:	Brindle; short
GROOMING:	
EXERCISE NEEDS:	
K-9 QUALITIES:	Sweet but fearless

In International Falls, Minnesota, U.S.A., it is **ILLEGAL FOR A CAT TO CHASE A DOG** up a telephone pole.

ADAPTABLE NORTH AMERICAN HOUNDS AND CURS

Among the American hounds are curs, versatile "treeing hounds" that were developed to chase their prey up trees. Like foxhounds, many curs "sing out" while trailing other animals. But curs aren't just hunters. These adaptable working dogs are also favorites on farms and ranches, and they make great pets, too.

AMERICAN FOXHOUND

One of the oldest American breeds—possibly even the first—these energetic pack dogs were developed in the mid-1600s in the American colonies. These rare dogs are loving and devoted pets, but they love to—actually, need to—run, so you might want to take up jogging.

FROM: U.S.A.

HEIGHT: 21–25 inches (53–64 cm)

WEIGHT: 40–66 pounds (18–30 kg)

COAT: Tricolor, and variety of other colors; short, close, hard

GROOMING:

EXERCISE NEEDS:

K-9 QUALITIES: Sweet and speedy

AMERICAN LEOPARD HOUND

FROM: U.S.A.

HEIGHT: 21–27 inches (53–69 cm)

WEIGHT: 35–75 pounds (16–34 kg)

COAT: Black, blue, brown, gray, red, yellow, possibly with markings; short, coarse or fine

GROOMING:

EXERCISE NEEDS:

K-9 QUALITIES: Affectionate and protective

One of the oldest treeing dog breeds in the Americas, some of these hounds' ancestors may have arrived in the Americas with Spanish conquistadors. Super sweet and loving toward their people, they're also protective of kids in their families.

TREEING TENNESSEE BRINDLE

These dogs were developed in the 1960s from brindle-coated curs found from the Appalachian Mountains to the Ozark Mountains. These sweet dogs are active and friendly. They love their families and even other dogs.

FROM: U.S.A.

HEIGHT: 16–24 inches (41–61 cm)

WEIGHT: 30–50 pounds (14–23 kg)

COAT: Brindle, black with brindle, possibly with white markings; short, smooth

GROOMING:

EXERCISE NEEDS:

K-9 QUALITIES: Loving and smart

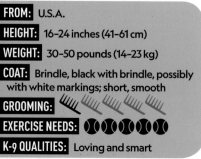

CATAHOULA LEOPARD DOG

FROM: U.S.A.

HEIGHT: 20–26 inches (51–66 cm)

WEIGHT: 50–90 pounds (23–41 kg)

COAT: Black, blue, brindle, chocolate, red, white, yellow, variety of merle; short to medium, tight

GROOMING:

EXERCISE NEEDS:

K-9 QUALITIES: Skilled and loyal

These versatile curs can have blue, green, brown, or amber eyes. Sometimes, each eye is a different color or even two colors! Catahoulas are mainly working dogs, but they're happy as pets, too. Affectionate and protective, they're better playmates for older kids.

BLACK MOUTH CUR

These curs, developed in the American South from hunting and herding dogs, are all-purpose working dogs and companions. With sweet and loyal personalities, they're great with kids of all ages as long as they're raised together, but maybe not with cats.

FROM: U.S.A.

HEIGHT: 16–25 inches (41–64 cm)

WEIGHT: 45–95 pounds (20–43 kg)

COAT: Red, yellow, fawn, buckskin (cream to red), brindle; short, dense

GROOMING:

EXERCISE NEEDS:

K-9 QUALITIES: Gentle and protective

MOUNTAIN CUR

These pioneer dogs, bred from various European hunting dogs and native dogs, protected American settlers and their livestock from wild animals or intruders. They were so important to settlers' survival that puppies rode in wagons or on pack animals—the horses, mules, and oxen that carried supplies—to keep the pups safe. These curs are tough guardians but not the best choice for family pet.

FROM: U.S.A.

HEIGHT: 18–26 inches (46–66 cm)

WEIGHT: 30–60 pounds (16–29 kg)

COAT: Black, blue, brindle, brown, red, yellow; short

GROOMING:

EXERCISE NEEDS:

K-9 QUALITIES: Courageous and protective

★ PUP STARS

The famous—but very sad—1957 movie *Old Yeller* stars a black mouth cur named Spike. The canine actor almost didn't get the role as Old Yeller, a dog who risks his life to save his family. Spike was too goofy and playful! But with extra training, he nailed the dramatic role and became a star.

DIVERSE CENTRAL EUROPEAN HUNTING HOUNDS

Throughout central Europe, many breeds of scent hounds were developed to hunt a variety of game in forests and mountainous regions, sometimes in harsh climates. In Germany and Austria, hounds known as brackes often have an ancestry that includes sight hounds as well as scent hounds.

POLISH HOUND

Popular in Poland, where their ancestors hunted alongside nobility as far back as the Middle Ages, these energetic working dogs are rare elsewhere. But they're affectionate with their families, especially kids, so they could be good pets for active owners.

FROM: Poland
HEIGHT: 22–26 inches (55–65 cm)
WEIGHT: 44–71 pounds (20–32 kg)
COAT: Black on fawn; short to medium
GROOMING:
EXERCISE NEEDS:
K-9 QUALITIES: Athletic and protective

AUSTRIAN BLACK AND TAN HOUND

FROM: Austria
HEIGHT: 19–22 inches (48–56 cm)
WEIGHT: 33–51 pounds (15–23 kg)
COAT: Black and tan; thick, short, smooth
GROOMING:
EXERCISE NEEDS:
K-9 QUALITIES: Energetic and skillful

Comfortable chasing foxes and rabbits in the high mountains, these rare hounds have reddish tan markings, giving them the nickname "fire hounds" (or "brandlbracke"). Though they're good natured, these dogs are kept as hunting companions, not pets.

STYRIAN COARSE-HAIRED MOUNTAIN HOUND

Developed by crossing Hanoverian scent hounds (p. 167) and Istrian wire-haired hounds (p. 145), these agile dogs are adapted to hunt in the steep, rugged mountains of Austria and Slovenia. They're also good-natured pets that get along well with older kids—but probably not your cat.

FROM: Austria
HEIGHT: 18–21 inches (45–53 cm)
WEIGHT: 33–40 pounds (15–18 kg)
COAT: Fawn, red, maybe with white on chest; rough, coarse
GROOMING:
EXERCISE NEEDS:
K-9 QUALITIES: Calm and protective

TYROLEAN HOUND

FROM:	Austria
HEIGHT:	16–20 inches (41–51 cm)
WEIGHT:	35–60 pounds (16–27 kg)
COAT:	Red, black and tan, tricolor; short, thick
GROOMING:	
EXERCISE NEEDS:	
K-9 QUALITIES:	Friendly and energetic

Evolved to hunt in high mountainous regions, these athletic dogs trace their ancestry to ancient Celtic hounds, bloodhounds, and foxhounds. Excellent at tracking game, they're mainly kept as hunting companions.

TRANSYLVANIAN HOUND

Tracing their heritage back 1,000 years, these capable hunting dogs were favorites of Hungarian royalty. Mainly known as hunting dogs, these sweet pups can also be loyal and protective family pets.

FROM:	Hungary
HEIGHT:	22–26 inches (56–65 cm)
WEIGHT:	55–77 pounds (25–35 kg)
COAT:	Black with tan markings; short, coarse
GROOMING:	
EXERCISE NEEDS:	
K-9 QUALITIES:	Friendly and watchful

SLOVENSKY KOPOV

These hunting dogs, with excellent senses of direction and smell, originated in the forests and foothills of central European mountain regions hundreds of years ago. Known also as Black Forest hounds, they're kept as hunting dogs, not pets.

FROM:	Slovakia
HEIGHT:	16–20 inches (41–51 cm)
WEIGHT:	33–44 pounds (15–20 kg)
COAT:	Black with tan markings; short, coarse
GROOMING:	
EXERCISE NEEDS:	
K-9 QUALITIES:	Athletic and independent

Dogs may **"TELL TIME"** by tracking how scents change throughout the day.

MAKING SENSE OF CANINE SENSES

Dogs have amazing senses. But of all of them, smell is supreme. Just as we rely on sight to figure out our surroundings, dogs sniff their way through their world.

SMELL

Dogs' incredible noses help them tell the difference among a staggering number of scents and smell things that we can't detect (like changes in your body chemicals that happen when you're sad or afraid). They draw in scents by breathing in through the front of their nostrils but out through slits on the sides, making air swirl around them. Even the moist, spongy outside of their noses helps trap scents! Inside their noses, they have up to 300 million scent receptors—60 times the amount we have—and, compared to us, they use a relatively larger part of their brains to make sense of scents.

TASTE

Despite that long tongue, dogs don't have a particularly good sense of taste compared to humans. They have about 2,000 taste detectors on their tongues, so they can tell the difference between sweet, sour, bitter, and salty. But with 9,000 taste detectors on our tongues, we're much better at it!

SIGHT

Dogs see better at night than we do—especially if something moves—but not as well during the day. They don't see as much detail or as many colors as humans do; their visual world is made of mainly grays, blues, and yellows.

TOUCH

Though dogs have touch receptors all over their bodies, they explore the tactile world through their mouths and muzzles. Their paws aren't that sensitive—good thing, since they walk on them.

HEARING

Dogs don't have superhuman hearing, but they do beat us in a couple of key areas. They can hear sounds much higher—even two octaves higher—than we can, so the high pitch of a dog whistle or mouse squeak gets their attention. They can also detect where a sound comes from better than we can.

THE SKILLED HOUNDS OF SOUTHERN EUROPE

In mountains and valleys throughout southern Europe, determined and agile hounds were developed as hunting dogs, able to handle any terrain. Most of these hounds are happy to remain working dogs and hunting companions, but with their devoted and sweet natures, more and more are becoming pets, content at home with their people.

SEGUGIO ITALIANO

Used for centuries to find wild boars for hunters, these good-natured Italian hounds are both fast sprinters and endurance runners. They're also quickly becoming popular family pets in their homeland because of their good nature. (Their name is pronounced si-GOO-djo ih-tahl-YAH-no.)

FROM:	Italy
HEIGHT:	19–23 inches (48–59 cm)
WEIGHT:	40–62 pounds (18–28 kg)
COAT:	Red, wheaten, black and tan; short and smooth or rough and wiry
GROOMING:	
EXERCISE NEEDS:	
K-9 QUALITIES:	Sweet and active

BOSNIAN COARSE-HAIRED HOUND

FROM:	Bosnia and Herzegovina
HEIGHT:	18–22 inches (45–56 cm)
WEIGHT:	35–55 pounds (16–25 kg)
COAT:	Black or gray on red or yellow, tricolor; long, wiry
GROOMING:	
EXERCISE NEEDS:	
K-9 QUALITIES:	Friendly and gentle

Descended from native dogs crossed with Italian hunting dogs, these loyal canines—previously called Illyrian hounds—are valued hunting dogs in their homeland but are rare elsewhere. They're affectionate toward their owners but not kept as pets. Their shaggy coats protect them from extremely cold weather.

Dogs have different **SNIFFING TACTICS—** sometimes sniffing the air, sometimes tracking along the ground. Newer scents are easier to pick up in the air.

ISTRIAN WIRE-HAIRED HOUND

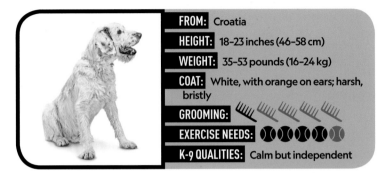

FROM: Croatia

HEIGHT: 18–23 inches (46–58 cm)

WEIGHT: 35–53 pounds (16–24 kg)

COAT: White, with orange on ears; harsh, bristly

GROOMING:

EXERCISE NEEDS:

K-9 QUALITIES: Calm but independent

Hailing from northwest Croatia's Istrian Peninsula, the largest peninsula in the Adriatic Sea, these hounds are determined hunters. They're lively in the field but, with good training and socialization, calm and gentle at home, where they can be patient playmates for kids.

ISTRIAN SMOOTH-COATED HOUND

Some of the oldest hounds found in the Balkans region of southeastern Europe, these all-purpose working dogs—originally bred to hunt foxes and hares—are mainly kept as hunting companions. But with their calm and good nature, they also settle in well as pets and get along great with kids.

FROM: Croatia

HEIGHT: 17–22 inches (44–56 cm)

WEIGHT: 31–44 pounds (14–20 kg)

COAT: White with orange markings; short, smooth

GROOMING:

EXERCISE NEEDS:

K-9 QUALITIES: Gentle and loyal

POSAVAC HOUND

FROM: Croatia

HEIGHT: 18–23 inches (46–58 cm)

WEIGHT: 35–53 pounds (16–24 kg)

COAT: Reddish wheaten with white markings; short, dense, straight

GROOMING:

EXERCISE NEEDS:

K-9 QUALITIES: Devoted and calm

These hounds have excellent stamina for hunting but also make gentle family pets and pals for kids—as long as their exercise needs are met. Their name means "scent hound from the Sava Valley."

SERBIAN HOUND

With ancestry going back a thousand years to early scent hounds in the Balkans, these friendly pack dogs will pursue any game, but they also make good watchdogs. At home, they're also energetic and friendly buddies for active families.

FROM: Serbia

HEIGHT: 17-22 inches (44-56 cm)

WEIGHT: 44-55 pounds (20-25 kg)

COAT: Black on tan; short, smooth

GROOMING:

EXERCISE NEEDS:

K-9 QUALITIES: Good-natured and protective

MONTENEGRIN MOUNTAIN HOUND

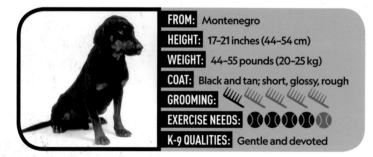

FROM: Montenegro

HEIGHT: 17-21 inches (44-54 cm)

WEIGHT: 44-55 pounds (20-25 kg)

COAT: Black and tan; short, glossy, rough

GROOMING:

EXERCISE NEEDS:

K-9 QUALITIES: Gentle and devoted

A rare breed from the Balkan Mountains, these hounds—sometimes called simply black hounds and formerly known as Yugoslavian mountain hounds—are capable hunters. But it's their calm and affectionate personalities that have made them valued as family pets.

SERBIAN TRICOLOR HOUND

Originally considered a variety of other Serbian scent hounds, these gentle dogs have been considered a separate breed since the mid-1900s. They're skilled hunters and sweet family dogs that are devoted to their people.

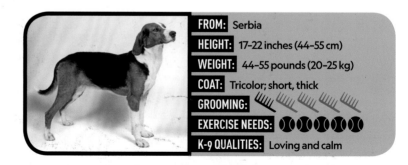

FROM: Serbia

HEIGHT: 17-22 inches (44-55 cm)

WEIGHT: 44-55 pounds (20-25 kg)

COAT: Tricolor; short, thick

GROOMING:

EXERCISE NEEDS:

K-9 QUALITIES: Loving and calm

HELLENIC HOUND

FROM: Greece

HEIGHT: 18–22 inches (45–55 cm)

WEIGHT: 37–44 pounds (17–20 kg)

COAT: Black and tan; short, smooth

GROOMING:

EXERCISE NEEDS:

K-9 QUALITIES: Outgoing and confident

With a heritage going back thousands of years to the scent hounds of ancient Greece, these rare working dogs are great trackers and can be great pets for experienced owners willing to put in the effort to train the strong-willed hounds.

SPANISH HOUND

Originating hundreds of years ago in the northern mountains of the Iberian Peninsula (the area of Spain and Portugal), these dogs, also known by the name sabueso Español, originally hunted all kinds of game, but now they specialize in tracking hares. Mainly kept as working dogs, their loving and devoted nature make them affectionate pets, happy to play with kids.

FROM: Spain

HEIGHT: 19–22 inches (48–57 cm)

WEIGHT: 44–55 pounds (20–25 kg)

COAT: White and orange; short, smooth

GROOMING:

EXERCISE NEEDS:

K-9 QUALITIES: Determined and strong-willed

FINNISH HOUND

Bred in the 1800s from French, German, and Swedish scent hounds, these pups—the most popular hunting dogs in Finland—can trail game for hours through deep snow and forests and then curl up next to their people at home.

FROM: Finland

HEIGHT: 20–24 inches (52–61 cm)

WEIGHT: 46–55 pounds (21–25 kg)

COAT: Tricolor; short, straight

GROOMING:

EXERCISE NEEDS:

K-9 QUALITIES: Affectionate and sociable

Ever see a dog **SPIN IN A CIRCLE** before settling down for a nap? It's part of their heritage, a **NESTING BEHAVIOR** that goes back to their wild ancestors.

FROM: Zimbabwe

HEIGHT: 24–27 inches (61–69 cm)

WEIGHT: 64–90 pounds (29–41 kg)

COAT: Red to wheaten, with small white markings; short, sleek

GROOMING:

EXERCISE NEEDS:

K-9 QUALITIES: Affectionate and smart

For years, **LEGENDS** about Rhodesian ridgebacks claimed that they actually had a **TRACE OF LION** in their background. (They don't.)

RHODESIAN RIDGEBACK

It's easy to pick out a "ridgie" from a pack. It's the one with the racing stripe running all the way down its backbone!

The hair along their spines sticks up because it points forward, the opposite direction from the rest of their coats. We can't say for sure that the cool look gives these dogs their confidence, but know this: They're not even afraid of lions! In fact, Rhodesian ridgebacks are also known as African lion hounds. They were developed in the early 18th century, when European settlers arriving in southern Africa needed versatile dogs that could hunt, protect them and their livestock, and handle the tough climate. So they crossed their own dogs—including mastiffs, greyhounds (p. 123), bloodhounds (p. 134), terriers, and Great Danes (p. 106)—with the native Khoekhoe peoples' dogs, which had ridges. The resulting dogs were hardy, smart, and brave enough to face down lions. The "Rhodesian" part of their name comes from the southern African state of Rhodesia—now called Zimbabwe—where they developed.

Don't let their "tough guy" image fool you. Ridgies are good-natured and affectionate family dogs that love to run, hike, or play with kids—though their size may make them better for older kids. They have a natural instinct to protect their families, and they need good obedience training, socialization, and exercise to be on their best behavior.

POOCH PROS: TRAINERS

If you love teaching dogs new tricks, then a career as a professional dog trainer may be for you. Most trainers don't actually spend their time teaching dogs to roll over or play dead. They use positive training—praise and treats—to teach dogs good manners, such as sitting or coming when called. A lot of the time, trainers teach dog owners how to train their own pets, or they work with families to correct bad habits that poorly trained dogs have learned. But some trainers specialize in teaching working dogs how to do their jobs, such as sniffing out illegal substances or guiding blind people. And a few teach dogs how to be actors in movies or TV shows! Many dog trainers learn on the job by working with more experienced trainers, but trainers can also become certified by a professional organization, such as the Certification Council for Professional Dog Trainers or the International Association of Animal Behavior Consultants, if they can demonstrate a certain level of experience, knowledge, and skill. The best place to start, of course, is by training your own pet!

HARDY SCANDINAVIAN HOUNDS

Scandinavia—the region that includes the countries of Norway, Sweden, and Denmark—has extremely varied climates and terrain, with lakes, mountains, forests, and coastlines. It takes hardy dogs to handle these extremes, and several hound breeds—often known as stövares (pronounced stuh-var-uh) in Sweden and støvers (stoh-ver) in Norway—have been developed to hunt in these lands.

HALDEN HOUND

Looking like a short version of the American foxhound, these medium-size hounds originated in southeastern Norway, where they love running through snow or romping with kids in their families. Valued as both hunting companions and pets in their homeland, they're rare elsewhere.

FROM:	Norway
HEIGHT:	20–24 inches (50–60 cm)
WEIGHT:	40–55 pounds (18–25 kg)
COAT:	White with black patches; short
GROOMING:	
EXERCISE NEEDS:	
K-9 QUALITIES:	Affectionate and athletic

HYGEN HOUND

FROM:	Norway
HEIGHT:	19–23 inches (47–58 cm)
WEIGHT:	44–55 pounds (20–25 kg)
COAT:	Black and tan, red-brown or yellow-red, with white markings; dense, harsh, shiny
GROOMING:	
EXERCISE NEEDS:	
K-9 QUALITIES:	Loyal and protective

Developed in the 1800s from multiple scent hounds, these lively dogs (whose name is pronounced HEE-gen) have the stamina to run across Arctic terrain for long periods. They bond with all members of a family, but they're suspicious of strangers.

NORWEGIAN HOUND

Descended from Norwegian and Russian hare hounds in the early 1800s, these beautiful hounds—also known as Dunkers, after Norwegian Captain Wilhelm Conrad Dunker, who first bred them—can tolerate the extreme cold. At home, they're affectionate pets, always up for playing with kids.

FROM:	Norway
HEIGHT:	19–22 inches (47–55 cm)
WEIGHT:	35–51 pounds (16–23 kg)
COAT:	Blue marbled with fawn and white markings, tricolor; dense, straight, harsh
GROOMING:	
EXERCISE NEEDS:	
K-9 QUALITIES:	Loving and calm

HAMILTONSTÖVARE

FROM: Sweden
HEIGHT: 18–24 inches (46–60 cm)
WEIGHT: 51–60 pounds (23–27 kg)
COAT: Tricolor; dense, short, flat
GROOMING:
EXERCISE NEEDS:
K-9 QUALITIES: Loyal and protective

These hounds—mixes of English fox-hounds and various German hounds—are Sweden's most popular hounds. They're not just skilled hunting companions and watchdogs, they're also devoted pets that love kids.

SCHILLERSTÖVARE

Developed in the late 1800s by crossing local Swedish dogs with English hounds, these rare, athletic dogs are the fastest Scandinavian hounds, even over snow. They tend to bond more strongly to one person, so they aren't the perfect family pets. (They will tolerate the rest of the family, though.)

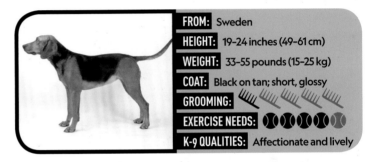

FROM: Sweden
HEIGHT: 19–24 inches (49–61 cm)
WEIGHT: 33–55 pounds (15–25 kg)
COAT: Black on tan; short, glossy
GROOMING:
EXERCISE NEEDS:
K-9 QUALITIES: Affectionate and lively

SMALAND HOUND

Believed to be the oldest scent hound breed native to Sweden, these hounds—bred from a variety of hounds and spitz-type dogs in the 16th century—are named for a forested region in southern Sweden. Popular hunting dogs (whose name is pronounce SMO-lon), they are also devoted and protective pets that do best with active families.

FROM: Sweden
HEIGHT: 17–21 inches (42–54 cm)
WEIGHT: 33–44 pounds (15–20 kg)
COAT: Black and tan; thick, shiny
GROOMING:
EXERCISE NEEDS:
K-9 QUALITIES: Gentle and watchful

Dogs caught getting into **MISCHIEF** may "look guilty." But that hangdog look is actually just a reaction to you being **UPSET** and their attempt to patch things up.

EUROPEAN HARE HUNTERS AND SHAGGY HOUNDS

Among the countless hounds originally bred to hunt in western Europe, some look strikingly similar, while others are definite individuals. Among the look-alikes are breeds that resemble supersized beagles—or downsized English foxhounds—bred originally to hunt hares and other small game. Among the most unusual breeds are the varied griffons, shaggy hounds with deep ancestries. What do they have in common? They're friendly, versatile dogs that make affectionate pets.

HARRIER

The name of these highly energetic hounds—whose background is uncertain—gives away their original prey: hares. Today, these sweet hounds make great companions for active owners.

FROM:	UK/England
HEIGHT:	19–22 inches (48–55 cm)
WEIGHT:	42–60 pounds (19–27 kg)
COAT:	White with black and tan markings; dense, short, hard
GROOMING:	
EXERCISE NEEDS:	
K-9 QUALITIES:	Affectionate and energetic

BEAGLE HARRIER

FROM:	France
HEIGHT:	18–20 inches (46–50 cm)
WEIGHT:	42–46 pounds (19–21 kg)
COAT:	Tricolor; thick, short
GROOMING:	
EXERCISE NEEDS:	
K-9 QUALITIES:	Devoted and calm

These hounds, which fall between harriers and beagles in size, have been around at least since the late 1800s in France. Excellent trackers, they're also affectionate family dogs.

BLUE GASCONY GRIFFON

Their shaggy coat isn't just fashionable; it protects them from bad weather. A versatile hunting companion—descended from other griffons—they have good stamina and also make devoted family dogs.

FROM:	France
HEIGHT:	19–22 inches (48–57 cm)
WEIGHT:	36–40 pounds (17–18 kg)
COAT:	Slate blue with black and tan markings; shaggy, harsh
GROOMING:	
EXERCISE NEEDS:	
K-9 QUALITIES:	Affectionate and lively

BRIQUET GRIFFON VENDÉEN

FROM: France

HEIGHT: 19–22 inches (48–55 cm)

WEIGHT: 35–53 pounds (16–24 kg)

COAT: Black on fawn, orange and white, black and white, black and tan, black, tan and white; long, wavy

GROOMING:

EXERCISE NEEDS:

K-9 QUALITIES: Cheerful and lively

Bred down in size from the grand griffon Vendéen (p. 132), these adaptable dogs (pronounced bree-kay gree-FOHN vehn-DAY-uhn) are happy running in a dog pack or playing with kids in a city.

FAWN BRITTANY GRIFFON

Originally bred as pack dogs to hunt wolves and wild boars, these hounds—also known by the name griffon fauve de Bretagne—are dedicated hunters but also devoted family dogs.

FROM: France

HEIGHT: 19–22 inches (47–56 cm)

WEIGHT: 40–49 pounds (18–22 kg)

COAT: Red-wheaten; wiry, very rough

GROOMING:

EXERCISE NEEDS:

K-9 QUALITIES: Affectionate and friendly

GRIFFON NIVERNAIS

FROM: France

HEIGHT: 21–25 inches (53–63 cm)

WEIGHT: 51–55 pounds (23–25 kg)

COAT: Black on sandy; dense, shaggy, rough

GROOMING:

EXERCISE NEEDS:

K-9 QUALITIES: Loyal and strong-willed

These cute pups (pronounced gree-FOHN nee-ver-NAY) are skilled hunters and wonderful family pets that like kids and maybe even cats—though they're always ready to run after wild critters outside. Their shaggy coats protect them as they run through thickets.

BEAGLE

It's a good thing beagles are so charming and cute, because these popular little scent hounds can be a bit mischievous.

They want to get their own way, and that means sniffing out food—whether it requires rooting around in your trash can, breaking into your pantry, or digging in your neighbor's garden. And if you ask them to do something they find "boring," they might just ignore you. Beagles also may "sing" with gusto when sirens pass by or strangers come to the door. But their happy, loving nature makes up for all that. With a bit of exercise and consistent training, these adaptable dogs can be happy in a small apartment or on a large estate. They love outdoor activity and playing with kids.

Beagles look like small English foxhounds, but their exact origins are unclear. What's known is that beagle-like pack hounds go back as far as 1475, when the name "beagle" caught on. The dogs were pack hunters, baying loudly when they caught the scent of their prey. In the early days, beagles varied a lot depending on where they hunted. Beagles in the rolling countryside of England were bigger and sniffed around slowly, while their cousins in the rugged terrain of Scotland tended to be more active. In the early 1800s, breeders worked to standardize the dogs, and beagles from that time look remarkably like the adorable pups of today.

PUP STARS

When it comes to mischief, no beagle matches the antics of Snoopy, the loyal but headstrong pet of Charlie Brown in the popular "Peanuts" comics and movies. Snoopy has incredible skills and creativity. He writes novels, plays baseball, does "happy dances," and imagines himself to be college student Joe Cool or a World War I flying ace battling the Red Baron. Charles M. Schulz, who created "Peanuts," modeled Snoopy on one of his childhood dogs, Spike. In the comic strip, Snoopy has a brother named Spike. He lives in the California, U.S.A., desert, wears a hat, and has droopy mustache-looking whiskers. Snoopy also has the loyal friendship of Woodstock, a bird.

FROM: UK/England

HEIGHT: 13–16 inches (33–40 cm)

WEIGHT: 20–24 pounds (9–11 kg)

COAT: Variety of colors; short

GROOMING:

EXERCISE NEEDS:

K-9 QUALITIES: Loving and mischievous

155

A MOSAIC OF FRENCH HOUNDS

Perhaps no country has contributed as many hound breeds as France. Sleek, shaggy, tall, and short, the French scent hounds are skilled and athletic trackers. Loyal and good-natured, many breeds also make good family dogs when given proper exercise, training, and socialization.

ARIÉGEOIS

Created in the early 1900s from crosses of other French hounds, these talented scent hounds (whose name is pronounced ah-ree-AYZH-wah) are named for the rocky region on France's border with Spain. Rare outside western Europe, these out-going pups love to play with kids and hang with their families.

FROM: France
HEIGHT: 20–23 inches (51–58 cm)
WEIGHT: 55–60 pounds (25–27 kg)
COAT: White with black markings and mottling; short
GROOMING:
EXERCISE NEEDS:
K-9 QUALITIES: Friendly and loyal

ARTOIS HOUND

FROM: France
HEIGHT: 21–23 inches (53–58 cm)
WEIGHT: 62–66 pounds (28–30 kg)
COAT: Tricolor; short
GROOMING:
EXERCISE NEEDS:
K-9 QUALITIES: Active and affectionate

These rare hounds, descendants of St. Hubert hounds and English breeds, always want to be on the go. A perfect day for an Artois (pronounced ar-TWAH) would include hiking with its family and playing with the kids.

POITEVIN

Named for the Poitou region of western France, these tireless hounds (whose name is pronounced pwet-van) can race over rough ground in a pack of hunting dogs. They originally hunted wolves but now pursue wild boars and deer. These awesome athletes are sometimes called the "greyhounds of the French hounds."

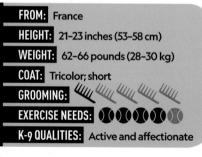

FROM: France
HEIGHT: 24–28 inches (61–71 cm)
WEIGHT: 65–75 pounds (30–34 kg)
COAT: Tricolor, white and orange; short, shiny, sleek
GROOMING:
EXERCISE NEEDS:
K-9 QUALITIES: Powerful and brave

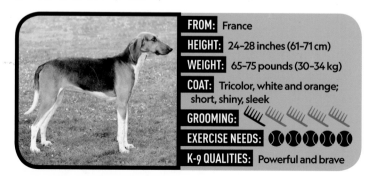

PORCELAINE

These friendly hunting hounds get their name from their shiny, slightly transparent coats, which look like enameled porcelain. Possibly the oldest of the French pack hounds, they're skilled hunters but also gentle and easygoing pups. With good training, they make fun pets for active families.

FROM: France
HEIGHT: 21–23 inches (53–58 cm)
WEIGHT: 55–62 pounds (25–28 kg)
COAT: White, showing black spots on skin; very short, fine
GROOMING:
EXERCISE NEEDS:
K-9 QUALITIES: Calm and devoted

PETIT BLEU DE GASCOGNE

FROM: France
HEIGHT: 20–23 inches (51–58 cm)
WEIGHT: 40–48 pounds (18–22 kg)
COAT: Blue with black patches and tan markings; short, thick
GROOMING:
EXERCISE NEEDS:
K-9 QUALITIES: Outgoing but stubborn

As their name suggests, these dogs were bred down in size from the grand bleu de Gascogne to hunt small game. They have the excellent sense of smell and musical voice of their ancestors and can work alone or in a pack. Though friendly, they're kept as working dogs, not pets.

ANGLO-FRANÇAIS
DE PETITE VÉNERIE

Rare outside their homeland, these hounds (pronounced ang-LO fron-SAY day pet-EET vay-neh-ree) are more often kept as pack hunting dogs than pets. Still, they are affectionate and good with kids.

FROM: France
HEIGHT: 19–22 inches (48–56 cm)
WEIGHT: 35–44 pounds (16–20 kg)
COAT: Tan and white, tricolor; dense, short, glossy
GROOMING:
EXERCISE NEEDS:
K-9 QUALITIES: Energetic but stubborn

BASSET FAUVE DE BRETAGNE

FROM: France
HEIGHT: 13–15 inches (32–38 cm)
WEIGHT: 35–40 pounds (16–18 kg)
COAT: Gold wheaten; thick, wiry
GROOMING:
EXERCISE NEEDS:
K-9 QUALITIES: Lively and charming

These spunky hounds (pronounced bas-SAY fove day bret-TAN-ye), derived from the grand fauve de Bretagne and other small hounds (p. 153), are agile hunters and cheerful family dogs. They get along great with kids.

BASSET BLEU DE GASCOGNE

These low-slung hounds may not be the fastest hunting dogs, but they're very determined, tracking prey for hours on end. Give them a job to do—even if it's sniffing out hidden treats—and they can be happy family pets. They love their people, including kids of all ages.

FROM: France
HEIGHT: 12–15 inches (30–38 cm)
WEIGHT: 35–44 pounds (16–20 kg)
COAT: Slate blue, with black and tan markings; short, dense
GROOMING:
EXERCISE NEEDS:
K-9 QUALITIES: Friendly and adaptable

GRAND BASSET GRIFFON VENDÉEN

FROM: France
HEIGHT: 15–17 inches (38–44 cm)
WEIGHT: 40–44 pounds (18–20 kg)
COAT: White with black and orange markings; thick, flat, hard
GROOMING:
EXERCISE NEEDS:
K-9 QUALITIES: Energetic and friendly

Brave hounds, these agile dogs (pronounced gron bas-SAY gree-FOHN vehn-DAY-uhn) were bred small to handle the thick undergrowth of the countryside in western France. These days, the cheerful dogs are more commonly kept as pets. They love staying close to their human packs, and they need to be kept active.

PETIT BASSET GRIFFON VENDÉEN

FROM: France
HEIGHT: 13–15 inches (33–38 cm)
WEIGHT: 24–42 pounds (11–19 kg)
COAT: White with dark markings; thick, coarse, rough
GROOMING:
EXERCISE NEEDS:
K-9 QUALITIES: Bold and happy

Slightly shorter than their grand relatives, these hounds have all the confidence, skill, and charm of the bigger dogs. Good family pets, they're still workers at heart and need active lifestyles. (Take a deep breath—their name is pronounced puh-TEE bas-SAY gree-FOHN vehn-DAY-uhn. But you can just call them "PBGVs".)

BASSET ARTÉSIEN NORMAND

Looking like light-weight basset hounds, these skilled hunters (whose name is pronounced bas-SAY ar-TAY-syen nor-mon) can track down small or large game and flush them out into the open. As pets, they're devoted to their families, which they view as their packs, but they need to be kept active. They're up for playing with kids.

FROM: France
HEIGHT: 12–14 inches (30–36 cm)
WEIGHT: 33–44 pounds (15–20 kg)
COAT: Tan and white, tricolor; short, smooth
GROOMING:
EXERCISE NEEDS:
K-9 QUALITIES: Good-natured and gentle

Some dogs use their **WHISKERS**—which are excellent touch detectors—to figure out if they can fit through **SMALL SPACES.**

DACHSHUND

 **American writer H. L. Mencken, known for his sharp wit, once described dachshunds (pronounced dahks-uhnd) as "a half-dog high and a dog-and-a-half long."**

Yes, "dachsies" are the famous "wiener dogs," the short-legged and low-slung hounds that are long on personality. Their unique shape is intentional, the result of selective breeding. Dachshunds were developed more than 300 years ago to hunt badgers. (*Dachs* means "badger" in German.) These little dogs needed to sniff out the animals, dig into their burrows, and then chase out the badgers, which can fight fiercely when cornered. It took a lot of determination and courage, and dachsies are still known as brave, bold, and feisty.

As pets, dachsies are spirited, active, and fun-loving. They're fine with kids, if they grow up with them, but it's important that kids learn to pick up and hold the dogs correctly. These dogs have long backs that can be hurt if held without proper support. Dachsies can be strong-willed and a little hard to housetrain. True to their nature, they love to dig. But they're also adaptable dogs that are as comfortable in an apartment as on an estate, as long as they get moderate exercise. With two different sizes and three coat types, there's a dachsund for everyone.

FROM:	Germany
HEIGHT:	5–6 inches (13–15 cm) for miniature; 8–9 inches (20–23 cm) for standard
WEIGHT:	9–11 pounds (4–5 kg) for miniature; 20–26 pounds (9–12 kg) for standard
COAT:	Variety of colors; smooth, wirehaired, or long-haired
GROOMING:	
EXERCISE NEEDS:	
K-9 QUALITIES:	Lively and strong-willed

★ PUP STARS

PICASSO & LUMP
A Dachshund's Odyssey
David Douglas Duncan

The famous artist Pablo Picasso loved dogs—even giving dogs to friends as gifts (partly to make sure there would be a dog around if he visited them). One day, a photographer from *Life* magazine, David Douglas Duncan, came to see Picasso and he brought along his dachshund, Lump (pronounced loomp; it's German for "rascal"). He couldn't leave Lump at home because his other, much larger dog was too rough with the dachshund. Lump immediately loved Picasso, and the feeling was mutual. When the photographer got ready to leave, Picasso held on to Lump and asked if Duncan would leave the dog. Though the photographer was fond of the dachsie, he realized Lump would have a better life someplace away from his larger dog. It was also hard to say "no" to the great artist! Picasso included Lump in several pieces of art, saying he liked to add Lump to his paintings "when they needed something to make them lighter and more amusing."

THE ADAPTABLE SMALL SWISS HOUNDS

Small Swiss hounds (known as Swiss neiderlaufhunds) are smaller versions of the Swiss laufhunds. The large laufhunds, talented as they were, tended to race from one place to another in pursuit of prey—even if that meant going outside the hunting grounds or onto other people's property. In the late 1800s, some Swiss regions of Switzerland banned hunting with large hounds. Hunters still wanted all the capabilities of the lauf-hunds, but they needed them in a smaller package. To downsize the dogs, breeders mixed French bassets into the hounds' lines. The results were excellent trackers that moved more slowly, allowing hunters on foot to keep up with them. Except for their size, these smaller hounds have the same skills and friendly natures of their larger rela-tives. They, too, vary by color depending on where each type was developed.

FROM: Switzerland

HEIGHT: 13–17 inches (33–43 cm)

WEIGHT: 18–33 pounds (8–15 kg)

COAT: Colors vary by type; short (and, for Bernese, rough as well)

GROOMING:

EXERCISE NEEDS:

K-9 QUALITIES: Sociable and loyal

SMALL BERNESE
HOUNDS

Small Bernese hounds, which can have either smooth or rough coats, come from west-central Switzerland.

SMALL LUCERNE
HOUNDS

Small Lucerne hounds hail from a German-speaking central Swiss region in the foothills of the Swiss Alps.

SMALL ST. HUBERT
JURA HOUNDS

Small St. Hubert Jura hounds are similar in appearance to Bruno Juras, but their coats tend to be smoother.

SMALL SCHWYZ
HOUNDS

Small Schwyz hounds were developed in central Switzerland.

SMALL BRUNO
JURA HOUNDS

Small Bruno Jura hounds hail from the northwestern Swiss Jura Mountains region.

Mainly kept as hunting dogs, the small Swiss hounds are very **LOVING** animals—so much that they'll bounce around you, wanting to **LICK AND PLAY.** With good training and socializing—and lots of exercise—they make playful pets that adore **KIDS** and grown-ups alike.

FROM: France

HEIGHT: 13–15 inches (33–38 cm)

WEIGHT: 40–60 pounds (18–27 kg)

COAT: Variety of colors; short

GROOMING:

EXERCISE NEEDS:

K-9 QUALITIES: Good-natured and charming but somewhat stubborn

"BASSET" comes from the French *bas*, which **MEANS "LOW."**

BASSET HOUND

 If you've seen a cartoon with a low-slung dog that keeps tripping over his long, floppy ears, that's a basset hound.

The adorable pups, with their big, sad eyes and mournful howls, are actually happy, intelligent dogs that have long been prized for their skills. Built close to the ground, with long ears that fan up scents, bassets are amazing trackers, probably second only to bloodhounds (p. 134). Don't let their height fool you: These are big dogs, with heavy bones and powerful legs that can carry them over rough terrain in dogged—but slow—pursuit of small animals. Bassets share their ancestry with the oldest of hounds developed at the St. Hubert abbey. While some St. Hubert hounds developed into bloodhounds, the slower, shorter-legged dogs are believed to be the bassets' ancestors.

Bassets like nothing better than to go on long, scent-filled walks and to hang out with their packs, especially if they include kids, whom bassets adore. These calm, friendly hounds get along with everyone: people, other dogs, and even cats. They're hounds to the core, following their noses wherever they lead—even if that's into mischief. But those big, pleading eyes and thumping tails usually get them out of trouble.

POOCH PROS: ANIMAL BEHAVIORISTS

We all want our pups to have happy, fulfilling lives with us. But sometimes dogs have problems that require the professional help of skilled animal behaviorists. Maybe your almost-perfect pal rips up your sofa when you leave the house, or your floppy-eared pup is afraid of dogs with pointed ears. Behaviorists are specially trained to figure out what's going on and how to help. They often study pets in their homes and with their families to look for reasons the pups may be acting up. They may suggest ways to help the pets through positive reinforcement or making changes in their environment or routines. Some animal behaviorists work as researchers or with zoo, farm, animal shelter, or even wild animals. But others work with pets and their owners. They have extensive training such as a master's degree or Ph.D.'s, or they specialize in behavior after veterinary school. All work to keep animals happy and healthy—and that's a great thing!

THE SKILLED BRACKE HUNTING DOGS

With roots going back centuries, the German brackes are still valued for their hunting skills. Unlike other hounds, they tend to have narrower heads, perhaps showing some common ancestry with greyhounds (p. 123) or ancient Celtic dogs.

GERMAN HOUND

Exceptional scent hounds and watchdogs, German hounds have a sweet-enough nature to be family pets, but they need a lot of socialization and physical activity to be happy with an indoor life.

FROM:	Germany
HEIGHT:	16–21 inches (40–53 cm)
WEIGHT:	35–40 pounds (16–18 kg)
COAT:	Tan with black and white markings; short, smooth
GROOMING:	
EXERCISE NEEDS:	
K-9 QUALITIES:	Gentle and loyal

WESTPHALIAN DACHSBRACKE

FROM:	Germany
HEIGHT:	12–15 inches (30–38 cm)
WEIGHT:	33–40 pounds (15–18 kg)
COAT:	Red with black and white markings; short, smooth
GROOMING:	
EXERCISE NEEDS:	
K-9 QUALITIES:	Playful and gentle and strong-willed

Smaller, short-legged versions of German hounds, these dogs can sneak into burrows or under overgrowth that stops larger breeds. Adaptable and good-natured, they also make good family dogs. (Dachsbracke is pronounced DOX-brack.)

ALPINE DACHSBRACKE

One of Austria's prized scent hounds, these hardy dogs were bred to handle the harsh mountainous terrain of their homeland. Though mainly kept as hunting dogs, these rare hounds are friendly enough to be good pets.

FROM:	Austria
HEIGHT:	13–17 inches (34–42 cm)
WEIGHT:	27–48 pounds (12–22 kg)
COAT:	Red with black, black and tan; dense
GROOMING:	
EXERCISE NEEDS:	
K-9 QUALITIES:	Fearless and friendly

DREVER

FROM: Sweden

HEIGHT: 12–15 inches (30–38 cm)

WEIGHT: 31–35 pounds (14–16 kg)

COAT: Variety of colors; smooth, thick

GROOMING:

EXERCISE NEEDS:

K-9 QUALITIES: Friendly and energetic

Drevers look a bit like beagles, but they actually were developed in the 1900s from Westphalian dachsbrackes and other hounds. These outgoing dogs are mainly kept as hunting companions, but they can be great pets, too. They're sweet, playful, and snuggly.

BAVARIAN MOUNTAIN SCENT HOUND

These dogs were developed in the 1870s to work in mountainous regions. They are calm hounds and excellent trackers. They can also be loving pets, but they need exercise and jobs, such as training for dog sports, to be happy.

FROM: Germany

HEIGHT: 17–20 inches (44–52 cm)

WEIGHT: 55–77 pounds (25–35 kg)

COAT: Red, fawn, tan, brindle; short, harsh, close-fitting

GROOMING:

EXERCISE NEEDS:

K-9 QUALITIES: Devoted and affectionate

HANOVERIAN SCENT HOUND

Skilled at tracking big game, hounds like these have been around since the Middle Ages. Hanoverians are bred to be working hunting dogs, not pets. They're loyal to their handlers but may be cautious around people they don't know. They're also independent, which makes training a challenge.

FROM: Germany

HEIGHT: 19–22 inches (48–55 cm)

WEIGHT: 55–88 pounds (25–40 kg)

COAT: Deer-red, brindle; short, thick, harsh

GROOMING:

EXERCISE NEEDS:

K-9 QUALITIES: Talented and strong-willed

Dogs' nostrils **SMELL SEPARATELY!** That helps them locate where **SCENTS** come from.

DALMATIAN

There's no mistaking a Dalmatian. The only spotted dog breed, "Dal" puppies are actually born white, with their black or liver-colored spots appearing at around two weeks and becoming more distinct as they get older.

These dogs are seriously athletic. Dalmatians were bred to run alongside carriages or horseback riders, so they have both speed and endurance. In the 1700s and 1800s, they had an important job: keeping the horses calm and protecting them and the carriages from stray dogs and robbers. For English aristocrats, it was a status symbol to have Dalmatians running beside their coaches. The more dogs, the higher the status.

Though they get their name from a coastal region of Croatia, there's no evidence suggesting Dalmatians actually came from there. Indeed, no one knows their true origins. European artwork from the 1300s—and also earlier art in Egyptian tombs and caves—depicts Dalmatian-like spotted dogs, but scientists have yet to figure out their heritage. The dogs often traveled through Europe with the nomadic Romany people before becoming popular carriage dogs.

Today's Dals are loving pets (which still get along great with horses), as long as they're well trained and socialized and get plenty of exercise. Seriously. No matter how much you loved *101 Dalmatians*, don't get one of these dogs unless you can promise to provide it with *lots* of exercise every single day. If they don't have outlets for their energy, they won't be happy pets.

HERO HOUNDS

You've seen the pictures: Dalmatians riding in fire trucks on the way to a fire. So, what's with that? Tradition. Back in the days when firefighters drove horse-drawn fire wagons, Dalmatians ran out of the firehouse, barking to get people out of the wagon's way once the fire alarm sounded. They'd run alongside the wagon to the fire, then stay with the wagon. They'd calm the horses—which are afraid of flames—and make sure no one stole the firefighters' equipment. After fire trucks replaced horse-drawn wagons, firefighters kept Dalmatians as companions, partly to protect their stuff and partly to keep the tradition going. The dogs remained popular through the 1930s, and dog shows even featured working firehouse Dalmatians. In the 1930s, one working Dalmatian named Jack was awarded a medal for pushing a child out of the path of a speeding fire truck. As the 1950s arrived, people increasingly wanted to protect the dogs from the dangers of firefighting, and the Dalmatians were retired from official duty. The few that remained in firehouses were just mascots. If they went anywhere with their firefighter friends, they didn't run alongside the fire trucks. They rode.

FROM:	Unknown
HEIGHT:	22–24 inches (56–61 cm)
WEIGHT:	40–60 pounds (18–27 kg)
COAT:	White with black or liver spots; short, dense, glossy
GROOMING:	
EXERCISE NEEDS:	
K-9 QUALITIES:	High-energy, smart, and loyal

SUPREME SPEEDSTERS

DALMATIANS even have spots in their **MOUTHS.**

POINTERS

Have you ever seen a dog freeze in place, staring straight ahead, one paw lifted, its tail thrust out straight behind? That dog has smelled an animal and is telling you where the critter is hiding. Just follow the dog's nose: It's saying, "Look, look! Over there!" That pose is called pointing. Though any dog may do it naturally, some dogs were selectively bred to emphasize this amazing skill. These dogs became known as pointers. Some pointing breeds perform a variation on this trick. They freeze into a crouching position—called setting—when they smell an animal. These pups are called setters. Among hunting dogs, pointing dogs are specialists in locating prey. Instead of snatching the prey themselves, they stand motionless—making sure not to scare away the animal—until hunters arrive. Talk about self-discipline! Dogs have helped hunters track and catch game for thousands of years, of course. But, as hunters began to carry guns, hunting dogs needed to adapt. They learned specific tasks: Pointers were bred to locate game, while other dogs were developed to scare prey out of hiding places (a skill called flushing) or to collect fallen game and bring it back (a skill called retrieving). Some hunting dogs continued to perform all these roles, but many breeds became specialists. Though they still show off their hunting expertise in the field or in competitions, most have developed another specialization: great family pet. Pointing dogs are devoted to their people, especially kids. They're always up for play, and they return all the love you can give them.

VERSATILE FRENCH POINTERS

Over centuries, various regions of France have developed an array of pointing dogs known for their versatility, athleticism, and loyalty. They're not only good hunting companions, capable of taking on a variety of tasks, but some also make gentle, loving pets.

ARIEGE POINTING DOG

Kept mainly by hunters, these rare dogs are a fairly recent breed. They can handle any hunting task and are playful and sweet—but they may have trouble settling into home life.

FROM:	France
HEIGHT:	22–26 inches (56–67 cm)
WEIGHT:	55–66 pounds (25–30 kg)
COAT:	Orange and white, brown shades and white, fawn or brown ticked; short, glossy
GROOMING:	
EXERCISE NEEDS:	
K-9 QUALITIES:	Loving and enthusiastic

AUVERGNE POINTER

FROM:	France
HEIGHT:	21–25 inches (53–63 cm)
WEIGHT:	49–62 pounds (22–28 kg)
COAT:	White with black markings and flecking; short, shiny
GROOMING:	
EXERCISE NEEDS:	
K-9 QUALITIES:	Lively and affectionate

One of the oldest of the French pointing dogs, developed in central France in the 1700s, these pointers' exact history is unknown. What is known is that they're talented, gentle dogs that love being with people and are great with kids. (Auvergne is pronounced oh-VERN-eh.)

BRAQUE DU BOURBONNAIS

Probably the oldest of the French pointers, these calm, affectionate dogs (whose name is pronounced brack doo bore-bon-nay) trace their heritage to the 1500s. They crave human attention and, when properly socialized, get along great with kids—but they may be too bouncy for young tots.

FROM:	France
HEIGHT:	19–22 inches (48–57 cm)
WEIGHT:	35–57 pounds (16–26 kg)
COAT:	White with brown markings and ticking; short, fine
GROOMING:	
EXERCISE NEEDS:	
K-9 QUALITIES:	Devoted and sweet

BRAQUE FRANÇAIS GASCOGNE

FROM:	France
HEIGHT:	22–27 inches (56–69 cm)
WEIGHT:	55–70 pounds (25–32 kg)
COAT:	White with red-brown markings and flecking; short, thick
GROOMING:	
EXERCISE NEEDS:	
K-9 QUALITIES:	Friendly and loyal

Developed in southwestern France in the 1600s, these French Gascony pointers are sweet, easygoing family pets, but they may play too roughly for toddlers. As hunters, they can do everything: tracking, pointing, and retrieving.

BRAQUE FRANÇAIS PYRENEAN

These French Pyrenean pointers are lighter and swifter—and more speckled—than their Gascony cousins, but they're every bit as athletic and affectionate. They're great family pets, always up for some active play.

FROM:	France
HEIGHT:	19–23 inches (47–58 cm)
WEIGHT:	40–53 pounds (18–24 kg)
COAT:	White with red-brown markings and flecking; short, fine
GROOMING:	
EXERCISE NEEDS:	
K-9 QUALITIES:	Devoted and active

BRAQUE SAINT-GERMAIN

These light-haired dogs have golden yellow eyes and pink noses. They're adaptable dogs that are happy working in all kinds of terrain or living in the city—as long as they're with their people. They like cuddles and kisses.

FROM:	France
HEIGHT:	21–24 inches (54–62 cm)
WEIGHT:	40–57 pounds (18–26 kg)
COAT:	White with orange markings; short, smooth
GROOMING:	
EXERCISE NEEDS:	
K-9 QUALITIES:	Sweet and skilled

In Galesburg, Illinois, U.S.A., you're **NOT ALLOWED** to keep a **SMELLY DOG.**

GERMAN
SHORTHAIRED POINTER

A dog that can do everything. That was the goal of German breeders in the mid to late 1800s, when they developed this breed from various German, Spanish, and English hunting dogs. They met their goal. "GSPs" are truly multipurpose dogs, skilled at any hunting task—whether tracking, pointing, or retrieving—in woods, fields, and water. But it gets even better: When the workday is over, these popular, intelligent dogs are eager to go home and play with the kids and cuddle with their people on the sofa.

FROM: Germany

HEIGHT: 21–25 inches (53–64 cm)

WEIGHT: 45–70 pounds (20–32 kg)

COAT: White, black, liver, with patches and ticking; short, coarse

GROOMING:

EXERCISE NEEDS:

K-9 QUALITIES: Loyal and affectionate

HERO HOUNDS

Not every dog takes a helicopter to work. But then, not every dog is Hertz, a member of the UK's Royal Air Force (RAF). Hertz, a German shorthaired pointer, loves flying and sports a special pair of doggie goggles—or "doggles"—so he can look out the helicopter window. He's been stationed with the RAF in Afghanistan, where he's made sure no civilian workers bring in cell phones, voice recorders, or any other electronics that could record secret information at the RAF base. His amazing nose even found a phone SIM card, which is about half the size of a postage stamp! Hertz is credited with keeping thousands of military men and women safe at the base. He became so famous that American and Danish forces asked for his help, and Hertz was happy to serve. When he isn't working, he likes to swim, play with his handlers, give them wet kisses—and occasionally get into mischief.

GERMAN
WIREHAIRED POINTER

A tiny bit taller and heavier than their German shorthaired relatives (GSPs), "GWPs" sport a water-resistant, harsh, wiry coat that protects them from bad weather and thorny underbrush. Their coat also creates a charmingly shaggy mustache, beard, and eyebrows! They are different from GSPs in looks, but not in their abilities and good nature. Devoted to their families— though sometimes one member more than others—they don't like to be separated from their people. Most enjoy playing with kids and soaking up their love. As working dogs, GWPs need plenty of exercise. If they don't get it, they will get into mischief.

FROM: Germany
HEIGHT: 22–26 inches (56–66 cm)
WEIGHT: 50–70 pounds (23–32 kg)
COAT: Liver, liver and white, black and white, with spots and ticking; straight, short- to medium-length, coarse, wiry
GROOMING:
EXERCISE NEEDS:
K-9 QUALITIES: Energetic and affectionate

WATER-RESISTANT COATS aren't the only reason GWPs are great swimmers. Their **PAWS** are webbed and spoon-shaped, forming perfect paddles!

GERMAN ROUGH-
HAIRED POINTER

These extremely rare dogs—one of the German wirehaired pointer's (p. 175) ancestors—are believed to be the oldest German rough-coated pointing breed. Also known as stichelhaars, they are brave working dogs but not the best pets—tending to be aggressive toward strangers.

FROM:	Germany
HEIGHT:	23–28 inches (58–70 cm)
WEIGHT:	44–75 pounds (20–34 kg)
COAT:	Brown, brown and white, roan, with ticking; coarse, wiry
GROOMING:	
EXERCISE NEEDS:	
K-9 QUALITIES:	Calm and courageous

PUDELPOINTER

What do you get when you cross a standard poodle (p. 206) and a pointer (p. 190)? These intelligent, friendly dogs with protective coats. They're versatile and eager to please, handling all types of hunting work in fields, woods, and water. They also make great, loving pets that enjoy hanging out with their people and get along great with kids of all ages.

FROM:	Germany
HEIGHT:	22–27 inches (55–68 cm)
WEIGHT:	44–66 pounds (20–30 kg)
COAT:	Black, brown/liver; rough
GROOMING:	
EXERCISE NEEDS:	
K-9 QUALITIES:	Sociable and calm

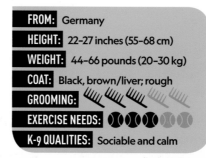

WEIMARANER

Nicknamed "gray ghosts" because of their shiny silver coats, these graceful dogs also have gray noses and distinctive gray, blue-gray, or amber-colored eyes.

Known for their speed and endurance, the dogs get their name from the Weimar region of central Germany, where aristocrats in the early 1800s worked to develop a unique, all-purpose "gentleman's hunting partner" by crossing several hunting breeds, possibly including the St. Hubert hound. Though they are still hunting companions, these eager-to-please dogs are also popular pets that are happy to romp with kids and hang with their families. Just don't expect them to enjoy being left alone too long!

FROM: Germany
HEIGHT: 23–27 inches (58–69 cm)
WEIGHT: 55–90 pounds (25–41 kg)
COAT: Silver-gray, blue, gray; short or long, silky, glossy
GROOMING:
EXERCISE NEEDS:
K-9 QUALITIES: Devoted and energetic

⭐ PUP STARS

If you recognize Weimaraners, it's probably thanks to the funny photos of William Wegman's pets. One day in the 1970s, Wegman was working in his art studio, and his pet Weimaraner, Man Ray, wanted to be part of the action. Wegman picked up his camera and snapped some photos of his pup. He created both eerie and funny portraits—and they were a big hit. Wegman never imagined his art career would focus on dogs, but his Weimaraners enjoy being in the limelight. Two dogs, Flo and Topper, inspired him to combine his photography and painting with storytelling. The result was the Flo & Wendell series of kids' books.

HOW TO
SPEAK DOG

Talking to your pooch pal can feel like a one-way conversation. We talk, they listen (and understand an amazing amount of what we say). But they don't talk back ... or do they? Dogs may not speak our language, but they do communicate with each other and with us. Pups use a nonverbal language, relying on their eyes, ears, mouth, tail, and overall body posture. So, listen up: Here's some basic dog vocabulary.

JUST CHILLIN'

- Body relaxed
- Tail in relaxed, natural position, maybe wagging gently
- Eyes "soft"—relaxed, a little squinty
- Ears carried naturally
- Mouth relaxed, closed, or panting slightly, corners turned slightly upward

LET'S PLAY!

- Play bow
- Loose and wiggly movements
- Wiggly, wagging tail, often making circles, and level with the dog's body
- Eyes bright but not staring
- Ears relaxed or held to side
- Relaxed mouth, open, maybe panting lightly

I'M SCARED

- Body low and tense, weight toward back or leaning away
- May roll onto side or back
- Tail tucked between legs
- Eyes rounder than normal, whites visible ("whale eye" or "half-moon eye")
- Ears flattened against head
- Mouth tightly closed or open wide, panting heavily and quickly
- May lick nose or lips, drool, or yawn

I'M ON ALERT

- Body tense and still, leaning slightly forward
- Head raised high above shoulders
- Tail held high and stiff, maybe wagging rigidly
- Hair raised across shoulders, spine, and tail
- Eyes hard and round, staring, pupils dilated
- Ears forward and up
- Mouth closed tightly, corners of mouth forward
- May wrinkle muzzle or curl lips up to expose teeth

WHAT'S THAT?

- Body still or leaning forward
- Head cocked to side
- Eyes bright
- Ears forward and alert
- Mouth closed

PLEASE DON'T BE MAD AT ME

- Body slightly lowered, weight evenly over legs
- Head lowered
- Tail wagging
- May squint or look to the side
- Ears back or to the side
- Licking or maybe displaying front teeth

179

EUROPEAN POINTING DOGS, OLD AND NEW

Pointing dogs may trace their heritage back to 17th-century Spanish dogs, such as the Old Spanish pointer, but breeders in several countries have developed national pointing breeds. These canines are well suited to hunting tasks in their homelands. Many European breeds are versatile dogs, bred to hunt, point, and retrieve. Others were bred to excel only at pointing.

OLD DANISH POINTER

In the early 1700s, a Danish breeder created these pointers by crossing local farm dogs with dogs that migrated into the region with nomadic people. High-spirited workers, they're even more popular as gentle, fun-loving pets for active families.

FROM:	Denmark
HEIGHT:	20–24 inches (50–60 cm)
WEIGHT:	57–77 pounds (26–35 kg)
COAT:	White with liver markings and flecking; short, smooth
GROOMING:	
EXERCISE NEEDS:	
K-9 QUALITIES:	Adaptable and good-natured

BRACCO ITALIANO

FROM:	Italy
HEIGHT:	22–26 inches (55–67 cm)
WEIGHT:	55–88 pounds (25–40 kg)
COAT:	White, white and orange, white and chestnut, white and amber, roan; short, smooth
GROOMING:	
EXERCISE NEEDS:	
K-9 QUALITIES:	Good-natured and playful

These large, lovable dogs, which are skilled at both pointing and retrieving, are devoted to their people. They make gentle pets that love to play with kids, but they need plenty of exercise to stay happy.

SLOVAKIAN ROUGH-HAIRED POINTER

A fairly new breed, which gets its rough coat from its Bohemian wirehaired pointing griffon (p. 188) ancestors and its color from its Weimaraner (p. 177) ancestors, these versatile, amber-eyed dogs are Slovakia's national pointer. With good training from puppyhood, these loving dogs enjoy family life, as long as they get plenty of daily exercise.

FROM:	Slovakia
HEIGHT:	22–27 inches (57–68 cm)
WEIGHT:	55–77 pounds (25–35 kg)
COAT:	Gray; flat, harsh
GROOMING:	
EXERCISE NEEDS:	
K-9 QUALITIES:	Energetic and loyal

BURGOS POINTER

Today's Burgos pointers, which look like a mix of scent hound and pointer, are descendants of Old Spanish pointers. Rare outside Spain, these gentle, quiet pups get along great with kids if they're raised together.

FROM: Spain
HEIGHT: 23–26 inches (59–67 cm)
WEIGHT: 55–66 pounds (25–30 kg)
COAT: White and liver, with patches; short
GROOMING:
EXERCISE NEEDS:
K-9 QUALITIES: Easygoing and intelligent

PORTUGUESE POINTER

Tracing their heritage to the 12th century, these dogs have been valued hunting companions for centuries—and still are. They're also devoted family pets that can keep kids busy all day playing fetch or hide-and-seek.

FROM: Portugal
HEIGHT: 20–22 inches (52–56 cm)
WEIGHT: 35–60 pounds (16–27 kg)
COAT: Reddish yellow, yellow, with white markings; short
GROOMING:
EXERCISE NEEDS:
K-9 QUALITIES: Affectionate and calm

Portuguese pointers teamed up with **FALCONS** to hunt in the 14th century. The pointers **SNIFFED OUT ANIMALS** and scared them out of their hiding places, and then the falcons swooped down to **CATCH THE PREY.**

VIZSLA

More than a thousand years ago, Magyar nomads—the ancestors of today's Hungarians—brought golden hunting dogs with them when they settled in central Europe. Some people believe that these dogs were the ancestors of today's vizslas. While it's impossible to know for sure, vizslas certainly have been treasured as hunting companions and family dogs for hundreds of years. The vizsla (pronounced VEEZH-la or VEESH-la and also known as the Hungarian shorthaired pointer) is considered a national treasure of Hungary—and with good reason. Athletic, intelligent, and devoted to their people, these dogs can do just about anything: pointing, retrieving, search and rescue, service, or sniffer detection work. And they make beloved pets. Channel their boundless energy into work or play, so they don't get into mischief. Vizslas love kids and will happily play fetch with you—all day, every day. They'll also return as much love as you can give them.

FROM:	Hungary
HEIGHT:	21–24 inches (53–61 cm)
WEIGHT:	44–60 pounds (20–27 kg)
COAT:	Golden red; short, sleek
GROOMING:	
EXERCISE NEEDS:	
K-9 QUALITIES:	Playful, gentle, and protective

SUPREME SPEEDSTERS

PUP STARS

A supersize dog that you can ride? Yes, please! We are, of course, talking about Clifford the Big Red Dog, the fictional star of books, television, and movies. As the story goes, Clifford was born extra small—the "runt" of his litter—but the love of Emily Elizabeth was so great that Clifford grew to be huge. But what breed is Clifford? Some fans say he's a giant vizsla, others say a vizsla/Labrador retriever mix. In early sketches—when Clifford was merely the size of a pony, instead of a house—he looked a bit more like a bloodhound. If it's a little unclear, that may be on purpose. Clifford's creator, Norman Bridwell, drew inspiration from the behavior of all types of dogs and wanted everyone to relate to the giant dog. What's clear is that Clifford's heart is as big as his body and his antics can keep us entertained for hours.

Clifford the Big Red Dog

BE BIG! BE A GOOD FRIEND

SCHOLASTIC   Norman Bridwell

WIREHAIRED VIZSLA

Wirehaired vizslas are not just shaggier versions of their sleek-coated kin. Though they share a similar coloring and skill set—excelling as hunters, agility and dock-diving competitors, or service and therapy dogs—they are a distinct breed. In the 1930s, Hungarian hunters and falconers wanted a dog like the vizsla, only with a coat that would protect it in tough field conditions and during the harsh winters of northern Hungary. They bred vizslas with solid-brown German wirehaired pointers (p. 175) and developed the wirehaired vizsla. These adaptable dogs have the calm, intelligent nature of their short-haired relatives—and just as much energy. Kept mainly as working dogs, they're becoming more popular as pets because of their devoted and affectionate personalities.

FROM: Hungary

HEIGHT: 21–25 inches (53–64 cm)

WEIGHT: 45–65 pounds (20–29 kg)

COAT: Golden red; medium-length, dense, wiry

GROOMING:

EXERCISE NEEDS:

K-9 QUALITIES: Active and loving

A **VIZSLA'S** golden red coat is the perfect camouflage, helping it **"DISAPPEAR"** in dried grasses and brush while it stalks its prey.

FRENCH SPANIEL

One of the first French spaniel-type dogs to be developed, in the late 1800s, these beautiful and adaptable dogs are as happy living in cities as they are bounding through fields—as long as they're with their people. They're affectionate pets that would be happy chasing a ball all day.

FROM: France

HEIGHT: 22–24 inches (55–61 cm)

WEIGHT: 44–55 pounds (20–25 kg)

COAT: White and brown, with spotting; medium-long, flat, silky

GROOMING:

EXERCISE NEEDS:

K-9 QUALITIES: Loyal and friendly

PICARDY SPANIEL

FROM: France

HEIGHT: 22–24 inches (55–61 cm)

WEIGHT: 44–55 pounds (20–25 kg)

COAT: Gray, brown, white, with patches and mottling; medium-length, dense, slightly wavy

GROOMING:

EXERCISE NEEDS:

K-9 QUALITIES: Calm and affectionate

These dogs are still hunters in their native homeland. They are also playful pets, and they love to romp through marshes or go swimming. Picardy spaniels can even adapt to city life, if they have enough exercise.

BLUE PICARDY SPANIEL

Similar to Picardy spaniels except in looks, these dogs probably get their distinctive blue coats from blue setters. They have the same friendly, adaptable nature of their relatives and make great family pets.

FROM: France

HEIGHT: 23–24 inches (57–60 cm)

WEIGHT: 44–46 pounds (20–21 kg)

COAT: Blue, with gray-black patches and speckling; medium-length, slightly wavy

GROOMING:

EXERCISE NEEDS:

K-9 QUALITIES: Gentle and playful

PONT-AUDEMER SPANIEL

These rare, scruffy-looking dogs may get their curly coats from Irish water spaniels (p. 208). Like those relatives, these dogs enjoy hunting in water and swamplands but also make good pets that enjoy playing with kids or going for a swim.

FROM: France
HEIGHT: 20–23 inches (51–58 cm)
WEIGHT: 40–53 pounds (18–24 kg)
COAT: Brown, with gray and brown mottling; curly
GROOMING:
EXERCISE NEEDS:
K-9 QUALITIES: Gentle and friendly

Pont-Audemer spaniels are so **FUN-LOVING** and fond of splashing around in water that they've been given the nickname **"LITTLE CLOWNS OF THE MARSHES."**

DRENTSCHE PATRIJSHOND

Related to the French spaniel (p. 184) and small Munsterlander (p. 189), "Drents" (their formal name is pronounced da-ringe puh-trice-hoon) are equally at home in the city or out hunting. They can have a bit of a stubborn streak, but they're loving family pets that want to stay by your side.

FROM: Netherlands
HEIGHT: 22–25 inches (55–63 cm)
WEIGHT: 44–55 pounds (20–25 kg)
COAT: White with brown markings and spots; medium-length, wavy
GROOMING:
EXERCISE NEEDS:
K-9 QUALITIES: Calm and loyal

STABYHOUN

FROM: The Netherlands
HEIGHT: 20–21 inches (50–53 cm)
WEIGHT: 42–55 pounds (19–25 kg)
COAT: Black with white markings, orange with white markings; long, straight, smooth
GROOMING:
EXERCISE NEEDS:
K-9 QUALITIES: Easygoing and loving

These Frisian pointing dogs are rare but versatile Dutch farm and hunting dogs. They track, point, and retrieve. These affectionate canines (whose name is pronounced sta-BAY-hoon) also love playing with kids, chasing balls, and cuddling.

BRITTANY

Energy and versatility are the name of the game when it comes to Brittanies, which take their name from the region of France where they were developed.

Bred to be pointers, they excel at finding game birds but can also handle retrieving duties. They are up for any terrain, whether dense brush or wide-open fields. Brittanies' exact ancestry is unknown, but some experts suspect it included various French spaniel breeds, Welsh springer spaniels (p. 200), and English setters (p. 190). Brittanies are beautiful, rugged, strong—and definitely not couch potatoes! To be happy companions, they need serious exercise, such as canine sports, hiking, running, or playing fetch (preferably all day). But if you provide them with enough exercise and training, you'll be rewarded with an enthusiastic playmate who's eager to take on a job and please you with their performance. Brittanies are affectionate family dogs that love kids and protect them. They can be good watchdogs, too. And, though they have strong hunting instincts, they'll get along with other pets if they're raised together. It's no wonder that these good-natured dogs have become popular companions.

Talk about talent and good looks! A lot of Brittanies become **DUAL CHAMPIONS,** racking up top honors in both dog show conformation events and field trials testing their skills.

POOCH PROS: PET PHOTOGRAPHERS, ARTISTS, AND WRITERS

Can't decide if you're an artsy person or an animal person? No need to choose between them! Some artistic animal lovers have jobs combining both their loves. Some professional photographers specialize in taking pictures of pets, often with their people. If you have an artist's eye, it may be a career for you! But if photography isn't your thing, maybe painting is? Painting animals is a time-honored tradition (pointers were favorite subjects in the past). If you're really good at it, you may find people who want to have you paint portraits of their pets. And if you have a way with words, you may be able to write about dogs for magazines, blogs, or books.

FROM: France

HEIGHT: 17–21 inches (43–53 cm)

WEIGHT: 30–40 pounds (14–18 kg)

COAT: Liver and white, orange and white, roan; medium-length, dense, slightly wavy

GROOMING:

EXERCISE NEEDS:

K-9 QUALITIES: Energetic, protective, and fun-loving

WIREHAIRED POINTING GRIFFON

These adorable, versatile dogs can point and retrieve on land or in the water. "WPGs" love to burn off their energy during the day and then hang out with their people in the evening.

FROM: Netherlands

HEIGHT: 20–24 inches (50–60 cm)

WEIGHT: 50–60 pounds (23–27 kg)

COAT: Brown and gray, chestnut and gray, with ticking, roan; long, dense, coarse

GROOMING:

EXERCISE NEEDS:

K-9 QUALITIES: Friendly, lively, and easygoing

BOHEMIAN WIREHAIRED POINTING GRIFFON

FROM: Czech Republic

HEIGHT: 23–26 inches (58–66 cm)

WEIGHT: 49–75 pounds (22–34 kg)

COAT: Dark roan with brown patches, brown; hard, wiry

GROOMING:

EXERCISE NEEDS:

K-9 QUALITIES: Loyal and eager to please

These mustached pups are gentle but also energetic family pets that thrive on active play, hiking, or other outdoor activities. Also known as the Cesky fousek (pronounced CHESS-kay fow-sek), these pointers are popular hunting companions in central Europe but rare elsewhere.

SPINONE ITALIANO

These big, shaggy dogs—popular hunting companions through the 1900s—are as huggable as they look. Calm and loving, the spinone Italiano (spin-oh-nay ih-tahl-YAH-no) is good with kids. Their ancestors probably include setters, mastiffs, and French griffon-type dogs.

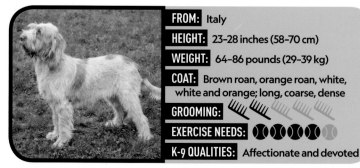

FROM: Italy

HEIGHT: 23–28 inches (58–70 cm)

WEIGHT: 64–86 pounds (29–39 kg)

COAT: Brown roan, orange roan, white, white and orange; long, coarse, dense

GROOMING:

EXERCISE NEEDS:

K-9 QUALITIES: Affectionate and devoted

GERMAN LONGHAIRED POINTER

FROM:	Germany
HEIGHT:	23–28 inches (58–70 cm)
WEIGHT:	60–71 pounds (27–32 kg)
COAT:	Brown roan, dark chocolate, white and chocolate, roan; long, dense
GROOMING:	
EXERCISE NEEDS:	
K-9 QUALITIES:	Good-natured and adaptable

With ancestry including various pointers, water dogs, and scent hounds, "GLPs"—also known as Deutsch langhaars—are versatile hunters. As long as they get enough exercise, they're great family pets that enjoy playing with kids.

SMALL MUNSTERLANDER

These quail dogs are valued hunting companions in Europe. They're affectionate and cheerful family companions, too. Their ancestors include German longhaired pointers (above) and longhaired spaniels. Despite their name, they're not related to large Munsterlanders (below).

FROM:	Germany
HEIGHT:	20–21 inches (52–54 cm)
WEIGHT:	40–60 pounds (18–27 kg)
COAT:	Brown with white and brown mottling; medium-length, thick, silky, wavy
GROOMING:	
EXERCISE NEEDS:	
K-9 QUALITIES:	Devoted and energetic

LARGE MUNSTERLANDER

FROM:	Germany
HEIGHT:	23–26 inches (58–65 cm)
WEIGHT:	64–68 pounds (29–31 kg)
COAT:	White with black mantle and flecking; medium-length, dense
GROOMING:	
EXERCISE NEEDS:	
K-9 QUALITIES:	Athletic and intelligent

Calm and versatile, these dogs are serious hunters, but they'll happily hang out with their families playing fetch, then more fetch, and finally chilling when the hunt is over. They're more related to German pointer breeds than to the small Munsterlander (above) and may have been around since the Middle Ages.

POINTER

These natural competitors—known as English pointers outside the United States and the United Kingdom—have long been valued by hunters for their pointing skills and often take the prizes in field trials, competitions that test their hunting skills. But when the workday is done, they're happy to play with kids or snuggle on the sofa.

FROM: UK/England
HEIGHT: 23–28 inches (58–71 cm)
WEIGHT: 45–75 pounds (20–34 kg)
COAT: Black, lemon, liver, orange, with or without white; short, fine
GROOMING:
EXERCISE NEEDS:
K-9 QUALITIES: Gentle and fun-loving

ENGLISH SETTER

FROM: UK/England
HEIGHT: 23–27 inches (58–69 cm)
WEIGHT: 45–80 pounds (20–36 kg)
COAT: Blue belton (speckled), blue belton and tan, lemon belton, liver belton, orange belton; long
GROOMING:
EXERCISE NEEDS:
K-9 QUALITIES: Sweet and easygoing

Elegant and gentle, English setters—developed by crossing pointing and spaniel breeds—are specialists in finding and pointing out game birds. At home, they're mellow family members and energetic playmates for kids.

GORDON SETTER

The brawniest of the setters, Gordons are built to handle the tough terrain and climate of their native Scotland. Originally used to track game birds, they're now more often devoted family pets. Gentle and protective, they're happy to get hugs from toddlers and play ball with older kids.

FROM: UK/Scotland
HEIGHT: 23–27 inches (58–69 cm)
WEIGHT: 45–80 pounds (20–36 kg)
COAT: Black with tan markings; long, silky
GROOMING:
EXERCISE NEEDS:
K-9 QUALITIES: Loving, good-natured, and energetic

IRISH SETTER

Irish setters' fiery red coats match their personalities. These are spirited dogs, always ready for a rollicking good time. They love being the center of attention and actively seek out opportunities to have fun, whether playing with kids or getting into mischief. They keep their puppylike zest for life well into doggy adulthood, so they need patient and persistent training. But if you don't make training fun, they may decide it's not worth their time, and you'll discover that they can be quite stubborn. With plenty of exercise, they're calm and loving companions.

FROM:	Ireland
HEIGHT:	24–27 inches (61–69 cm)
WEIGHT:	35–70 pounds (16–32 kg)
COAT:	Red; long, glossy
GROOMING:	
EXERCISE NEEDS:	
K-9 QUALITIES:	Sweet, fun-loving, and spirited

IRISH RED AND WHITE SETTER

After a century of watching their solid-red Irish setter relatives get most of the attention, these beautiful dogs—which share their cousins' bouncy personalities and skills—are slowly becoming more popular as playful and loving family pets.

FROM:	Ireland
HEIGHT:	22–26 inches (56–66 cm)
WEIGHT:	35–60 pounds (16–27 kg)
COAT:	Red and white; long, fine, wavy
GROOMING:	
EXERCISE NEEDS:	
K-9 QUALITIES:	Affectionate and energetic

Ireland's setters started out **RED AND WHITE**—an easy combo to spot in the field. But in the early 1800s, an **IRISH NOBLEMAN** spied a solid-red setter and got so excited that he started to raise them—lots of them! By the end of the century, red Irish setters were **ALL THE RAGE.**

RETRIEVERS, FLUSHING DOGS & WATER DOGS

If you want to guarantee a great game of fetch—you know, one where your dog actually brings the ball back to you—think about adopting a retriever. Lots of dogs like to play fetch, of course. But of all the specialized breeds, retrievers were developed specifically to go after something, grab it, and bring it back to their people. Back when they originated, retrieving was a hunting skill used mainly for bringing back waterfowl to hunters. The dogs would leap into the water and swim out, even in crashing waves and icy-cold temperatures.

Retrievers are water dogs, a grouping that includes many spaniels and some other breeds, too. Many have water-resistant coats that protect the dogs in blustery weather and chilly lakes. A long time ago, most water dogs were called water spaniels, but that's not really accurate. Not all the water dogs are spaniels, and not all spaniels are water dogs! Some "land spaniels" specialize in finding and flushing (driving out) small game from their hiding places. What do these dogs have in common? They're loving, huggable, playful, and smart—among the most popular family pets. Any would be a great partner for a game of fetch!

LABRADOR RETRIEVER

"Labs" are the total package: awesome athletes and water retrievers; skilled search-and-rescue, service, and sniffer dogs; and, most of all, devoted and playful family pets. These superpopular pooches love romping with kids (though when they're young, they may be too rowdy for toddlers). Despite their name, they're not from Labrador, Canada, but from neighboring Newfoundland, where fishermen in the 1700s bred small, black canines, known as St. John's water dogs, to help them haul in their nets and catch any fish that escaped. Though St. John's dogs have died out, they were the ancestors of today's Labs. Labs want to stay with you and do whatever you do, especially if it's active (and involves water). If you don't provide outlets for their energy, they'll find their own—digging holes, chomping on furniture legs, eating your toys. But with enough exercise, Labs can adapt to almost any living situation: city apartment, suburban home, doesn't matter. If they're with you, they're happy!

In 1979, Jimpa, a Lab/boxer cross who had gone missing while on a trip with his owner, **TRAVELED 2,000 MILES** (3,218 km) to find his way to his people in Australia.

FROM:	Canada
HEIGHT:	22–25 inches (55–62 cm)
WEIGHT:	55–80 pounds (25–36 kg)
COAT:	Yellow, black, chocolate; short
GROOMING:	
EXERCISE NEEDS:	
K-9 QUALITIES:	Outgoing and versatile

GOLDEN RETRIEVER

If any dogs are going to compete with Labs for "most popular" honors, they'd probably be goldens. These dogs are wonderful pets—gentle, eager to please, loving, and playful. And did we say active? They'll play fetch until your arm feels like it's going to fall off, and they're always up for a hike or swim. Developed in the mid to late 1800s by Lord Tweedmouth of Scotland, goldens descend from various retrievers, setters, and spaniels. These smart pups were designed to retrieve both small game and waterbirds, and they're still valued hunting companions and strong competitors in field trials that test dogs' skills. Like other working dogs, if they don't get enough socialization, training, and exercise, they'll amuse themselves—and you (and your home) may not like what they dream up. Don't bother getting a golden if you want a good guard dog. They're way too friendly for that job.

FROM:	UK/Scotland
HEIGHT:	21–24 inches (53–61 cm)
WEIGHT:	55–75 pounds (25–34 kg)
COAT:	Golden (light to dark); long, silky
GROOMING:	
EXERCISE NEEDS:	
K-9 QUALITIES:	Loving and energetic

CANINE EINSTEINS

HERO HOUNDS

Ricochet was destined to help people. She just found an unusual way to do it: riding a surfboard! The water-loving golden retriever first used her skills to help Patrick Ivison, a paralyzed teen who loved to surf. After riding the waves side-by-side, Ricochet ran over to Patrick on the shore. She wanted to surf together—and Patrick did, too! Ricochet senses what people need. While surfing, she shifts her weight to balance the board for surfers with special needs. This surfer girl is a natural therapy dog.

CHESAPEAKE
BAY RETRIEVER

With their waterproof coats and determined attitudes, the powerfully built "Chessies" are superb water dogs, ready and willing to brave the rough, icy waves of the Chesapeake Bay in pursuit of ducks. The origins of the breed were two Newfoundland dogs (p. 98) saved from a shipwreck off the coast of Maryland, U.S.A., in 1807 and bred with local retrievers, other hounds, and probably Irish water spaniels (p. 208). Chessies are affectionate at home and protective of their people.

FROM: U.S.A.
HEIGHT: 21–26 inches (53–66 cm)
WEIGHT: 55–80 pounds (25–36 kg)
COAT: Browns (light to dark), deadgrass (light to dark straw colored), tan, sedge (red-gold); wavy, oily
GROOMING:
EXERCISE NEEDS:
K-9 QUALITIES: Independent and loyal

NOVA SCOTIA DUCK
TOLLING RETRIEVER

"Tolling" is an old word that means to attract or lure something in, and that's what makes "tollers" effective retrievers. They playfully toss a stick around at the water's edge, arousing the curiosity of ducks, which swim in close to check them out. (Bad idea, ducks!) The dogs' playful nature also makes them fun companions, happy to hang out with active families.

FROM: Canada
HEIGHT: 17–21 inches (43–53 cm)
WEIGHT: 35–50 pounds (16–23 kg)
COAT: Red, red-gold, with white markings; long, dense
GROOMING:
EXERCISE NEEDS:
K-9 QUALITIES: Tireless and playful

CURLY-COATED
RETRIEVER

Developed in the late 18th century—probably from now extinct English water spaniels and St. John's water dogs, with a bit of poodle (p. 206) mixed in later—"curlies" don't think twice about plunging into icy water to retrieve game. They're happy to take on a variety of roles, such as assistance dogs, and they form strong attachments with their people. Energetic and fairly independent, curlies are always up for an outdoor adventure or play.

FROM: UK
HEIGHT: 23–27 inches (58–69 cm)
WEIGHT: 60–95 pounds (27–43 kg)
COAT: Black, liver; tightly curled

GROOMING:
EXERCISE NEEDS:
K-9 QUALITIES: Smart and energetic

FLAT-COATED RETRIEVER

"Flat-coats" were once the most popular retrievers. These adorable dogs were developed from a mix of Newfoundlands (p. 98) and various setters, sheepdogs, and water spaniels. They love to retrieve, especially from water. They keep a puppylike enthusiasm throughout their entire lives and adore their families, wanting to stay close to them. Among the most active breeds, flat-coats need plenty of exercise and relish outdoor adventures or swimming.

FROM: UK
HEIGHT: 22–25 inches (56–63 cm)
WEIGHT: 60–70 pounds (27–32 kg)
COAT: Black, liver; long, dense, straight

GROOMING:
EXERCISE NEEDS:
K-9 QUALITIES: Friendly and energetic

COCKER SPANIEL

Talk about puppy eyes! Cockers have them in abundance. These small spaniels, also known as American cocker spaniels, are among the most popular family dogs for good reason. Well-bred cockers are delightful: beautiful, sweet, and athletic. Yes, pamper them if you wish, but never forget these are working dogs, bred to run all day and find birds hiding in brush. Give them jobs, plenty of exercise and training, and active play sessions. You'll be rewarded with a happy, playful pet.

FROM: U.S.A.
HEIGHT: 13–15 inches (34–39 cm)
WEIGHT: 20–30 pounds (9–14 kg)
COAT: Black or brown (solid or with tan and/or white), buff or red (solid or with white), silver; long, wavy

GROOMING:
EXERCISE NEEDS:
K-9 QUALITIES: Affectionate and athletic

DEUTSCHER WACHTELHUND

These athletic, water-loving German spaniels (whose name is pronounced doyt-cher VACH-tel-hoond) are excellent retrievers that are happiest when working—even if their job is bringing a ball back to you over and over. They're great family companions for experienced owners who can provide plenty of exercise and training.

FROM: Germany
HEIGHT: 17–21 inches (44–54 cm)
WEIGHT: 40–55 pounds (18–25 kg)
COAT: Brown, brown roan, red, red roan; medium-length, dense, wavy

GROOMING:
EXERCISE NEEDS:
K-9 QUALITIES: Athletic and friendly

ENGLISH
COCKER SPANIEL

English and American cocker spaniels used to be one breed (along with English springer spaniels, p. 202), but they grew apart—literally. English cockers are slightly larger than their American cousins (p. 198); those bred for fieldwork also have shorter coats. English cockers—known simply as cockers in the United Kingdom—are just as affectionate and cheerful as their cousins across the ocean and make playful and snuggly pets.

FROM: UK/England
HEIGHT: 15-17 inches (38–43 cm)
WEIGHT: 26-34 pounds (12–15 kg)
COAT: Black, blue roan, gold, lemon roan, liver, orange, red (solid, roan, or with tan and/or white); long or moderate, silky

GROOMING:
EXERCISE NEEDS:
K-9 QUALITIES: Devoted and athletic

CLUMBER
SPANIEL

They're big, muscular, and low-slung, with heads that'd look just fine on St. Bernards. But, yes, Clumbers are spaniels—though some dog experts have their doubts. What's more certain is Clumbers are playful and sweet pets, and they can be great friends to kids when they grow up together.

FROM: France
HEIGHT: 17-20 inches (43–51 cm)
WEIGHT: 55-80 pounds (25–34 kg)
COAT: White with orange or lemon markings; long

GROOMING:
EXERCISE NEEDS:
K-9 QUALITIES: Gentle and playful but a bit slobbery

FIELD SPANIEL

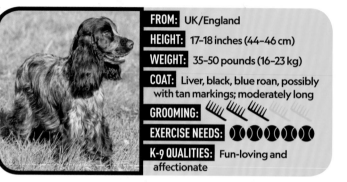

FROM: UK/England
HEIGHT: 17–18 inches (44–46 cm)
WEIGHT: 35–50 pounds (16–23 kg)
COAT: Liver, black, blue roan, possibly with tan markings; moderately long
GROOMING:
EXERCISE NEEDS:
K-9 QUALITIES: Fun-loving and affectionate

During the "dog fancy" years of the late 1800s, field spaniels were bred to be extremely long and low simply to win dog shows. It wasn't good for the dogs so, after public criticism, breeders revived the breed to produce the beautiful and energetic dogs we see today. Sweet and playful, they're great pets for families with kids.

SUSSEX SPANIEL

Sussex spaniels have the heavy bones and strength to carry their long, low-built bodies at a slow-and-steady pace through thick undergrowth—typical of the region in England where they originated in the late 1700s. Despite their serious expressions, these dogs are happy, friendly family dogs, though fond of barking and howling.

FROM: UK/England
HEIGHT: 15–16 inches (38–41 cm)
WEIGHT: 40–51 pounds (18–23 kg)
COAT: Golden liver; long, rich
GROOMING:
EXERCISE NEEDS:
K-9 QUALITIES: Cheerful and smart but a bit stubborn

WELSH SPRINGER SPANIEL

FROM: UK/Wales
HEIGHT: 17–19 inches (43–48 cm)
WEIGHT: 35–51 pounds (16–23 kg)
COAT: Red and white; long, soft, straight
GROOMING:
EXERCISE NEEDS:
K-9 QUALITIES: Devoted and gentle

Slightly smaller and more laid-back than their cousins, the English springer spaniels (p. 202), "Welshies" were bred to flush birds and retrieve them. They're hard workers but equally loving family dogs that want to stay close to their people. Somewhat protective, they also make good watchdogs.

KOOIKERHONDJE

"Kooikers" were bred to lure water-birds into traps. The dogs (their name is pronounced COY-ker-HUND-yeh but they're also known as Dutch decoy spaniels) pranced around near water, playing with sticks and wagging their fluffy tails. Curious waterbirds would swim in and follow the dogs into a trap. These skills make kooikers playful pets that are also happy just to chill out with their families.

Kooikerhondjes lure waterbirds to shore, so **CONSERVATION GROUPS** and researchers can tag and release the birds without harming them.

FROM: Netherlands
HEIGHT: 14–16 inches (35–40 cm)
WEIGHT: 20–24 pounds (9–11 kg)
COAT: White with orange-red patches; long, sleek, slightly wavy
GROOMING:
EXERCISE NEEDS:
K-9 QUALITIES: Smart and fun-loving

BOYKIN SPANIEL

The official state dog of South Carolina, U.S.A., these friendly retrievers were developed to help hunt from small boats, so they love anything to do with water: retrieving, boating, kayaking, swimming, you name it. These cheerful and inquisitive spaniels make devoted members of active families.

FROM: U.S.A.
HEIGHT: 14–18 inches (36–46 cm)
WEIGHT: 24–40 pounds (11–18 kg)
COAT: Dark chocolate, liver; curly
GROOMING:
EXERCISE NEEDS:
K-9 QUALITIES: Energetic and easygoing

ENGLISH
SPRINGER SPANIEL

Long, fluffy ears? Speckled nose? Eyes that seem to peer into your soul? It must be an English springer spaniel! These lively spaniels love their people, kids included, and are happy to hang out with them wherever they go or live—as long as they get enough exercise. Back before the 1900s, springer and cocker spaniels were considered the same breed, with springers being more than 28 pounds (13 kg) and cockers smaller. Both kinds of spaniels might even come from the same litter of puppies! In 1902, the Kennel Club of England declared the two breeds separate. These days, breeders emphasize different qualities depending on whether the springers are destined for the show ring or the hunting grounds. Both types are great companions.

FROM: UK/England

HEIGHT: 18–22 inches (46–56 cm)

WEIGHT: 40–50 pounds (18–23 kg)

COAT: Black and white, liver and white, possibly with tan markings; medium to long

GROOMING:

EXERCISE NEEDS:

K-9 QUALITIES: Lively and affectionate

Springer spaniels got their name from their skill in **STARTLING OTHER ANIMALS.** They jump out—or spring—to flush out hiding game.

PORTUGUESE
WATER DOG

Whenever you see "Porties," they're running or bounding somewhere. Maybe they're chasing a flying disc, playing soccer with kids, or—even better—jumping into a lake. The key for Porties is play. And if it involves water, all the better. Porties, an ancient breed depicted as far back as the 13th century, developed along Portugal's coast, where they helped fishermen by retrieving broken nets or lost tackle, driving fish into nets, or carrying messages from one ship to another. They have the strength and stamina to swim all day in either icy or warm water, thanks to their curly or wavy coats, which are waterproof and insulate them. These adaptable, high-energy dogs delight in active fun with their families, especially kids, and they fit into any type of home—as long as you're willing to provide enough exercise, socialization, and training for them. Good chance you'll tire out long before they do!

FROM: Portugal
HEIGHT: 17-23 inches (43–58 cm)
WEIGHT: 35–60 pounds (16–27 kg)
COAT: Black, brown, white, or with white markings; curly or wavy
GROOMING: 🖌🖌🖌
EXERCISE NEEDS: ⚾⚾⚾⚾⚾
K-9 QUALITIES: Energetic and loving

⭐ PUP STARS

In 2000, the San Francisco Giants baseball team moved into a new waterfront stadium. It was so close to San Francisco Bay, in California, U.S.A., that batters could slug a homer over the right-field wall and into the water. There was only one problem: Someone had to retrieve those "splash hits." So who'd want to play catch in the water? It was a no-brainer: Porties! The Giants put together the Baseball Aquatic Retrieval Korps—BARK, for short—a squad of six Porties to retrieve the balls. Splash-hit balls quickly became coveted collectors' items. Unfortunately, BARK Porties faced competition from souvenir seekers in boats, so stadium officials pulled the plug on BARK to keep the dogs safe.

DESIGNER DOGS

Designer dogs—or crossbreeds—rank among today's most popular pets. The goal is to combine two popular breeds' best qualities (and, with any luck, not their worst traits instead!). With oodles of doodles, huggly pugglies, and other cutie-poos, designer dogs could fill an entire book. Here are half a dozen particularly popular pooches.

PEKEAPOO

A Pekingese/poodle cross, these adorable little dogs, which can have either curly or straight coats, are friendly, affectionate, and brave.

PUGGLE

A pug/beagle cross, these sturdy little dogs can be a bit independent, but mostly they're affectionate and playful.

CHIWEENIE

A Chihuahua/dachshund cross, these teeny pups can be a bit stubborn to train, but they make up for it with their cuteness and playful energy.

LABRADOODLE

A Labrador retriever/poodle cross, this original doodle was created to be a service dog for people with allergies. Smart, affectionate, and versatile, they're popular pets in many sizes and colors.

COCKAPOO

A cocker spaniel/poodle cross, these adorably scruffy dogs tend to be friendly, devoted pets that are easy to train.

GOLDENDOODLE

A golden retriever/poodle cross, these beloved pets—which come in several sizes—are smart and affectionate and also make good therapy and service dogs.

POODLE

Combine Einstein-like intelligence, water-dog athleticism, and a streak of mischief and you've got one of the most popular curly coated canine companions: the standard poodles. The standard is the original size of the breed. They sometimes get a bad rap as silly, frou-frou dogs because of the exaggerated puffy coats they wear in the show ring. But, like other water dogs, poodles were bred to be working dogs and water retrievers. And those froufrou coats? They're a really fancy version of a practical haircut that helped the dogs as they worked in cold water. The fluffy manes kept the poodles' hearts and lungs warm, and thick "rosettes" on their hips insulated their kidneys. The puffs on their legs protected their joints from the cold, and long hair at the end of their tails acted like rudders to help them swim. The rest of the coat was clipped short to lighten their loads, avoid tangles, and let them swim faster. The dogs often are called French poodles—a name that reflects their popularity as companions ever since the 1700s in France. But the dogs, also popular in England and Spain back then, probably originated in Germany. The word "poodle" derives from the Low German word *pudel*, "puddle," or *pudeln*, "to splash."

Poodles are smart and eager to please and are capable of doing multiple jobs. Besides hunting companions, they've worked as herders, pulled carts, and even raced in the grueling 1,049-mile (1,688-km) Iditarod dog-sled race. (see p. 42). These days, they're more often seen competing in obedience and agility trials, working as therapy or even search-and-rescue dogs, or showing off those froufrou coats in conformation classes. Most of all, they're affectionate and good-natured pets who enjoy playing with kids and having jobs to do. They love to learn, and it's good to keep their minds busy so they stay out of mischief. Otherwise, you may find your poodle outwitting you.

CORDED POODLE

Any poodle's coat can "cord," wrapping into dreadlocks, if it gets long enough. But some breeders have selectively bred certain lines of standard poodles for years to get the distinctive coat. Corded poodles are just as smart, loving, and athletic as other standard poodles, but they have an unusual coat. The look was popular in the 19th century but is rare today, more often found on herding dogs. Once a coat cords, it's surprisingly easy to care for.

FROM:	Germany
HEIGHT:	15–24 inches (38–61 cm)
WEIGHT:	40–70 pounds (18–32 kg)
COAT:	Apricot, black, blue, brown, cream, gray, red, silver, silver-beige (faded brown), white; curly
GROOMING:	
EXERCISE NEEDS:	
K-9 QUALITIES:	Lively and devoted

CANINE EINSTEINS

POODLES HAVE HAIR, NOT FUR. It keeps growing, like yours, and requires regular trips to the groomer for haircuts. But there's an upside to all that care: Unlike some other breeds, poodles don't have a strong "doggy smell."

WORLDLY WATER DOGS

A lot of dogs love splashing around in water. But some breeds were selectively bred to work in water, to help either fishermen or hunters. These athletic pups have special coats—often tightly curled or water-resistant—to protect them from icy waters. Many also have webbed toes to help them swim. As pets, they love nothing more than playing fetch in the water.

BARBET

These friendly French water dogs (their name is pronounced bar-BAY) are ancestors of many other water-loving dogs, including poodles (p. 206), otterhounds (p. 133), and Newfoundlands (p. 98). Smart and sweet, these athletic pups love kids and make playful pets.

FROM: France

HEIGHT: 21–26 inches (53–65 cm)

WEIGHT: 35–60 pounds (16–27 kg)

COAT: Black, brown, fawn, gray, white, with markings; densely curled ringlets

GROOMING:

EXERCISE NEEDS:

K-9 QUALITIES: Fun-loving and affectionate

IRISH WATER SPANIEL

FROM: Ireland

HEIGHT: 20–23 inches (51–58 cm)

WEIGHT: 44–66 pounds (20–30 kg)

COAT: Dark liver; densely curled ringlets

GROOMING:

EXERCISE NEEDS:

K-9 QUALITIES: Active and faithful

Nicknamed "bogdogs" because they love to leap into the icy-cold water of their native Ireland, these dogs are cheerful and gentle. They make great companions for people who can keep them busy, preferably outdoors near water. They need early and consistent training and socializing to fit in well in homes with children or other pets.

LAGOTTO ROMAGNOLO

These smart dogs (pronounced la-goh-toe ro-man-yo-lo) make lively and sweet pets, especially for kids, and love having jobs to keep them busy. They originally worked as retrievers in northern Italian marshlands but also learned to sniff out truffles, a mushroom-like delicacy that grows in forests.

FROM: Italy

HEIGHT: 16–19 inches (41–48 cm)

WEIGHT: 24–35 pounds (11–16 kg)

COAT: White, brown, orange, roan, with markings; woolly, curly ringlets

GROOMING:

EXERCISE NEEDS:

K-9 QUALITIES: Active and affectionate

SPANISH WATER DOG

FROM: Spain

HEIGHT: 16–20 inches (40–50 cm)

WEIGHT: 31–49 pounds (14–22 kg)

COAT: Brown, brown and white, black, black and white, white; thick, woolly, sometimes corded

GROOMING:

EXERCISE NEEDS:

K-9 QUALITIES: Versatile and faithful

Believed to have been brought to the Spanish region of Andalusia by merchants, these smart dogs helped tow boats for fishermen, retrieve waterfowl for hunters, and herd sheep for farmers. They are suspicious of strangers and may be impatient with kids, so they're best with experienced owners.

WETTERHOUN

These rugged dogs, also known as Frisian water dogs, originally helped fishermen keep otters from eating their catch. The versatile dogs (pronounced vet-eh-hoon) are still valued as hunting companions, farm dogs, and guardians. To be good pets, they need early training, socialization, and jobs to do.

FROM: Netherlands

HEIGHT: 22–23 inches (55–59 cm)

WEIGHT: 33–44 pounds (15–20 kg)

COAT: Black, dark brown, with white chest markings; curly

GROOMING:

EXERCISE NEEDS:

K-9 QUALITIES: Adaptable, faithful, but a bit strong-willed

AMERICAN WATER SPANIEL

These rare spaniels, the state dog of Wisconsin, U.S.A., are skilled retrievers and small enough to fit into a boat—traits that made them popular hunting companions in the 19th century. They're outdoorsy athletes and loving pets, always up for a swim, hike, or game of fetch with kids.

FROM: U.S.A.

HEIGHT: 15–18 inches (38–45 cm)

WEIGHT: 25–45 pounds (11–20 kg)

COAT: Liver, brown, dark chocolate; tightly curled or very wavy

GROOMING:

EXERCISE NEEDS:

K-9 QUALITIES: Eager to please and cheerful

American Water Spaniels go ape over **BANANAS!** The sweet fruit is the pup's favorite **PEOPLE FOOD,** according to many owners. The potassium- and fiber-rich fruit is a **HEALTHY TREAT** for dogs.

PINSCHERS &
SCHNAUZERS

It may not seem like pinscher and schnauzer breeds have much in common. After all, most pinschers have sleek coats and pointy noses, while schnauzers sport bushy beards and mustaches. But until the late 1800s, they were considered varieties of the same breed! The dogs developed in central Europe, mainly Germany, in the 1700s and 1800s to be working farm dogs, killing rats that tried to eat (and spoil) grain. They later took on other duties, such as herding livestock and guarding the farm and home. The smooth-haired pinschers eventually were named German pinschers, and the bearded wire-haired pinschers became known as standard schnauzers. Over the next century, breeders developed them into several breeds in a variety of sizes. But all schnauzers and pinschers tend to be smart, brave, and athletic—traits that have also helped them excel in military and police work, search and rescue, and as guard dogs. With all that versatility, most pinschers and schnauzers also make great watchdogs and affectionate family pets. They're happy to throw their energy into all sorts of jobs, including dog sports or playing ball. Some of the dogs can be a bit independent and strong-willed—so good training and socialization are important—but they make up for it with their playfulness and devotion.

FROM:	Germany
HEIGHT:	24–28 inches (61–71 cm)
WEIGHT:	60–100 pounds (27–45 kg)
COAT:	Black, blue, fawn (Isabella), red, with rust markings; short, smooth
GROOMING:	
EXERCISE NEEDS:	
K-9 QUALITIES:	Loyal, loving, and protective

CANINE
EINSTEINS

Starting in the late 1950s, **DOBERMAN DRILL TEAMS** amazed crowds at dog shows, celebrations, and sporting events, where they marched in various formations and performed tricks showcasing their intelligence and agility.

DOBERMAN PINSCHER

Speedy, smart, and loyal, "Dobes" (or "Dobies") are affectionate and good-natured companions.

They are often thought of as having attitude problems and quick to react aggressively to the slightest affront. True, Dobermans were developed to be guard dogs, but their bad reputation comes from poor breeding, training, and socialization, not the breed's actual qualities. Properly bred and trained Dobermans are sweet, trustworthy companions that form deep bonds with their families. They're smart, eager to please, gentle with kids, and playful. It's their devotion that makes them loving protectors, ready to defend their people if the need arises. But most days, they just want to wow you with their skill at various jobs, spend time playing with you, then snuggle close to you in your home.

Dobermans get their name from Louis Dobermann, a German official who created the breed in the late 1800s so he'd have a companion and guard dog to accompany him as he collected taxes, a sometimes dangerous task. Many dogs are believed to have contributed to the Doberman: mixed breeds, black and tan Manchester terriers (p. 231), greyhounds (p. 123), German shepherds (p. 62), German pinschers (p. 215), Weimaraners (p. 177), and Rottweilers (p. 107). The result was a hardy, intelligent, and courageous dog with excellent guarding and tracking abilities, quick reflexes, speed, and stamina. Dobermans distinguished themselves as K-9 messengers and scouts for the U.S. Marine Corps in World War II. These days, they also excel as search-and-rescue dogs and, most of all, as wonderful companions.

POOCH PROS: DOG HANDLERS

In the show ring, where a dog's conformation—its build and movement—is judged to see how closely it matches the ideal for the breed, dog handlers get the pups ready to strut their stuff and show off their best qualities. They also help get the dogs ready to compete, making sure they're in top shape physically and perfectly groomed. In field trials for hunting dogs, handlers train the dogs and cue them during the competitions, which test the hunting dogs' abilities to track, point, flush out game, or retrieve. To become a professional dog handler for show dogs and athletes, many people start as a handler's assistant. But kids can also get experience in the show ring by competing in junior showmanship classes, which judge your skill in handling your dog.

AUSTRIAN PINSCHER

Developed from German pinschers (p. 215) and native Austrian dogs, these alert and loyal dogs originally worked as farm dogs, herding livestock and protecting the farm. These days, they're still reliable guard dogs but also loving family companions, especially devoted to and protective of kids.

FROM: Austria

HEIGHT: 17–20 inches (42–50 cm)

WEIGHT: 26–40 pounds (12–18 kg)

COAT: Stag red, russet gold, brownish yellow, black and tan, with white markings; dense, short

GROOMING:

EXERCISE NEEDS:

K-9 QUALITIES: Faithful and protective

AFFENPINSCHER

These scruffy little canines are big on personality. Considered to be among the most ancient toy dogs, "affens" were bred to rid homes and barns of rodents—a job they're still happy to perform. Devoted and affectionate pets, they're always up for play or an adventure.

FROM: Germany

HEIGHT: 9–11 inches (24–28 cm)

WEIGHT: 7–9 pounds (3–4 kg)

COAT: Black, possibly with silver or tan, belge (black and reddish brown), red; shaggy, wiry

GROOMING:

EXERCISE NEEDS:

K-9 QUALITIES: Bold, alert, and amusing

GERMAN PINSCHER

They look like small Dobermans (p. 212), but German pinschers actually are an older breed, one of the Dobe's ancestors. They're more closely related to schnauzer breeds than other pinschers are. Bred to be farm dogs, German pinschers are protective guardians. Strong-willed and bold, they need consistent training and exercise, and they do better with older kids.

FROM: Germany
HEIGHT: 17–19 inches (43–48 cm)
WEIGHT: 24–35 pounds (11–16 kg)
COAT: Black, blue, brown, fawn (Isabella), red, with markings; short, smooth, sleek

GROOMING:
EXERCISE NEEDS:
K-9 QUALITIES: Watchful and alert

MINIATURE PINSCHER

"Min pins" are lively and fearless, willing to protect their families from strangers many times their size. Known as the "king of the toys," these spirited dogs—originally bred down from German pinschers to hunt rats on farms—are known for prancing, lifting their legs high as they walk or trot. They need experienced owners who can handle their strong wills and are best with older kids.

FROM: Germany
HEIGHT: 10–12 inches (25–30 cm)
WEIGHT: 8–10 pounds (4–5 kg)
COAT: Black and rust or tan, chocolate and rust or tan, red, stag red; short, smooth

GROOMING:
EXERCISE NEEDS:
K-9 QUALITIES: Lively, curious, and devoted

GIANT SCHNAUZER

The largest of the schnauzer breeds, the powerful "giants" were developed probably centuries ago by German farmers who needed larger dogs to drive cattle to market for sale. To supersize the schnauzers, breeders crossed standard schnauzers with larger, smooth-coated dogs, rough-coated sheepdogs, and black Great Danes (p. 106). Adaptable and intelligent, giants worked in breweries, stockyards, and butcher shops in the 1900s and then as police dogs throughout Europe. Friendly and confident, bold and energetic, they're happiest when they have jobs to do around the house. They're also dependable watchdogs, but they're not "all work." They also love to play—but may be a bit too rowdy for younger kids—and are affectionate family members that happily compete in dog sports or play games of fetch.

FROM: Germany
HEIGHT: 24–28 inches (60–70 cm)
WEIGHT: 55–85 pounds (25–39 kg)
COAT: Black, pepper and salt; dense, wiry
GROOMING:
EXERCISE NEEDS:
K-9 QUALITIES: Lively and protective

Despite their name, giant schnauzers are not a **"GIANT DOG BREED"**—a rough classification that usually includes dogs, such as mastiffs (p. 115) and Great Danes (p. 106), that grow heavier than 100 pounds (50 kg).

MINIATURE
SCHNAUZER

"Minis" are the most popular of the schnauzer breeds. These little dogs were bred down from standard schnauzers (p. 218) probably by crossing small members of that breed with affenpinschers (p. 214) and small poodles (p. 253). Developed to rid farms of rodents, they're serious squirrel chasers—and not the dogs you want to leave alone with your pet hamster! When you provide proper training, socialization, and exercise, minis are delightful pets. They are smart and lively dogs that enjoy being part of family life. Sometimes they prefer one member of the family, and they do best when they grow up together with kids in the family. They'll follow you around, bark loudly to make sure you don't miss someone at the front door, and happily compete in any type of dog sport.

FROM:	Germany
HEIGHT:	12–14 inches (30–36 cm)
WEIGHT:	11–20 pounds (5–9 kg)
COAT:	Pepper and salt, black and silver, black; dense, wiry
GROOMING:	
EXERCISE NEEDS:	
K-9 QUALITIES:	Energetic and playful

The **BUSHY BEARD AND MUSTACHE** aren't just fashion statements. Thick facial hair **PROTECTED** schnauzers from getting bitten by the rats they hunted on farms.

STANDARD
SCHNAUZER

Medium-size schnauzer-like dogs with rough coats were common in Europe in the Middle Ages and shown in German artwork from the 15th and 16th centuries. Those dogs are believed to be the ancestors of today's standard schnauzer, the first schnauzer breed. Standards were developed to be farm dogs, keeping rodents away from grain stores, as well as watchdogs and hunting dogs. They're smart, curious, and friendly—traits that make them devoted, if slightly mischievous, family pets.

FROM: Germany

HEIGHT: 17–20 inches (44–50 cm)

WEIGHT: 35–50 pounds (16–23 kg)

COAT: Black, pepper and salt; wiry, tight-fitting

GROOMING:

EXERCISE NEEDS:

K-9 QUALITIES: Friendly, active, vocal, and protective

"SCHNAUZER" comes from the German word *schnauze*, meaning **"SNOUT."**

DUTCH SMOUSHOND

These little working dogs adapted to several roles: watchdog, ratcatcher, and coachman's dog, companions that ran behind a horse and carriage. Today, they're rare but make energetic and affectionate pets.

FROM:	Netherlands
HEIGHT:	14–17 inches (35–42 cm)
WEIGHT:	20–22 pounds (9–10 kg)
COAT:	Yellow; shaggy, coarse, wiry

GROOMING:

EXERCISE NEEDS:

K-9 QUALITIES: Lively and adaptable

BLACK RUSSIAN TERRIER

These giant dogs were developed by the Soviet Army in the 1940s to be guard dogs in the frigid Russian winters. Their ancestors include giant schnauzers (p. 216), Rottweilers (p. 107), and Airedales (p. 224). Though protective, they can be friendly pets if they receive patient training and socialization from puppyhood.

FROM:	Russia
HEIGHT:	26–30 inches (66–77 cm)
WEIGHT:	83–143 pounds (38–65 kg)
COAT:	Black; thick, wavy

GROOMING:

EXERCISE NEEDS:

K-9 QUALITIES: Devoted and protective

TERRIERS

Few breeds are as spunky as terriers. These dogs, whose name comes from the Latin word for "earth," often seem like they're on a mission to tunnel to the center of it! Digging is a natural trait for dogs originally bred to hunt vermin and dive into underground burrows. Getting to their prey required tremendous persistence—and terriers have it in abundance—plus the right anatomy: Many terriers are small, and sturdy, with short, strong legs ideally suited for digging. Of course, not all terriers are small. Bigger terriers with longer legs were developed to hunt larger game aboveground, too, and to guard herds of livestock. Most, but not all, terriers were developed in the United Kingdom or Ireland, and they're often named for the regions where they originated, the types of critters they hunted, or the breeders who developed them. Terriers are bright, determined dogs that usually have winning personalities; they're friendly and affectionate—and sometimes feisty. Because they were bred to go after critters, they often need a lot of training and socialization to get along well with other dogs and pets. (Even then, it's probably best not to leave them alone with your pet hamster!) And don't be surprised if they try to excavate your garden.

BORDER TERRIER

With unusual otter-shaped heads and longer legs, border terriers stand out from the crowd. These intelligent dogs, which originated along the English-Scottish border to rid farms of foxes, have the usual terrier bravery combined with a laid-back, loving attitude that makes them popular pets that are happy to hang out with kids.

FROM:	UK
HEIGHT:	11–16 inches (28–41 cm)
WEIGHT:	11–16 pounds (5–7 kg)
COAT:	Blue and tan, grizzle and tan, red, wheaten; dense, hard, wiry

GROOMING:
EXERCISE NEEDS:
K-9 QUALITIES: Affectionate and obedient

BRAZILIAN TERRIER

Eager to chase little critters—underground, if needed!—these terriers, the result of European terriers crossed with Brazilian farm dogs, are both determined hunters and spunky pets with a mind of their own.

FROM:	Brazil
HEIGHT:	13–16 inches (33–40 cm)
WEIGHT:	15–22 pounds (7–10 kg)
COAT:	White with black and brown markings; short, smooth

GROOMING:
EXERCISE NEEDS:
K-9 QUALITIES: Frisky and devoted

BEDLINGTON
TERRIER

A dog in sheep's clothing? Yup, that's what a Bedlington looks like. These terriers, named for the mining town that bears their name, probably have an ancestry that includes whippets (p. 123) as well as terriers. They were bred in the mid-1800s to rid the mines of rodents and are masters at both endurance and speed. Capable hunters, they excel at a variety of dog sports. More mellow than many kinds of terriers, they're affectionate and lively playmates that are also happy to snuggle up next to their people.

Bedlington terriers are born with dark **COATS THAT GROW LIGHTER** as they get older. If they suffer an injury that damages their coat, the spot fills in with black fur.

FROM: UK/England
HEIGHT: 15–17 inches (38–43 cm)
WEIGHT: 17–23 pounds (8–10 kg)
COAT: Whitish blue, liver, sandy, possibly with tan; thick, woolly, curly

GROOMING:
EXERCISE NEEDS:
K-9 QUALITIES: Sweet and energetic

JAGDTERRIER

These terriers—both fearless and tireless—can hunt across any terrain. Seriously, any. Nothing stops these scrappy little dogs, which were bred from a variety of English and Welsh terriers. Jagdterriers (pronounced YAHK-terrier) are also known as German hunting terriers—with good reason. They're friendly, but they're too intent on hunting to be ideal family pets.

FROM: Germany
HEIGHT: 13–16 inches (33–40 cm)
WEIGHT: 19–22 pounds (8–10 kg)
COAT: Black and tan; rough-coated or smooth-coated

GROOMING:
EXERCISE NEEDS:
K-9 QUALITIES: Relentless and athletic

AIREDALE TERRIER

In the mid-1800s, breeders in the Aire Valley of Yorkshire, England, about 100 miles (160 km) south of the Scottish border, needed a terrier capable of hunting not just rats but larger game, too.

They bred the now extinct Old English black and tan terrier with otterhounds (p. 133) and other breeds to get a large terrier with great hunting ability. Originally called waterside or Bingley terriers, Airedales became known for their versatility, excelling not only as hunters but also herders, all-around farm workers, guard dogs, and eventually police and military K-9s.

Airedales are one of the largest terrier breeds, but they earned their nickname "king of the terriers" for more than their size and strength. They're also friendly and intelligent—which can lead the dogs into mischief if they don't have exercise and jobs to keep them busy. Like other working dogs, Airedales also need persistent training—and it better be fun to keep their attention—and socialization from an early age. These athletic terriers do everything with enthusiasm, whether competing in dog sports, digging up flowers in your garden, or loving you.

HERO HOUNDS

No one knew why the big Airedale showed up alone that day in 1928 at the waterfront in Wellington, New Zealand. The seamen and dockworkers didn't know that the dog had often visited the wharves before—or that he had run away from home after his companion, Elsie, died from a terrible illness just before her fourth birthday. Paddy the Wanderer, as he became known, soon became a much loved fixture on the waterfront. Seamen, dockworkers, taxi drivers, and harbor workers chipped in to pay his annual dog license. They looked the other way when Paddy stowed away on a ship or hopped a tram or taxi for a free ride. He even got to ride in a Gipsy Moth biplane! The Harbour Board, which managed the harbor and boat traffic, named the well-traveled pooch "assistant night watchman responsible for pirates, smugglers, and rodents." When Paddy died in 1939, a fleet of taxis formed a long funeral procession. Queens Wharf in Wellington placed a memorial plaque to Paddy the Wanderer next to a special drinking fountain—regular height for people, plus two fountains at ground level for dogs.

FROM:	UK/England
HEIGHT:	22–24 inches (56–61 cm)
WEIGHT:	50–70 pounds (23–32 kg)
COAT:	Tan and black, tan and grizzle (black/brown mix); wavy, wiry
GROOMING:	
EXERCISE NEEDS:	
K-9 QUALITIES:	Devoted and energetic

Airedales served with the **BRITISH MILITARY** and Red Cross during **WORLD WAR I.** They carried messages, warned troops when enemy forces were approaching, and rescued the injured.

FEARLESS FOX TERRIERS

Though they have different ancestries stretching back to the late 18th century, wire fox terriers and smooth fox terriers were long considered two varieties of one breed and, in early years, interbred. Carried in saddlebags by horse-riding hunters, fox terriers would dig out foxes that hounds had driven into underground hiding places. Fox terriers are energetic, natural-born diggers, and they're happy to uproot your garden. But well-trained and socialized fox terriers can be delightful pets and alert watchdogs. They love the limelight and excel as competitors in obedience and agility trials; as sniffer, search-and-rescue, and therapy dogs; and as television performers. They're adoring dogs that will learn tricks, play with you, and—if you manage to tire them out—snuggle with you on the sofa.

SMOOTH
FOX TERRIER

Besides their smooth coats, smooths' heads are more V-shaped than the wires'.

WIRE FOX TERRIER

These rough-coated terriers are also "wired" to spring into action.

FROM:	UK/England
HEIGHT:	Up to 15 inches (39 cm)
WEIGHT:	Up to 18 pounds (8 kg)
COAT:	White, with tan and/or black markings; wiry or smooth
GROOMING:	/////
EXERCISE NEEDS:	●●●●●
K-9 QUALITIES:	Active, outgoing, and affectionate

LAKELAND TERRIER

FROM: UK

HEIGHT: 13–15 inches (33–37 cm)

WEIGHT: 15–18 pounds (7–8 kg)

COAT: Blue, black, liver, red, wheaten, grizzle, possibly with "saddle" patch; dense, wiry

GROOMING:

EXERCISE NEEDS:

K-9 QUALITIES: Devoted and lively

One of the oldest working terrier breeds, "Lakeys" used to be known as Patterdale terriers. With boundless energy and love for their people, they're playful companions that have a zest for life, especially if it involves digging or chasing cats.

WELSH TERRIER

Larger than Lakeland terriers but smaller than Airedales (p. 224), Welsh terriers share their cousins' Old English black and tan terrier ancestry. These sturdy, outgoing dogs are a bit mellower than other terriers, but they're still happy to do some digging and remodel your garden if they don't get enough exercise and training.

FROM: UK/Wales

HEIGHT: Up to 15 inches (39 cm)

WEIGHT: 20–22 pounds (9–10 kg)

COAT: Black and tan, grizzle (bluish gray); wiry

GROOMING:

EXERCISE NEEDS:

K-9 QUALITIES: Friendly and playful

DANDIE DINMONT TERRIER

These rare short-legged, long-bodied terriers make lovable pets that enjoy romping and cuddling with kids. They have a surprisingly deep bark for a small dog and have a distinctive haircut with a poofy topknot of hair on their heads.

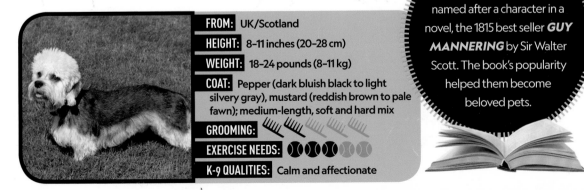

FROM: UK/Scotland

HEIGHT: 8–11 inches (20–28 cm)

WEIGHT: 18–24 pounds (8–11 kg)

COAT: Pepper (dark bluish black to light silvery gray), mustard (reddish brown to pale fawn); medium-length, soft and hard mix

GROOMING:

EXERCISE NEEDS:

K-9 QUALITIES: Calm and affectionate

The **DANDIE** is the only breed named after a character in a novel, the 1815 best seller *GUY MANNERING* by Sir Walter Scott. The book's popularity helped them become beloved pets.

VERSATILE AND VARIED TERRIERS OF IRELAND

Unlike many of the super-specialized terriers of their neighbors, Ireland's small terriers were bred more often to be all-purpose dogs, ridding farms of vermin, serving as guards and watchdogs, and even herding livestock. They are slightly more mellow than the average terrier. With proper exercise, training, and socialization, the Emerald Isle's terriers make playful, loving family companions.

SOFT-COATED WHEATEN TERRIER

Wheatens do everything with enthusiasm. If you leave the house even for only a few minutes, they'll welcome you back with a "wheaten greetin'," jumping and twirling with happiness. Their puppylike playfulness stays with them into adulthood, and their good-natured personalities combine terrier

FROM	Ireland
HEIGHT	17-19 inches (43-48 cm)
WEIGHT	30-40 pounds (14-18 kg)
COAT	Wheaten; soft, silky, gently wavy
GROOMING	
EXERCISE NEEDS	
K-9 QUALITIES	Lively, adaptable, and loving

alertness with working-dog steadiness. That makes them great watchdogs and family dogs, more than happy to romp with older kids. References to terriers that fit the wheaten's description go back to the days before official records were kept, fueling speculation that these terriers may be one of Ireland's oldest breeds. They share a common ancestry with Kerry blue and Irish terriers.

GLEN OF IMAAL TERRIER

FROM:	Ireland
HEIGHT:	12-14 inches (30–36 cm)
WEIGHT:	32-40 pounds (15–18 kg)
COAT:	Wheaten, blue brindle; medium-length
GROOMING:	
EXERCISE NEEDS:	
K-9 QUALITIES:	Active and devoted

Scruffy and cute, these little-known Glens developed in an isolated valley in the Wicklow Mountains. In addition to being farm and hunting dogs, these strong, sturdy terriers had a unique job: turnspit dogs, running on little treadmills that turned meat over the fire so it would cook evenly. Today, Glens are brave and loving pets.

IRISH TERRIER

FROM:	Ireland
HEIGHT:	18–19 inches (46–48 cm)
WEIGHT:	25-27 pounds (11-12 kg)
COAT:	Red, wheaten; tight
GROOMING:	
EXERCISE NEEDS:	
K-9 QUALITIES:	Intelligent and devoted

When fans say "ITs" are fiery, it's not just because they're the only all-red terriers. These long-legged dogs from County Cork are spirited and brave daredevils. But they're also delightful, charming family dogs that get along well with kids.

KERRY BLUE TERRIER

With roots going back a century in Ireland's County Kerry, these smart and athletic terriers are multipurpose dogs, herding sheep and cattle on farms, guarding the homestead, and trailing and retrieving. Loving pets, they still like having jobs to do.

FROM:	Ireland
HEIGHT:	18–19 inches (46–48 cm)
WEIGHT:	33–40 pounds (15–18 kg)
COAT:	Light to dark blue; soft, dense, wavy
GROOMING:	
EXERCISE NEEDS:	
K-9 QUALITIES:	Lively and devoted

Kerry blue puppies are born black, with their **COATS FADING TO BLUE** over the following 18 months.

RAT TERRIER

These strong and fearless little terriers were common farm dogs in America a century ago, bred to protect farms from vermin that could spoil grain stores. Now they're enjoying a resurgence in popularity in a new role: friendly family dogs. A bit calmer and more easily trained than the average terrier, "RTs," or "ratties," are pleasant, outgoing, devoted, and up for almost anything—playing with kids, hiking, agility competitions, or snuggling on the sofa.

FROM: U.S.A.

HEIGHT: 10–13 inches (25–33 cm) for miniature; 13–18 inches (33–46 cm) for standard

WEIGHT: 10–25 pounds (5–11 kg)

COAT: Variety of colors, with large white or colored patches; short, smooth

GROOMING:

EXERCISE NEEDS:

K-9 QUALITIES: Inquisitive and loving

TEDDY ROOSEVELT TERRIER

"TRTs" share a common ancestry and working history with their rat terrier cousins, but TRTs are shorter-legged. These energetic and affectionate dogs—named for the U.S. president believed to have owned such terriers to combat the rat infestation in the White House—can adapt to a variety of lifestyles.

FROM: U.S.A.

HEIGHT: 8–15 inches (20–38 cm)

WEIGHT: 10–25 pounds (5–11 kg)

COAT: White, bicolor, tricolor; short

GROOMING:

EXERCISE NEEDS:

K-9 QUALITIES: Watchful, bold, and friendly

AMERICAN HAIRLESS TERRIER

Created in 1972, when a litter of rat terriers included a hairless puppy, "AHTs" are the result of a genetic mutation. Since developed into their own breed, they're cheerful pets that get along with kids and enjoy family activities. They need sweaters in the winter and sunscreen in sunny weather.

FROM: U.S.A.
HEIGHT: 10–18 inches (25–46 cm)
WEIGHT: 10–25 pounds (5–11 kg)
COAT: Variety of skin colors, usually with freckles or spots; hairless

GROOMING:
EXERCISE NEEDS:
K-9 QUALITIES: Energetic and friendly

MANCHESTER TERRIER

Manchester terriers were developed in the 19th century to kill rats and to race, and they have some whippet (p. 123) in their backgrounds. These days, the elegant dogs are loving family companions, as at home in cities as in the countryside, as long as they get enough exercise. The American Kennel Club recognizes both standard and toy sizes, with the toys being very similar to English toy terriers (p. 246). The larger dogs are better family pets, as the toy terriers can be too delicate for play.

FROM: UK
HEIGHT: 10–12 inches (25–30 cm) for toy; 15 to 16 inches (38–41 cm) for standard
WEIGHT: Up to 12 pounds (5 kg) for toy; 12 to 22 pounds (5–10 kg) for standard

COAT: Black and tan; short
GROOMING:
EXERCISE NEEDS:
K-9 QUALITIES: Alert, watchful, and loyal

WEST HIGHLAND
WHITE TERRIER

These little white bundles of scruffy adorableness could probably out-cute your favorite plush toy animals. But make no mistake: There's serious terrier inside them.

"Westies" are energetic and inquisitive terriers, bred to handle the rugged terrain and unforgiving environment of the Scottish Highlands, where they originally were hunting companions. They share their ancestry with other short-legged Scottish terrier breeds, including Skye (p. 235), cairn (p. 238), and Dandie Dinmont (p. 227) terriers.

These days, Westies are more often family dogs—a role they fulfill with energy and cheerfulness. They love their people, including kids. Give them jobs—agility, flyball, rally, and obedience competitions are great choices—to keep their terrier brains busy. Consistent exercise, training, and socialization will keep their digging and barking within tolerable limits. Westies adore being part of family activities, but think of them more as playmates than couch potatoes. They have a lot of spunk and are always up for fun.

POOCH PROS: DOG BEHAVIOR RESEARCHERS

Ever wonder what your pup is thinking when she stares at you with those big brown puppy eyes? Or how he senses your moods even if you're trying to keep them to yourself? Or whether she feels guilty after scattering trash all over your living room? If these questions keep you up at night, consider a career as a dog behavior and cognition (understanding) researcher. In recent years, researchers have gained a lot of insight into how dogs understand us, their world, and themselves. But it's just the tip of the iceberg. There's a lot more to learn!

Westies are standouts in many ways—and looks are one of them. They were first bred to have **SNOW-WHITE COATS** so they'd be easy to see running through foliage during hunts.

FROM: UK/Scotland

HEIGHT: 10–11 inches (25–28 cm)

WEIGHT: 15–20 pounds (7–9 kg)

COAT: White; thick, hard

GROOMING:

EXERCISE NEEDS:

K-9 QUALITIES: Spunky and devoted

AUSTRALIAN TERRIER

These shaggy little "Aussies," descendants of dogs brought by British settlers to the land down under in the 1800s, were the first breed developed in Australia and recognized by other kennel clubs. Clever and good-natured terriers, they make good watchdogs as well as family pets.

FROM:	Australia
HEIGHT:	10–11 inches (25–28 cm)
WEIGHT:	14–16 pounds (6–7 kg)
COAT:	Red, blue with tan; straight, dense, harsh

GROOMING:
EXERCISE NEEDS:
K-9 QUALITIES: Spirited and upbeat

CESKY TERRIER

These terriers (whose name is pronounced CHESS-kay), still used as working dogs and watchdogs, are more laid-back than some terriers. But they still want to be on the go, either hunting, digging in your garden, or playing catch with you until your arm feels like it wants to drop off!

FROM:	Czech Republic
HEIGHT:	10–13 inches (25–32 cm)
WEIGHT:	13–22 pounds (6–10 kg)
COAT:	Gray-blue, liver; wavy, silky, shiny
GROOMING:	
EXERCISE NEEDS:	
K-9 QUALITIES:	Playful andfearless, but sometimes stubborn

SEALYHAM TERRIER

FROM: UK/Wales
HEIGHT: 10–12 inches (25–30 cm)
WEIGHT: 18–20 pounds (8–9 kg)
COAT: White; long, hard
GROOMING:
EXERCISE NEEDS:
K-9 QUALITIES: Loving, playful, and watchful

A bit more relaxed than some other terriers, "Sealys" can be happy in the city or countryside. These powerful pups are curious and devoted to their people, happy to snuggle on the couch if they get enough exercise. Originally bred in the mid-1800s to tackle badgers, otters, and fox, these days they're family pets.

SKYE TERRIER

Taking their name from Scotland's rugged Isle of Skye, these adorable, low-slung terriers originally were powerful hunters, but now they're spirited pets with minds of their own.

FROM: UK/Scotland
HEIGHT: 9–10 inches (23–25 cm)
WEIGHT: 24–40 pounds (11–18 kg)
COAT: Gray, black, cream, fawn; long, silky
GROOMING:
EXERCISE NEEDS:
K-9 QUALITIES: Devoted and good-natured

JAPANESE TERRIER

Cheerful and playful, these rare dogs, almost unknown outside of Japan, are probably descended from English toy terriers (p.246) and now extinct toy bull terriers. They are one of the few terrier breeds that are honest-to-goodness lapdogs, originally bred to be loving pets, not workers. But, like any terrier, they're ready for (and need) active time, too.

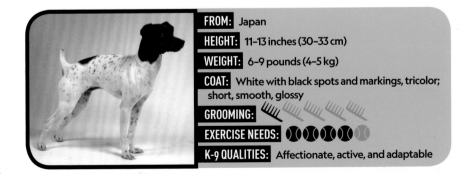

FROM: Japan
HEIGHT: 11–13 inches (30–33 cm)
WEIGHT: 6–9 pounds (4–5 kg)
COAT: White with black spots and markings, tricolor; short, smooth, glossy
GROOMING:
EXERCISE NEEDS:
K-9 QUALITIES: Affectionate, active, and adaptable

PARSON JACK RUSSELL'S TENACIOUS TERRIERS

In the mid-1800s, the Reverend John "Jack" Russell, known as "the sporting parson," bred sturdy, mostly white working terriers—probably from now extinct Old English white terriers and black and tan terriers—with the drive to hunt foxes both above and belowground. Soon afterward, pretty much any earth-working terrier was called a "Jack Russell" in honor of the reverend. But things eventually got sorted, and a definite breed of Jack Russell terrier emerged—or, depending on whom you ask, two or three definite breeds. (It's a heated debate.) True to their working-dog background, they can be a handful and need to be kept busy. But the fearless and lively terriers are also friendly, playful, and loving.

FROM: UK/England

HEIGHT: 10–12 inches (25–31 cm) for Russells; 13–15 inches (32–38 cm) for Parsons

WEIGHT: 9–15 pounds (4–7 kg) for Russells; 13–18 pounds (6–8 kg) for Parsons

COAT: White with tan and/or black markings; smooth or rough

GROOMING:

EXERCISE NEEDS:

K-9 QUALITIES: High-energy and devoted

RUSSELL TERRIER

The popular Russells—still called Jack Russells outside the United States—are the smaller breed.

The first Jack Russells were bred to fit in **SADDLEBAGS** so their owners could carry them on **HORSEBACK.**

PARSON
RUSSELL TERRIER

Parsons are the longer-legged breed.

THE "PERFECT DEMONS" FROM TRUMPINGTON STREET

Around the turn of the 20th century, students from England's prestigious Cambridge University got little terriers, crosses of Yorkshire (p. 244) and Irish terriers (p. 229), to rid their dormitories of rats. One of those "perfect demons"—a nickname early breeders used to describe the energetic pups' vermin-chasing—was crossed with a Scottish-type terrier to rid a stable on Trumpington Street of rats. These Trumpington terriers were then crossed with small red Irish terriers to produce Norfolk terriers, and with a little white terrier, a Dandie Dinmont (p. 227) and Fox terrier (p. 226) mix, to create Norwich terriers. At first, they were considered the same breed, but then later were recognized as distinct. Some of the smallest working terriers, these robust canines have big, bold personalities. Charming and friendly, they're some of the best terriers for families. They're sturdy and playful, always up for a romp with older kids.

UNIVERSITY OF CAMBRIDGE

HERE'S A TRICK to help keep these cousins straight: A Norfolk's ears fold, a Norwich's are pointy like a witch's hat.

NORFOLK TERRIER

Norfolk terriers have drop ears and slightly longer backs than their cousins.

FROM: UK/England

HEIGHT: 9–10 inches (23–25 cm)

WEIGHT: 11–12 pounds (5–6 kg)

COAT: Red, wheaten, black and tan, grizzle; wiry, water-resistant

GROOMING:

EXERCISE NEEDS:

K-9 QUALITIES: Plucky and charming

NORWICH TERRIER

Norwich terriers have pointy ears that stand up.

CAIRN TERRIER

FROM:	UK/Scotland
HEIGHT:	11–12 inches (28–31 cm)
WEIGHT:	13–18 pounds (6–8 kg)
COAT:	Wheaten, cream, red, silver, black, brindle; hard, harsh outer coat
GROOMING:	
EXERCISE NEEDS:	
K-9 QUALITIES:	Bright and affectionate

Cairns may be small, but they're not delicate little dogs. These scraggly terriers have big personalities and plenty of energy. They're always up for romping with the kids, going on hikes, or protecting your house from squirrels. But if you do manage to tire them out, they're happy to snuggle with you on the sofa. They're adaptable little dogs, happy both on farms and in city apartments—as long as they get some quality exercise. Of course, if they're good at squirrel patrol, that also means you shouldn't trust them around your gerbils. These popular pets share a working-dog ancestry with their Scottish cousins, Westies (p. 232), Dandie Dinmonts (p. 227) and, of course, Skye terriers (p. 235). Cairns get their name from the Scottish Gaelic term for a stack of stones that served as a memorial or marker—or, for little rodents, a hiding place. With their well-padded front paws, cairns were only happy to dig through piles of rock to get at them.

⭐ PUP STARS

"Toto, I've a feeling we're not in Kansas anymore." The 1939 movie *The Wizard of Oz* gave us that famous line, and a little cairn terrier gave us many of the story's thrilling and *awww*-inspiring moments. A debate rages, however, over whether the dog in the book the movie was based on was a cairn or a Yorkie (p. 244). Like the character she played (or, some might say, like any terrier), Terry, the canine actress, had a talent for getting into trouble. Her owners couldn't housetrain the pup, so they dropped her off at a dog trainer—and never came back. It turns out the trainer was one of Hollywood's top dog trainers, and he saw a lot of star potential in Terry. There was no going back to Kansas for that cairn.

SCOTTISH TERRIER

"Scottish terrier" was once a catchall name for all short-legged terriers from Scotland, but these "Scotties" are the real deal, the originals—a breed that has changed little since the mid-1800s. Once the favorites of King James VI of Scotland in the 17th century and Queen Victoria of England in the 19th century, Scotties are now popular pets. They're instantly recognizable with their long, low-slung bodies and bushy beards and brows. Though black is the classic Scottie color, their coats actually come in a variety of shades. These are true terriers—rugged, determined, and a bit willful. On the outside, Scotties seem to be all business, alert and watchful, always ready to chase off an invading squirrel or tunnel after a mole. But on the inside, they're softies, devoted to their people and ready for fun … as long as it's dignified.

FROM: Scotland

HEIGHT: 10–11 inches (25–28 cm)

WEIGHT: 18–22 pounds (8–10 kg)

COAT: Black, wheaten, brindle, silver, red; long, hard, wiry

GROOMING:

EXERCISE NEEDS:

K-9 QUALITIES: Affectionate and watchful, but stubborn

When the makers of the classic board game **MONOPOLY** asked members of the public to vote in 2013 on which **GAME PIECES** would get to stay as part of the set, the little Scottie dog game piece got the **MOST VOTES,** beating the top hat, battleship, and even the race car. Sadly, for fans of housework, the iron was voted out of the game.

BULL TERRIER

These muscular dogs look tough, like they could be professional wrestlers, but "bullies" are actually supersweet, playful dogs that have reputations as mischievous clowns and form deep bonds with their people. They'll delight you with the energy they put into activities that amuse them—but that might not include lying peacefully at your feet. As their name suggests, bullies were developed in the mid-1800s from crosses of bulldogs (p. 112) and various terriers. The result was a dog with a bulldog's courage and a terrier's intensity and agility. Bullies aren't yappy dogs, so if they bark, pay attention. Befitting a dog whose head looks like a medieval battering ram, Bullies can be headstrong, seeing little reason to listen to you. The powerful dogs are also infamous leash-pullers and overly protective at times. But all that can be soothed with early, patient, and persistent training—preferably with food and toy rewards—and socialization to make them the well-mannered, gentle pets that they can be.

FROM: UK
HEIGHT: 21–22 inches (53–56 cm)
WEIGHT: 50–70 pounds (23–32 kg)
COAT: White, red, black, brindle; short, glossy
GROOMING:
EXERCISE NEEDS:
K-9 QUALITIES: Energetic and affectionate

MINIATURE
BULL TERRIER

All that bully personality in a smaller package—that's what a "mini" is. Fans say the breed, bred down in size from bull terriers, could claim the title of "clown prince of dogdom."

FROM: UK
HEIGHT: 10–14 inches (25–36 cm)
WEIGHT: 24–33 pounds (11–15 kg)
COAT: White, red, black, fawn, brindle; short, glossy
GROOMING:
EXERCISE NEEDS: ⚾⚾⚾⚾⚾
K-9 QUALITIES: Energetic and mischievous

⭐ PUP STARS

Talk about salesmanship! We're talking about a bully named Patsy Ann, born in 1929, who helped Juneau, Alaska, U.S.A., earn a reputation as a friendly port. Patsy Ann was born deaf, but she had such an uncanny sense of when ships were arriving that some people swore she heard their whistles. She greeted all the arriving ships, and she visited local businesses when no ships were in dock. In 1934, the town's mayor gave Patsy Ann the title of "official greeter of Juneau, Alaska." Loved by all, a bronze statue of Patsy Ann now welcomes hundreds of thousands of tourists to Juneau's wharf.

STAFFORDSHIRE BULL TERRIER

Bred in the 1800s from various bulldogs and terriers, "Staffies" are powerful and agile. These brave dogs adore their people—but maybe not other dogs or cats.

FROM: UK
HEIGHT: 14–16 inches (36–41 cm)
WEIGHT: 24–37 pounds (11–17 kg)
COAT: Variety of colors; short, glossy
GROOMING:
EXERCISE NEEDS:
K-9 QUALITIES: Brave and devoted

PATTERDALE TERRIER

American bully breeds were symbols of **NATIONAL PRIDE** during World Wars I and II.

These little terriers from England's Lake District, bred to be working dogs, are energetic and determined hunters. These pups are at their best with experienced owners who can give them proper training, exercise, and socialization.

FROM: UK/England
HEIGHT: 10–15 inches (25–38 cm)
WEIGHT: 11–13 pounds (5–6 kg)
COAT: Black, red, bronze (brownish-black), black and tan; smooth, coarse, or rough
GROOMING:
EXERCISE NEEDS:
K-9 QUALITIES: Active and skilled

AMERICAN STAFFORDSHIRE TERRIER

Developed from Staffordshire bull terriers (p. 242), "Am Staffs" are larger than their British cousins. Friendly and affectionate, these people-oriented dogs can be great family dogs when properly raised. Like their British cousins, they are probably not the best dogs to have with cats and other small pets.

FROM: U.S.A.
HEIGHT: 17–19 inches (43–48 cm)
WEIGHT: 62–88 pounds (28–40 kg)
COAT: Variety of colors; short, glossy
GROOMING:
EXERCISE NEEDS:
K-9 QUALITIES: Sweet, devoted, and courageous

AMERICAN PIT BULL TERRIER

In the past, "APBTs"—or "pitties"— were popular farm and family dogs and military mascots. In the hands of loving families who raise, train, and socialize them properly, these friendly and playful dogs can be great pets.

FROM: U.S.A.
HEIGHT: 18–22 inches (46 to 56 cm)
WEIGHT: 30–60 pounds (14–27 kg)
COAT: Variety of colors; short, glossy
GROOMING:
EXERCISE NEEDS:
K-9 QUALITIES: Powerful and devoted

GETTING A BAD RAP

Pit bulls and other bully breeds get unfairly accused of being "aggressive" dogs. It's true that these breeds were originally developed for fighting and that pit bulls selectively bred for their fighting ability may be more likely than other breeds to fight with dogs. But it doesn't mean they'll be aggressive toward people—or that they can't be socialized to be around other dogs. If bred for work and companionship, they're gentle, devoted pets.

FROM:	UK/England, Scotland
HEIGHT:	7–9 inches (18–23 cm)
WEIGHT:	4–7 pounds (2–3 kg)
COAT:	Black/blue with gold/tan; long, silky
GROOMING:	
EXERCISE NEEDS:	
K-9 QUALITIES:	Spirited and affectionate

SUPER SMALLS

Yorkies' hair—like yours—**WILL KEEP GROWING** and can reach **TWO FEET** (60 cm) long. Show dogs often sport long, flowing coats, but most pet Yorkies have shorter, spunkier "puppy cuts."

YORKSHIRE TERRIER

Don't be fooled by their elegant looks. "Yorkies" were developed as working dogs, to eradicate rats and mice from wool mills and mine shafts in northern England, and they still have the courage, intelligence, and energy to go with such work.

They trace their ancestry to a variety of Scottish and English terriers, crossed when Scottish weavers moved into the Yorkshire area of England in the mid-1800s. Originally called broken-haired Scottish terriers, they were slightly larger than today's Yorkies but small enough that they didn't cost too much to feed. As Yorkies became companion dogs—favorites of high society—breeders selectively bred them for smaller size.

Today, Yorkies are considered a toy breed, but they still have the bold, fearless personality of a typical terrier. It's quite possible they don't realize how little they are, because they don't hesitate to take on dogs many times their size. Some Yorkies are cuddlier than others, but all prefer to walk instead of ride in a puppy purse. Intelligent and curious, they like to investigate their surroundings. If you have Yorkies, you need to love combing their long, silky coats, but they're worth the effort. And, yes, you can put bows in their hair (but only if they're OK with it!).

HERO HOUNDS

When Bill Wynne first saw the little Yorkshire terrier in March 1944 in an abandoned army foxhole, she was scrawny and underfed, with hair badly cut, weighing a mere four pounds (1.8 kg) and standing only seven inches (18 cm) tall. But Bill didn't think twice about keeping her. He named her Smoky, and she became the U.S. Army Air Corps corporal's constant companion during World War II, surviving air raids, a dozen combat missions, and typhoons. One time, she scampered through a long pipe to help servicemen string an underground telephone wire. Smoky's help got communications established days faster, and she was credited with saving 250 men and 40 planes that day. When Bill got sick and had to go to an army hospital, Smoky went with him. She cheered up all the sick and injured patients by performing tricks that Bill had taught her. Without any special training, she had become one of the first therapy dogs.

SILKY TERRIER

No, they're not big Yorkies—but it's easy to tell that they're related. A cross between Yorkies (p. 244) and Australian terriers (p. 234), silkys are typical terriers, spirited and fond of digging. Despite their size—they're a toy breed—they're usually not content being lapdogs, but they're always up for playing. They'll happily take up residence in the city or countryside.

FROM:	Australia
HEIGHT:	9–10 inches (23–25 cm)
WEIGHT:	8–10 pounds (4–5 kg)
COAT:	Gray-blue and tan, black and tan; long, silky

GROOMING:	
EXERCISE NEEDS:	
K-9 QUALITIES:	Friendly and lively

ENGLISH TOY TERRIER

Originally called miniature black and tan terriers, English toys are similar to Manchester terriers (p. 231) but are smaller and have ears that stand up. Formerly ratters, they became popular town pets during the "dog fancy" years of the late 1800s. Lively and watchful, these terriers are also loving, playful, and sometimes cuddly pets.

FROM:	UK/England
HEIGHT:	10–12 inches (25–30 cm)
WEIGHT:	7–9 pounds (3–4 kg)
COAT:	Black and tan; thick, glossy

GROOMING:	
EXERCISE NEEDS:	
K-9 QUALITIES:	Affectionate and adaptable

TOY FOX TERRIER

Bred to rid farms of rats, "TFTs" are a cross between smooth fox terriers (p. 226) and several toy breeds, including miniature pinschers (p. 215), Italian greyhounds (p. 123), Chihuahuas (p. 268), and Manchester terriers (p. 231). They have all the terrier drive and playfulness—and make good watchdogs—but some also may be happy cuddling in laps of adults and older kids. (They're a bit too delicate for young kids.)

SUPER SMALLS

FROM:	U.S.A.
HEIGHT:	9–12 inches (23–30 cm)
WEIGHT:	4–7 pounds (2–3 kg)
COAT:	White with black and/or tan; short, satiny

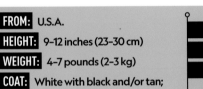

GROOMING:
EXERCISE NEEDS:
K-9 QUALITIES: Playful and fearless

BIEWER TERRIER

Named for their breeder, Biewers originated in the mid-1980s, when a little blue-white-and-gold puppy was born in a litter of Yorkies. Since developed into their own breed, these friendly terriers (whose name is pronounced BEE-vair) are devoted to their families, though they have a mischievous streak typical of terriers.

FROM:	Germany
HEIGHT:	7–11 inches (18–28 cm)
WEIGHT:	4–8 pounds (2–4 kg)
COAT:	Tricolor; long, soft, silky

GROOMING:
EXERCISE NEEDS:
K-9 QUALITIES: Playful and affectionate

COMPANION & TOY DOGS

Almost any dog can be a great companion, of course. Even if the breed originally was developed to hunt, herd, or guard, most working dogs have made the move into our homes—and hearts—where they've become our best buddies. But there are several breeds that took the express route straight to our laps and couches.

Most of these dogs did not rid our ancestors' barns of rats or watch over their sheep. Developed solely to be companions, they were the pampered pets of royals and aristocrats through the late 1800s. They were selectively bred to hang out with people, sitting on laps, entertaining or loving them, or just looking decorative. Companion dogs often were bred to emphasize different features that people thought looked cool—even if they didn't serve any useful purpose. Many companion dogs are "toy" breeds, small dogs ideally suited for cuddling on our laps or carrying in our arms. Today, of course, they're not only playthings of the rich. These "nonworking" breeds may take on worthwhile jobs, such as service or therapy dogs. But most of all, many of these companion dogs make terrific family pets. Pamper them if you want, but make sure to engage them in active play and exercise. These are, after all, the descendants of wolves.

BICHON FRISE

Little, playful fluff balls of wonderfulness: That pretty much sums up the bichon frise (pronounced BEE-shon Free-ZAY). Their name means something like "small dog with curly hair" in French, but most people translate it as "fluffy white dog." Because, you know … they are. They're also gentle, affectionate, and playful companions that can burst into excited romps that fans call the "bichon blitz." These toy dogs are not only playmates, they're also smart and easy to train; some have found jobs as service or therapy dogs. If these popular dogs sound absolutely perfect, it's because they are—well, almost. They can be a bit difficult to housetrain and require a lot of grooming. (But, if you're into bows and bling, that may be good thing!) These spunky little dogs have a deep history. Small white dogs described as bichons—descended from larger, curly coated water dogs—were known for centuries in the Mediterranean region and accompanied Spanish and Italian sailors on their voyages. Bichons' charming personalities were so valued, the dogs were bartered internationally.

FROM: Mediterranean, possibly Spain
HEIGHT: 9–12 inches (23–30 cm)
WEIGHT: 10–18 pounds (5–8 kg)
COAT: White, possibly with apricot, buff, or cream; long, fluffy
GROOMING:
EXERCISE NEEDS:
K-9 QUALITIES: Adoring and adorable

Bichons have won adoring fans throughout the ages. One of the biggest was the 16th-century French king **HENRY III,** who, as the legend goes, dangled a basket around his neck to carry his pet bichon so they'd never be separated.

MALTESE

Picture this: a playful pup racing toward you, her long, luxurious coat flowing behind her, dazzling white in the sun. If that's your image of the perfect pet, then the Maltese may be the dog for you. Not just sweet and adorable, these toy dogs are hardy, vigorous canines that are happy to learn tricks and compete in dog sports such as agility and obedience. Most of all, they want to play and hang out with their people. One of the breeds that developed simply as companions, Maltese are happy cuddling in your lap. But, whew, is that coat a commitment! It takes daily grooming to keep Maltese looking their best. Many people have professional groomers clip the dogs' fur short into a "puppy clip" to make the job easier, but even those cuts need daily care. Maltese dogs' charming personalities and hardy athleticism have made them prized companions for centuries, with art and stories from long ago depicting the dogs. In ancient times, Maltese were often sold or traded internationally, ensuring their spread around the world. By the Middle Ages, they were living in the laps of luxury—quite literally. European aristocrats fell in love with the cheerful pets, with women tucking them in a sleeve or blouse to carry them around.

Leona Helmsley, the rich **"HOTEL QUEEN"** and real estate tycoon, so loved her pet Maltese, Trouble, that the dog received a **$2 MILLION** inheritance after the businesswoman died!

FROM: Malta
HEIGHT: 8–10 inches (20–25 cm)
WEIGHT: 6–8 pounds (3–4 kg)
COAT: White; long, silky
GROOMING:
EXERCISE NEEDS:
K-9 QUALITIES: Lively and affectionate

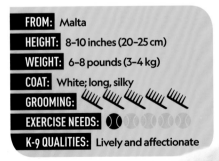

COTON DE TULEAR

Cotons (pronounced co-TAWN day two-LEE-are) do, indeed, have cottony-soft coats. Related to bichons (p. 250), these sturdy and athletic "cotton dogs" are highly sociable. They love their families, including kids and other pets, but do not like to be left alone. They're happy as lapdogs but active enough to compete in dog sports.

FROM: Madagascar
HEIGHT: 10–13 inches (25–32 cm)
WEIGHT: 9–13 pounds (4–6 kg)
COAT: White; long, soft, cottony

GROOMING:
EXERCISE NEEDS:
K-9 QUALITIES: Friendly, loyal, and lively

LÖWCHEN

These affectionate "little lion" dogs, named for their distinctive trims, have been around for 400 years. They're bold as lions around other dogs, but they're charming little clowns around their people. (Their name is pronounced LEUV-chen.)

FROM: France, Germany
HEIGHT: 10–13 inches (25–33 cm)
WEIGHT: 8–18 pounds (4–8 kg)
COAT: Variety of colors; long, wavy

GROOMING:
EXERCISE NEEDS:
K-9 QUALITIES: Affectionate and lively

BOLOGNESE

A little shier than their bichon (p. 250) cousins, Bolognese (pronounced bo-luh-NAZE) love people—but are sometimes one-person dogs.

FROM: Italy
HEIGHT: 10–12 inches (26–31 cm)
WEIGHT: 7–9 pounds (3–4 kg)
COAT: White; long

GROOMING:
EXERCISE NEEDS:
K-9 QUALITIES: Laid-back and intelligent

POODLE
(TOY AND MINIATURE)

Bred down in size from the water-retriever standard poodles (p. 206), these smaller varieties have always been just companion dogs. The midsize minis are the most popular poodles, with energy to match their high regard. They love being right in the middle of family activities and may follow you around looking for attention or to play. Toys are the ultimate lapdogs, though they're playful and energetic enough that they need to get out for a good walk or romp in the yard. In the 1700s, French king Louis XVI became enamored with toy poodles, earning them the nickname "French poodle." And through the next century, the upper crust of society kept the dogs as pampered pets, often styling their coats in fanciful ways. One of the most intelligent dog breeds, poodles need jobs to keep their minds busy so they don't plot ways of getting into mischief.

FROM: Germany
HEIGHT: Up to 10 (25 cm) inches for toy; 10–15 inches (25–38 cm) for miniature
WEIGHT: 7–9 pounds (3–4 kg) for toy; 15–18 pounds (7–8 kg) for miniature

COAT: Apricot, black, blue, brown, cream, gray, red, silver, silver-beige (faded brown), white; curly
GROOMING:
EXERCISE NEEDS:
K-9 QUALITIES: Smart and affectionate

BRUSSELS GRIFFON

SUPER SMALLS

Depending on whom you ask, the Brussels griffon is one or three breeds, with distinct coats and names (Brussels griffon, Belgian griffon, and smooth-coated Brussels griffon). Athletic and amusing, smart and active, these little pups may demand to be the center of attention, and they want to stick close to their favorite person. But they may not like hugs and kisses from kids—or to be around rowdy play.

FROM: Belgium

HEIGHT: 9–11 inches (23–28 cm)

WEIGHT: 7–11 pounds (3–5 kg)

COAT: Varies by breed/type. Brussels griffon: red; medium-length, rough, wiry; Belgian griffon: black, black and tan; medium-length, rough, wiry; smooth-coated Brussels griffon: red, black and tan, black; short, straight, smooth

GROOMING:

EXERCISE NEEDS:

K-9 QUALITIES: Devoted and mischievous

HIMALAYAN SHEEPDOG

These rare canines, also known as Bhotia, are definitely not little lapdogs! Related to the larger Tibetan mastiff (p. 101), they come from the foothills of the Himalaya, where they've been watchdogs and loyal companions for active, outdoorsy families.

FROM: Nepal

HEIGHT: 20–25 inches (51–63 cm)

WEIGHT: 50–60 pounds (23–27 kg)

COAT: White, gold, black, possibly with markings; long, harsh

GROOMING:

EXERCISE NEEDS:

K-9 QUALITIES: Watchful, adaptable, and somewhat reserved

DANISH-SWEDISH FARMDOG

A working dog and happy companion, these friendly dogs are always up for a romp with the kids. They've been around since the 1700s—and probably have pinscher-type ancestry—but only got their name in the mid-1980s.

FROM: Denmark, Sweden
HEIGHT: 13–15 inches (32–37 cm)
WEIGHT: 15–26 pounds (7–12 kg)
COAT: White with tan and/or black; short, smooth

GROOMING:
EXERCISE NEEDS:
K-9 QUALITIES: Adaptable and active

KROMFOHRLANDER

Named for the region in Germany where they were developed in the 1950s, the Kromfohrländer (pronounced KROME-fore-lahn-dair) probably has terrier, hound, and herding-dog background. These cute dogs are playful and loving.

One of the Kromfohrländer's ancestors is believed to be a mixed-breed dog named Peter, who was **A MASCOT FOR U.S. TROOPS** stationed in Germany after World War II.

FROM: Germany
HEIGHT: 15–18 inches (38–46 cm)
WEIGHT: 20–35 pounds (9–16 kg)
COAT: White with tan markings and speckles; smooth or rough
GROOMING:
EXERCISE NEEDS:
K-9 QUALITIES: Good-natured and eager to please

HAVANESE

If it's possible for a dog to be *too* cute, Havanese are serious contenders for the title.

The popular dogs always seem to have a spring in their steps and a mischievous twinkle in their eyes. They're famous for loving to play with kids, but they're also content to snuggle on your lap. Havanese look like fluffy little mops of dogs (and, yes, their coats do have a tendency to mop up leaves as they walk along), and they require a lot of care, even if their coats are clipped short. Havanese also have deeper, decidedly not-yappy barks, which they reserve for alerting their people to strangers. Easy to train and cheerful, these dogs have the stamina for dog sports and also make good therapy dogs.

The national dog of Cuba—and its only native dog breed—Havanese are named for the country's capital. They have a history almost as colorful as their coats. Long ago, the Spanish brought bichon-type dogs to Cuba from Tenerife, the largest of Spain's Canary Islands, off West Africa. The dogs adapted to Cuba's climate, becoming smaller and growing white silky coats. Known as the blanquito de la Habana, or Havana silk dog, those dogs were crossed with poodles (p. 206) in the 19th century to produce slightly larger bichon-type dogs with silky coats of various colors—today's Havanese. Breeders of Havanese tried to develop the ideal pet—and they pretty much succeeded. At least until they come up with a self-grooming variety.

POOCH PROS: GROOMERS

You want to keep your pets looking their best. You bathe them when they're dirty, clip their nails, and clean their ears. And, of course, you comb or brush their coats. But some dogs, such as the Havanese and several other long- and curly-haired breeds, need even more attention. They have coats that continue to grow—just like your hair—and they need regular trims. Professional dog groomers have the styling skills to handle the job. Like hairstylists in fancy salons, groomers learn all the styles that various breeds wear. For most family pets, they can do easy-care clips. Where their skills really shine are with show dogs, which often require superfancy trims. Many dog groomers learn on their own or by working as assistants to experienced groomers. Others take short courses in dog grooming. If you have an eye for style and the patience to work with pups, a career as a dog groomer may be for you.

FROM:	Cuba
HEIGHT:	9–11 inches (23–28 cm)
WEIGHT:	7–13 pounds (3–6 kg)
COAT:	Variety of colors; long, soft, fine, silky (sometimes corded)
GROOMING:	
EXERCISE NEEDS:	
K-9 QUALITIES:	Devoted and adaptable

Though it looks like Havanese would get too hot in the **WARM SUNSHINE** of Cuba, their fluffy coats are actually fine and **LIGHTWEIGHT** and insulate them from the sun and overheating.

CHINESE CRESTED

Long, flowing mane and tail, feathered legs—is it a small pony? No, it's a Chinese crested, and it is one unique-looking dog! Believed to be descended from African hairless dogs traded among sailors, these cheery companions are always up for a cuddle on your lap or for playing with their toys. Though they like kids, they're too little for rough-and-tumble play. They're smart, sensitive, and amusing pets, but they take some extra care. Their skin needs to be protected from both cold and from sun—yes, that means putting on sunscreen!—and they're among the hardest breeds to housetrain. But if you're up to the work, they make charming and loving pets.

FROM: Africa, China
HEIGHT: 9–13 inches (23–33 cm)
WEIGHT: 8–12 pounds (4–5 kg)
COAT: Variety of colors; hairless with long mane, tail, and feathered legs, or fully covered with long, soft hair
GROOMING:
EXERCISE NEEDS:
K-9 QUALITIES: Gentle and affectionate

POWDERPUFF CHINESE CRESTED

Not into the pony look? Hairless coats are the result of a genetic mutation, and not all puppies get the gene. If you like your dogs fluffier, consider the powderpuff. They're born in the same litters as their hairless siblings, but they grow long, soft coats.

PEKINGESE

Named for the ancient city of Peking, now Beijing, these sacred dogs (whose name is pronounced PEEK-in-eeze) have been depicted in art going back to the Tang dynasty of the seventh to 10th centuries. According to legend, these little "lion dogs" trace their origins to a lion that fell in love with a marmoset, but we suspect genetic testing won't back that up. One of the oldest of dog breeds, these dogs were developed to be companions to royalty. "Pekes" aren't the easiest to train or housetrain, and they're better with adults and older kids, but they can be as happy in an apartment as a palace.

FROM:	China
HEIGHT:	6–9 inches (15–23 cm)
WEIGHT:	Up to 12 pounds (5 kg)
COAT:	Variety of colors; long, straight

GROOMING:	
EXERCISE NEEDS:	
K-9 QUALITIES:	Bold and good-natured

JAPANESE CHIN

Sharing ancestry with the Pekingese, "chins" probably came to Japan as royal gifts from the Chinese emperor. In Japan, the royal chin were considered distinct from "dogs," the working inu breeds. Generally calm, they're also naturals at tricks, sometimes turning in rapid circles known as the "chin spin."

FROM:	Japan, China
HEIGHT:	8–11 inches (20–28 cm)
WEIGHT:	4–9 pounds (2–4 kg)
COAT:	Black and white, sable and white, lemon and white; long, straight, silky
GROOMING:	
EXERCISE NEEDS:	
K-9 QUALITIES:	Cheerful and mischievous

SHIH TZU

These little "lion dogs" were once the prized lapdogs of Chinese emperors, but their royal past didn't go to their heads.

Shih tzu (pronounced SHEED-zoo, meaning "lion" in Mandarin), are sweet, playful dogs whose goal in life is to soak up love and dish it back out. Developed as companion dogs, these popular pets tend to like kids, other dogs, and even cats. They also make great therapy dogs. Shih tzu can adapt to any indoor living arrangement, as long as they're with their people. For a toy breed, they're sturdy and athletic, and are able to compete in agility or play fetch. They can be a bit stubborn when it comes to training, including house training, and their coats, of course, require a lot of effort.

Everyone agrees that shih tzu have an ancient history, but the dogs' exact origins are a mystery—and a matter of fierce debate. The dogs may have originated in Tibet, bred by Tibetan monks to be lion-looking companions and watchdogs, and then been given as tributes in the mid-1600s to China's emperors, who further developed the breed. Or their history may go back much further in China, as paintings and artwork dating from the first century depict dogs that look like shih tzu. Either way, they became prized pets of the Chinese imperial royalty. The breed survived the 1949 Chinese Communist Revolution—which saw the end of the royalty and their hobbies—thanks to foreign diplomats who had acquired several of the dogs and brought them back to Europe.

HERO HOUNDS

Early one morning in 2014, Richard Harris collapsed in his home in Calgary, Canada. Lucky for him, a resourceful shih tzu named Timmy was nearby. Timmy ran into the bedroom where Richard's adult daughter, Pauline, was sleeping. He pestered her until she woke up. But Pauline, who had only recently moved into her father's home, thought Timmy just wanted to play, and she sent him away. Timmy didn't give up. He ran downstairs for reinforcements: a big husky named Bella. With Timmy leading, the two ran back into Pauline's room. Bella jumped up on the bed and pushed Pauline out of it, then helped her up. Now awake—and alarmed by the dogs' behavior—Pauline followed the canine heroes downstairs and found her father unconscious on the floor. She called emergency responders, who rushed him to the hospital. The brainy shih tzu and brawny husky were lifesavers that day.

FROM:	Tibet, China
HEIGHT:	8–11 inches (20–28 cm)
WEIGHT:	9–16 pounds (4–7 kg)
COAT:	Variety of colors; long, dense
GROOMING:	
EXERCISE NEEDS:	
K-9 QUALITIES:	Outgoing and loving

SHIH TZU ARE CALLED "CHRYSANTHEMUM DOGS" because their hair frames their faces like chrysanthemum flower petals.

LHASA APSO

Lhasas come by their furry manes intentionally. They were bred by Tibetan monks to look like ferocious little lions to guard temples and monasteries. *Apso* means "bearded," referring to their furry manes. Still good watchdogs, they're affectionate with their families, but they can be a bit stubborn and mischievous.

FROM: Tibet, China
HEIGHT: 10–11 inches (25–28 cm)
WEIGHT: 12–18 pounds (5–8 kg)
COAT: Variety of colors; long, heavy, straight

GROOMING:
EXERCISE NEEDS:
K-9 QUALITIES: Watchful, independent, and amusing

In Tibet , China, the Lhasa apso is known as the **ABSO SENG KYE,** which means "bark lion sentiment dog."

KYI-LEO

The name of these playful dogs gives away their origins. *Kyi*, Tibetan for "dog," honors its Lhasa apso heritage, while *Leo*, Latin for "lion," refers to its Maltese ancestors. Good watchdogs, kyi-leo are also affectionate pets. (*Kyi* is pronounced KI as in "kite.")

FROM: U.S.A.
HEIGHT: 9–11 inches (23–28 cm)
WEIGHT: 9–13 pounds (4–6 kg)
COAT: Variety of colors; long, thick, silky

GROOMING:
EXERCISE NEEDS:
K-9 QUALITIES: Gentle and devoted

TIBETAN TERRIER

Despite their names, these sheep-dogs aren't terriers, just terrier size. They're actually related to the Lhasa apso (p. 262.) "TTs" have thick coats and wide "snowshoe" feet that help them travel the mountainous terrain of their native land. They're athletic pets for active families.

FROM: Tibet, China
HEIGHT: 14–16 inches (36–41 cm)
WEIGHT: 18–31 pounds (8–14 kg)
COAT: Variety of colors; long, silky

GROOMING:
EXERCISE NEEDS:
K-9 QUALITIES: Devoted and energetic

KNOWN AS LUCK BRINGERS in their native country, Tibetan terriers were never sold, lest it risk bad luck. But they could be given as special gifts or in return for favors.

TIBETAN SPANIEL

Described by fans as part terrier, part monkey, and part cat, these dogs were bred by Tibetan monks as watchdogs for monasteries. "Tibbies" are not true spaniels; they got their name because, like small spaniels, they're known for providing comfort to their people. They love snuggling and going on walks with their families.

FROM: Tibet, China
HEIGHT: 8–10 inches (21–26 cm)
WEIGHT: 9–15 pounds (4–7 kg)
COAT: Variety of colors; long, sleek

GROOMING:
EXERCISE NEEDS:
K-9 QUALITIES: Good-natured, loving, and bold

AFFECTIONATE "COMFORTER DOGS" OF THE UK

Spaniels have been favorite companions for centuries in Europe, especially in the United Kingdom. The larger, working spaniels were developed into land spaniels or water spaniels, depending on their hunting roles. But the smallest spaniels were valued for their "lap-ability." At first merely decorations and amusements, people soon discovered that the dogs' affection made them feel better. Ever since, these small spaniels—the foundations of today's "toy" varieties—have been known as comforter dogs.

CAVALIER KING
CHARLES SPANIEL

One of the larger toy breeds, Cavaliers—or "Cavies"— enjoy long walks and playing fetch as much as snuggling with you on the couch. Today's Cavaliers are re-creations of the royal pets of the 15th to 19th centuries, which were both lapdogs and companions of estate owners. Hardy enough to follow a horseback rider all day back then, these popular pets are still sturdy companions whose exercise needs adapt to their people's lifestyles. Just make sure they get some quality lap time at the end of the day.

In the **MIDDLE AGES**, when people's hygiene was a bit less attended to than it is today, one of the unpleasant "duties" of lapdogs was to **ATTRACT FLEAS** off of their people.

FROM: UK
HEIGHT: 12–13 inches (30–33 cm)
WEIGHT: 11–18 pounds (5–8 kg)
COAT: Red and white (Blenheim), black and tan, black and white, ruby; long, silky

GROOMING:
EXERCISE NEEDS:
K-9 QUALITIES: Playful and devoted

ENGLISH TOY SPANIEL

Favorites of King Charles II of England in the mid-1600s, "Charlies"—known as King Charles spaniels in some countries—were already favorites in England by the 1500s. Adaptable dogs, they're happy playing with you or snuggling by your side, and they're equally at home in apartments or on large estates. These affectionate pets probably got their pug noses and domed heads from being crossed with Asian toys, such as the Pekingese (p. 259) and Japanese chin (p. 259) along the way.

FROM: UK/England

HEIGHT: 10–11 inches (25–27 cm)

WEIGHT: 9–13 pounds (4–6 kg)

COAT: Black and tan (King Charles), black, white and tan (Prince Charles), red (Ruby), red and white (Bleinheim); long, silky

GROOMING:

EXERCISE NEEDS:

K-9 QUALITIES: Cheerful and gentle

KING CHARLES II, who ruled England in the mid-1600s, was so fond of his spaniels that he decreed they should be welcomed in any public place. That included the **BRITISH HOUSE OF PARLIAMENT,** where animals usually weren't allowed. The decree is still in place.

PAPILLON

Papillon **is French for "butterfly," and a quick look at these dogs' winglike ears shows that it's the perfect name for them.** Descended from dwarf spaniels popular in the 16th century, papillons (pronounced pa-pee-YONE) were favorites of the French aristocracy up through the early 1700s, but they also owe much of their popularity to Spanish and Italian breeders. Papillons may look dainty, but they're bundles of energy. Like their namesakes, they're always on the move, flitting from one place to another. They love exercise and play—and kids as playmates, as long as they're old enough to play gently with the petite pups. Intelligent and easy to train (except maybe for housetraining), papillons excel at agility and learning tricks—both great ways to keep their minds busy. If you manage to tire them out, they'll happily snuggle up next to you in the evening.

FROM:	France, Belgium
HEIGHT:	8–11 inches (20–28 cm)
WEIGHT:	4–11 pounds (2–5 kg)
COAT:	White and either black, lemon, red or sable, tricolor; long, full, soft
GROOMING:	⫷⫷⫷⫷
EXERCISE NEEDS:	⬤⬤⬤⬤⬤
K-9 QUALITIES:	Affectionate and energetic

PHALÈNE

Phalènes are identical to papillons in all ways except one: They have long, droopy ears. Papillons and phalènes (pronounced FAH-len) are born in the same litters. *Phalène* is French for "moth"!

RUSSIAN TSVETNAYA BOLONKA

When dogs curl up to sleep, it's not just to keep warm—or to look incredibly cute! Their **INSTINCTS TELL THEM TO PROTECT** their soft bellies from any predators lurking in the night.

These adorably scruffy dogs get along great with kids and other pets, but they can't handle vigorous play. Developed from various toy-size breeds, including bichon-type dogs and dogs given to Russian nobility by Louis XIV of France, the breed only became established in the mid-1900s. They're alert and intelligent, ready to perform watchdog duties or tackle obedience or agility competitions. (Their name is pronounced SVET-nie-yuh bah-LONE-kuh.)

FROM:	Russia
HEIGHT:	7–10 inches (18–25 cm)
WEIGHT:	5–11 pounds (2–5 kg)
COAT:	Variety of colors, except white; thick, wavy or curly

GROOMING:

EXERCISE NEEDS:

K-9 QUALITIES: Easygoing and devoted

RUSSIAN TOY

One of the smallest dog breeds in the world, these Chihuahua look-alikes actually developed in the 1800s from English toy terriers (p. 246), which were popular pets of the Russian aristocracy. These rare dogs are playful and friendly pets and are also good candidates for dog sports or therapy work.

SUPER SMALLS

FROM:	Russia
HEIGHT:	8–11 inches (20–28 cm)
WEIGHT:	3–7 pounds (1–3 kg)
COAT:	Black and tan, blue and tan, brown and tan, red, red and brown, red-sable; short, shiny, smooth or long, slightly wavy

GROOMING:

EXERCISE NEEDS:

K-9 QUALITIES: Lively and happy

Chihuahuas are **BRAINY** little dogs—literally! When you look at dogs' brains relative to their **BODY SIZE**, Chihuahuas have the **BIGGEST.**

SUPER SMALLS

FROM:	Mexico
HEIGHT:	6–9 inches (15–23 cm)
WEIGHT:	4–6 pounds (2–3 kg)
COAT:	Variety of colors; short or long and soft
GROOMING:	
EXERCISE NEEDS:	
K-9 QUALITIES:	Smart and devoted

CHIHUAHUA

They may be the smallest of all breeds, but Chihuahuas have huge personalities (and ears to match).

The ultimate "purse puppies," Chihuahuas are extremely portable. And that suits them just fine, because they are devoted to their people—sometimes one member of the family more than others—and want to be with them always. They're superb lapdogs, but they're too small and fragile to play with kids and may even feel the need to defend themselves from rambunctious playmates.

Chihuahuas (pronounced chee-WA-wa) don't seem to know they're little. They'll stand up for themselves and their people against foes many times their size. The popular dogs are intelligent and easily trained (though housetraining may take a while). Most Chihuahuas are short-haired, but a litter can include long-haired puppies, too.

Depictions of Chihuahua-like dogs have popped up in ancient art all over the world, but today's Chihuahua comes from Mexico and is named for a northwestern state in that country. The little dogs are believed to be descendants of now extinct Techichi dogs kept by the Toltecs back in the ninth century. When the Aztecs became the dominant civilization in early 14th century Mesoamerica, they probably crossed their small, hairless breeds with the Techichi dogs, producing the Chihuahua.

HERO HOUNDS

Zoey may have weighed in at only five pounds (2.3 kg), but she proved she was just as brave as any Doberman. The little Chihuahua was hanging out with her owners' one-year-old grandson, Booker, in Colorado, U.S.A. The little boy was having a great time, splashing his hands in a birdbath in his grandparents' backyard. No one—at least, no person—saw the danger approaching: A rattlesnake had slithered up to the toddler! It rattled its tail and then struck. Zoey jumped in front of Booker, shielding him and taking the rattlesnake's bite herself. The brave little Chihuahua got sick from the snake's venom, but she pulled through after being treated by veterinarians. After she recovered, Zoey pranced around the home just like she did earlier—maybe with a little extra pride. Zoey proved that even if you're little, you can do big things.

PUG

There's no mistaking a pug. From their wrinkly muzzles to their curly tails, these popular dogs command attention. And once they have your attention, they'll charm you with their playful and loving nature. For pugs, life doesn't get any better than spending time with their people, playing with kids, and cuddling on laps. Muscular and sturdy, they can even handle a little more romping than most toy breeds. Pugs have a long history of being affectionate pets. Centuries ago, they were pampered companions of nobles in China, where they lived in the lap of luxury, often guarded by soldiers. Today, they're as happy in a palace as they are in an apartment...as long as it's air-conditioned. With their shortened muzzles and airways, these dogs don't handle heat well, and that rules out strenuous exercise, too. But they're all too happy to tag along with their people on walks, picnics, or jaunts about town, or even to compete in dog sports—on a cool day.

FROM: China
HEIGHT: 10–13 inches (25–33 cm)
WEIGHT: 14–18 pounds (6–8 kg)
COAT: Fawn, black; short, smooth, glossy
GROOMING:
EXERCISE NEEDS:
K-9 QUALITIES: Fun-loving and adaptable

Pugs probably got their name from their facial expressions, which were similar to those of **MARMOSET MONKEYS,** also known as "pug monkeys." The monkeys were popular pets in the 1700s.

FRENCH BULLDOG

With their bat-wing ears and chunky build, "Frenchies" have a distinctive look. Descended from now extinct English toy bulldogs brought to France by lacemakers in the 1800s, these sturdy little pups can adapt to any home (as long as it's kept cool). They are tremendously popular pets—and with good reason. They love people, enjoy some fun, and happily curl up in your lap.

FROM: France
HEIGHT: 11–13 inches (28–33 cm)
WEIGHT: 24–29 pounds (11–13 kg)
COAT: Fawn, cream, brindle, white, possibly with markings; short

GROOMING:
EXERCISE NEEDS:
K-9 QUALITIES: Charming and loving

BOSTON TERRIER

Nicknamed the "American gentleman" because of their gentle nature and "tuxedo" coat, these popular pets love to be with their people, including kids. Playing fetch, training for agility, cuddling on laps—whatever: If it's something you can do together, these pups are all in! A cross between bulldogs and now extinct white English Terriers, this breed is sturdy and intelligent—the perfect pet.

It took a few tries to get the right name for **BOSTON TERRIERS.** Before being named in 1889 for the city of their origin, the dogs were called round heads, bullet heads, and Bull Terriers.

FROM: U.S.A.
HEIGHT: 15–17 inches (38–43 cm)
WEIGHT: 11–24 pounds (5–11 kg)
COAT: Black and white, brindle and white; short

GROOMING:
EXERCISE NEEDS:
K-9 QUALITIES: Loving and adaptable

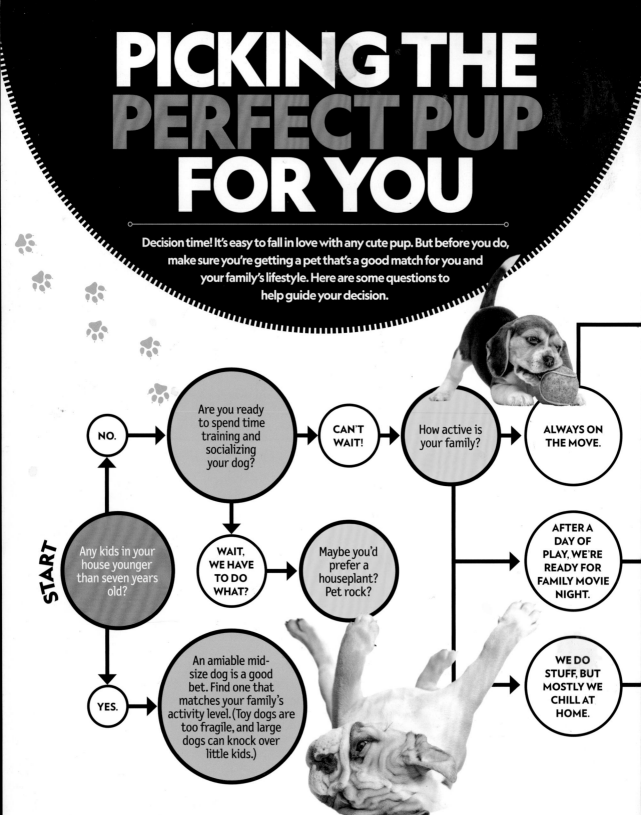

PICKING THE PERFECT PUP FOR YOU

Decision time! It's easy to fall in love with any cute pup. But before you do, make sure you're getting a pet that's a good match for you and your family's lifestyle. Here are some questions to help guide your decision.

START

Any kids in your house younger than seven years old?

NO. → **Are you ready to spend time training and socializing your dog?** → CAN'T WAIT! → **How active is your family?** → ALWAYS ON THE MOVE.

Are you ready to spend time training and socializing your dog? ↓ **WAIT, WE HAVE TO DO WHAT?** → **Maybe you'd prefer a houseplant? Pet rock?**

AFTER A DAY OF PLAY, WE'RE READY FOR FAMILY MOVIE NIGHT.

YES. → **An amiable mid-size dog is a good bet. Find one that matches your family's activity level. (Toy dogs are too fragile, and large dogs can knock over little kids.)**

WE DO STUFF, BUT MOSTLY WE CHILL AT HOME.

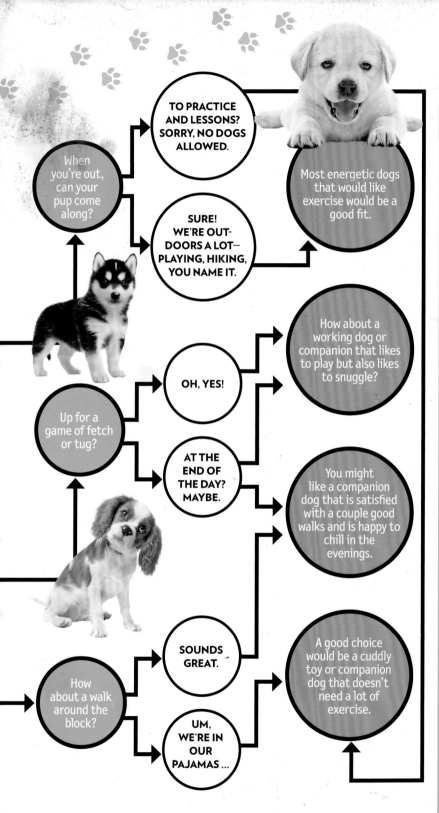

When you're out, can your pup come along?

- **TO PRACTICE AND LESSONS? SORRY, NO DOGS ALLOWED.** → Most energetic dogs that would like exercise would be a good fit.
- **SURE! WE'RE OUTDOORS A LOT— PLAYING, HIKING, YOU NAME IT.** → Most energetic dogs that would like exercise would be a good fit.

Up for a game of fetch or tug?

- **OH, YES!** → How about a working dog or companion that likes to play but also likes to snuggle?
- **AT THE END OF THE DAY? MAYBE.** → You might like a companion dog that is satisfied with a couple good walks and is happy to chill in the evenings.

How about a walk around the block?

- **SOUNDS GREAT.** → A good choice would be a cuddly toy or companion dog that doesn't need a lot of exercise.
- **UM, WE'RE IN OUR PAJAMAS ...** → A good choice would be a cuddly toy or companion dog that doesn't need a lot of exercise.

"HYPOALLERGENIC" DOGS

The truth is, all dogs (and other animals) produce allergens, which can cause some people to sneeze, get itchy eyes, break out in hives, wheeze, or have asthma attacks. Dogs produce six allergens, found in different mixes in their dander (skin flakes), saliva, and urine. People with dog allergies may be more sensitive to one dog than another, even within the same breed! Some dogs—those with curly or wiry coats, hair instead of fur, or hairless skin—are referred to as hypoallergenic because they don't shed, so they leave less dander lying around. But they still produce allergens. "Hypo" just means less; there are no "nonallergenic" dogs. If you're allergic to dogs, talk to your doctor before getting a pet. You don't want to adopt a furry friend and then discover you can't live together.

FINDING FIDO

The most important thing you can do when choosing your new forever friend is to spend time with them in person.

Only adopt from a rescue group, an animal shelter, or a good breeder that carefully matches dogs with families. A pup's early life and their parents' background affect their personality, behavior, and health forever. Never buy from an online breeder, "puppy farm", or pet store. With an adult, learn more at PupQuest (www.pupquest.org).

With as many as 5.5 million dogs entering shelters each year in the United States alone, there are lots of pups that need good homes. Talk to your parents about considering a rescue dog. Rescue groups and shelters usually have adult or young dogs—both purebreds and mixes—and many have puppies. Many need new homes because their owners couldn't take care of them anymore; others have an unknown or traumatic history and may have behavioral problems that require owners with special skills. Make sure you talk to the rescue organizations about a dog's background and temperament. Some dogs may not be good choices for families with kids.

SHELTERS AND RESCUES

A GOOD SHELTER OR RESCUE GROUP...

☐ Requires you to fill out an application and meets you to discuss the best pet for your family.

☐ Requires you to meet the pup in person before you adopt.

☐ Knows about dogs' personalities, how easy they are to handle, how well socialized they are, and how they react to different situations, kids, and other animals.

☐ Has veterinarians examine, vaccinate, treat, microchip, and spay or neuter the dogs.

☐ Will take the pup back at any time and for any reason.

☐ Has clean facilities.

BREEDERS

A GOOD BREEDER...

☐ Usually raises only one or a few breeds of dog, knows a lot about those breeds, and has pedigreed puppies available to good homes.

☐ Insists on meeting you and learning about your family, home, and plans for the pup.

☐ Requires you to meet the puppy in person and lets you see where he spends his time.

☐ Lets you meet the pup's parents.

☐ Raises pups with their mother in a home.

☐ Socializes the puppies to different people, places, and things.

☐ Won't let the puppies go home until they're at least 8 to 12 weeks old.

☐ Knows the personalities and health histories, including screenings, of the parent dogs.

☐ Has veterinary records proving each puppy has been examined and vaccinated.

☐ Will take the puppy back at any time and for any reason.

☐ Makes your family sign a contract.

PREPARING FOR
YOUR POOCH

Before you bring your new friend home, you have some work to do. You need to find a vet to take care of your pup's health and "puppy-proof" her environment. After all, it'll be your pup's new forever home!

CHECK OUT VETS

Before you select a pet, select a vet. Ask pet-owning friends for recommendations. You may even like to meet with the vet to get feedback about breeds you're considering. Make an appointment for right after you get your puppy so you can make sure your new friend is healthy and up to date on vaccinations.

PUPPY-PROOF

Puppy-proofing means making your home safe for your puppy—not just from the little chewing machine (though it's that, too). Pretend you're a puppy. Get low and snoop around your house and yard. What could a puppy chew on, knock over, or slip through? Remove anything that shouldn't be chewed or eaten or that could fall on the puppy. Look out for electrical cords; household cleaners, chemicals, fertilizers, and weed killers; people food; possible choking hazards; things that are easy to knock over; and plants, which could be toxic if your puppy chews on them. Outside, also look for gaps under gates, fences, and hedges.

GEAR UP

Part of preparing for your new friend means having the right pet supplies to take care of the pup. And, yes, that means puppy toys! Here's the gear you need:

Gate (optional): A dog- or child-safety gate can keep your puppy away from unwanted areas.

Crate or play/exercise pen: Your puppy needs a safe place to stay when you're not in the room. Leave it open when you're around. Fashion it with a bed, puppy pad, water, and toys or chewies appropriate for the puppy.

Bed: Use a crate pad or something that's cheap and washable—and expect the puppy to chew it and possibly have accidents on it. Save the cushy bed for an older pup or adult dog that's house-trained and won't rip it up.

Dog bowls: Get two bowls; stainless steel is easiest to keep clean. The water bowl needs to always be full.

Collar and ID tag: Get a small, light, comfortable puppy collar with a clasp or buckle, not a choke-style. (Yes, you'll need another when your puppy outgrows it.) Add a tag with your dog's name and your contact information.

Harness (optional): Some people and dogs prefer harnesses that fit around the dog's body, taking pressure off their neck. The front clip harnesses can also be a great tool to start teaching your puppy not to pull on his leash.

Leash: A basic six-foot (1.8-m)-long leash with a sturdy clasp is best. A retractable leash gives you too little control over your dog (not good for training), and a strong dog may be able to snap it.

Grooming tools: A rubber grooming glove works well for smooth-haired breeds, but a slicker brush or comb is better for longer-coated breeds. You also need a dog nail clipper, toothbrush, and doggy toothpaste. (Never use people toothpaste.)

Toys: Make sure toys are specially designed for puppies or dogs. Puppies need soft toys, ropelike tug toys, and harder chew toys. Adult dogs appreciate toys with a variety of textures.

Puppy food: Ask your vet to recommend a good-quality puppy or dog food. If you get your pup from a shelter, they will probably recommend the food your pup has been eating.

DOG'S BEST FRIEND

Friendship is a two-way street. You can show your friendship by making sure your pup is happy, playful, and healthful. Here's how:

SOCIALIZATION

Puppies' early experiences, when they're only 8 to 12 weeks old, affect whether they become good-natured grown-up dogs that are comfortable around all sorts of people, animals, and new experiences. Introduce your puppy early on to people of all sizes, ages, and hair and skin colors—even some wearing funny hats. Let your puppy choose to approach them and get a treat and pat on the back. A week after your puppy gets her first set of vaccinations, introduce your furry friend to friendly dogs of all different sizes, shapes, and colors. Check out a puppy training class or "puppy play-dates" organized by a dog trainer. Take your pup to different places and to see new things. Let your puppy observe loud noises, like vacuum cleaners, from across the room at first. Pet your friend—and provide treats. When a puppy gets a treat around someone or something, that good feeling lasts. And socialization doesn't stop at 12 weeks: Exposing your growing puppy or adult dog to positive and safe experiences; introducing him to new and exciting people, places, and things; and avoiding negative experiences will help your pup develop into a well-mannered canine. Finally, watch out for body language that indicates your dog is fearful. It's best to remove her from situations causing fear to avoid her developing negative feelings toward that situation, person, place, or thing.

EXERCISE

Dogs are perfect exercise buddies. They like to play and do active things. Make sure your pup gets enough daily exercise (see the ball ratings in the quick fact box for your dog's breed).

HEALTH CARE AND GROOMING

Regular veterinary checkups and grooming sessions keep pups healthy and looking their best. Your vet or dog's breeder can show you how to clip your dog's nails and clean their ears. Don't forget to brush your friend as often as the breed needs it (see comb ratings). It can be a great way to bond.

FOOD

Feed your puppy three healthful meals each day until he's four months old, then start feeding him twice a day and continue that through adulthood. A good-quality kibble (dry dog food) provides all the nutrition your pup needs. The bag lists how much to feed each day. You can also add canned food or make your own—as long as it's good for dogs. No table scraps! Some people foods can make dogs sick.

DOGGY DAY CARE

If your pup's alone during the school and work day, have a dog walker come to give your pup some exercise or see if there's a good doggy day care nearby.

DOG TRAINING
DOS AND DON'TS

Training dogs isn't just fun, it's a great way to bond with your buddy.

Training also keeps dogs' brains busy so they stay out of mischief, and it helps them become great family members. All dogs should know some basic obedience skills, such as sitting and lying down on cue, staying and coming when called, and walking on a leash without pulling. Beyond those basics, you can teach your pup all sorts of fun tricks. Taking your puppy to puppy training classes is a terrific way for your furry friend to socialize with other pups—and for you to learn how to teach your dog. But whether you decide to train your friend by yourself or go to classes led by a professional dog trainer, researchers have found that dogs learn best when you use positive, rewards-based training. If dogs do something that you want to see again and immediately get a reward—a process called learning by association—they'll do it again. With practice, they'll master the new skill.

DO

☐ Find out what motivates your dog to show off his skills. Hint: It's almost always food, so use little dog treats for training. But also use plenty of praise and see if a favorite toy works, too.

☐ Before teaching a skill, get your pup's attention. Calling his name and holding a treat next to your eyes usually does it—but remember to reward him so that he learns to do it again!

☐ Another way to train your dog is to think of the treat as a magnet attached to your dog's nose! Lure your dog into doing what you want by holding a treat in front of her nose and moving it in the direction you want her to go.

☐ As your dog performs the skill, give him a special hand signal for the skill so your pup connects the signal to his action.

☐ Keep training sessions short and fun.

☐ As soon as your pup does what you want, immediately reward her with a treat, pat, and praise in a happy voice.

☐ When your pup starts to get good at the skill, add a verbal cue to the hand signal. Here's how: Make the hand signal, say the verbal cue, wait for his response, and then reinforce the skill with a treat and praise.

☐ Start with easy skills and build up to more advanced tricks, such as "sit," then "lie down."

☐ If your dog makes a mistake, just say something simple like "oops" in a sweet voice and try again.

☐ Remember, dogs like to learn and to please their people.

DON'T

☐ Force your dog into the position you want him to take. He won't understand why you're shoving him.

☐ Confine your dog in his crate as punishment. Your pup's crate should only be a happy, safe, and relaxing den.

☐ Jerk your dog's collar or use a choke collar or shock collar to control him.

☐ Pin your puppy down to "show her who's the boss." Some trainers may recommend doing this, but researchers have found that it's not effective and can hurt your dog's trust in you.

☐ Yell, spank, or punish your dog, even if she does something wrong. It's mean, and it can cause behavior problems, such as anxiety or even aggression.

PUTTING IT INTO PRACTICE

A great way to start training your puppy is to teach her to sit when you ask her. Here's how:

1. Stand facing your puppy and get her attention. Call her name, make a kissy noise, and, if necessary, hold a treat by your eyes so she looks at your face.

2. Start by holding the treat right in front of her nose (remember, like a magnet) but high enough that she won't snatch it. Slowly move your hand back over her head.

3. As your puppy raises her nose to follow the treat, she'll naturally sit down. If she jumps up, you might be holding the treat too high or moving too fast. The second she sits, say "yes," give her the treat, and praise her in a happy voice.

4. Practice this skill three to four times and then try it without the treat in your hand. Do this by holding your hand out with an open palm facing up, move your hand toward your shoulder as you bend your elbow. Keep rewarding her successes.

5. Once she gets good at sitting with the hand signal, add a verbal cue. Show her the hand signal, then say "sit," wait for her to respond, and reward her for getting it right.

6. After practicing with both the hand signal and "sit," work on using only the verbal cue. Keep rewarding her when she gets it right.

7. Now you have a dog who can sit when you ask or signal her.

FIND OUT MORE

BOOKS

Barron's Dog Bibles series, by various authors (Barron's) Each volume of this superinformative series focuses on a specific breed and provides in-depth information on its looks, behavior, health, and more.

Dog Heroes series, by various authors (Bearport Publishing) A series of gripping stories about dogs that help people in so many ways, including search and rescue, sled dogs, conservation, therapy, even skydiving.

How to Speak Dog: A Guide to Decoding Dog Language, by Aline Alexander Newman and Gary Weitzman (National Geographic Kids, 2013) A fun look at what a dog's body language and behavior is trying to tell us.

WEBSITES

Kennel clubs include the official breed standards, information about dog competitions, and other helpful articles.

American Kennel Club, www.akc.org

Australian National Kennel Council, www.ankc .org.au

Canadian Kennel Club, www.ckc.ca

DogTime, www.dogtime.com/dog-breeds

EasyPetMD, www.easypetmd.com

Fédération Cynologique Internationale, www.fci.be

Kennel Club, UK, www.thekennelclub.org.uk

These websites provide in-depth profiles of dog breeds and articles on a wide range of topics.

VetStreet, www.vetstreet.com

GLOSSARY

aerodynamic—a streamlined shape that reduces the drag from air as something moves

aristocracy—the highest class in a society, usually the wealthy upper classes or nobility

Celts—an ancient people who spread across Europe starting in the seventh or eighth century B.C.

game—wild mammals or birds that are hunted

gene—the basic unit of a living thing's makeup; holding codes with instructions for various traits

genetics—the study of genes and heredity

genomics—the study of genes within a living being and their functions

litter—the group of baby animals, such as puppies, born to one mother at the same time

musher—the driver of a dog sled

mutation—a genetic change that dramatically alters an inherited trait

nomad—a member of a people who travel from place to place, usually to find fresh pasture for their livestock, and have no permanent home

Phoenicia—an ancient civilization, existing between 1500 B.C. and 300 B.C., on the coast of the Mediterranean Sea where Syria, Lebanon, and northern Israel now exist

sarcophagus—a stone coffin, usually with etchings or sculptures

socialization—introducing a dog or puppy to many new people, animals, things, and experiences in a safe and positive way so the dog feels comfortable around them

toy dogs—tiny small dogs selectively bred to be pets for people to carry or cuddle on their laps

INDEX

PHOTO CREDITS

COVER

Cover (UP RT), cynoclub/GI; (havanese), Dorottya Mathe/SS; (CTR RT), Artsilense/SS; (Papillon), Sergey Lavrentev/SS; (LO RT), Rosa Jay/SS; (bone), Ingram; (LO LE), BG-FOTO/SS; (collar), Perutskyi Petro/SS; (ball), Eric Isselee/SS; (CTR LE), Eric Isselee/SS; (toy), 9dream studio/SS; (UP LE), cynoclub/GI; **Back cover** (UP RT), Anna Hoychuk/SS; (LO RT), Viorel Sima/SS; (LO CTR), Liliya Kulianionak/SS; (LO LE), BW Folsom/SS; (UP LE), SikorskiFotografie/SS; **Spine**, BG-FOTO/SS

FRONT MATTER

1 (CTR), Cynoclub/SS; 2-3 (LE), Ammit Jack/SS; 3 (LO LE), Gillmar/SS; 4 (UP), Miraswonderland/SS; 4 (CTR), Kasefoto/SS; 5 (UP CTR), Richard Peterson/SS; 5 (UP RT), Susan Schmitz/SS; 5 (LO LE), Cynoclub/SS

WHAT IS A DOG?

6 (UP RT), Maila Facchini/SS; 6 (LO LE), Susan Schmitz/SS; 7 (CTR), San Diego Humane Society; 8 (LO LE), Csanad Kiss/SS; 9 (Ancient), Artur Balytskyi/SS; 9 (Island Fox), Russ Bishop/ASP; 9 (Coyote), Jim Cumming/SS; 9 (Dhole), Iakov Filimonov/SS; 9 (Bush Dog) (Arctic Fox) (Red), Eric Isselee/SS; 9 (Gray Fox), Roee Fung/SS; 9 (Fennec Fox), Lifetimestock/SS; 9 (Maned Wolf), Anan Kaewkhammul/SS; 9 (Crab-Eating Fox), Ondrej Prosicky/SS; 9 (Gray Wolf), mariait/SS; 9 (Golden Jackal), Martin Mecnarowski/SS; 9 (African Wild Dog), Rich Carey/SS; 9 (Domestic), Papilio/ASP; 10 (LO LE), Michelle Lalancette/SS; 11 (LO RT), Toloubaev Stanislav/SS; 15 (UP LE), Jagodka/SS; 15 (UP CTR), Jenson/SS; 15 (CTR RT), Agcuesta/SS; 15 (LO RT), Emily Skeels/SS; 16 (UP RT), Eric Isselee/SS; 16 (LO LE), Csandad Kiss/SS; 16 (LO CTR), Jagodka/SS; 16 (LO RT), Willeecole Photography/SS; 17 (Candle-Flame Ears) (Pendant Ears), Dorling Kindersley Ltd/ASP; 17 (Bat Ears), Csanad Kiss/SS; 17 (Rose Ears), Daniel Heighton/SS; 17 (Erect Ears), Eric Isselee/SS; 17 (Butterfly Ears), Jiri Vaclavek/SS; 17 (Folded Ears), Willeecole Photography/SS; 17 (Button Ears), Erik Lam/SS; 18 (UP LE), Willeecole Photography/SS; 18 (UP RT), Eric Isselee/SS; 19 (Full Double), Eve Photography/SS; 19 (Wirehaired), Mykolamoriev/SS; 19 (Stand-Off), Smart-Foto/SS; 19 (Long), Sasastock/SS; 19 (Curly), Joseph Gaul/SS; 19 (Powderpuff), Volofin/SS; 19 (Smooth), Grigorita Ko/SS; 19 (Short), Jpagetrfphotos/SS; 19 (Corded), Borina Olga/SS; 20 (UP RT), Jagodka/SS; 20 (LO LE), Debby Wong/SS; 21 (LO LE), Cat'chy Images/SS

PRIMITIVE DOGS

22-23 (CTR), Aneta Jungerova/SS; 24 (LO CTR), Masarik/SS; 25 (UP LE), Monica Doallo/ASP; 25 (LO RT), Alice Van Kempen/SS; 26 (UP LE), Papilio/ASP; 26 (LO LE), Jogodka/SS; 27 (UP RT), Ming-Nan Chen, Formosan Mountain Dog Conservation Center/Hsiao Wu Fong Kennel; 27 (LO LE), Keattikorn/SS; 28 (LO RT), Anetapics/SS; 29 (LO RT), Jannarong/SS; 30 (CTR RT), Otsphoto/SS; 30 (LO LE), Ivonne Wierink/SS; 31 (UP LE), Blickwinkel/ASP; 31 (LO LE), Kuznetsov Alexey/SS; 32 (CTR), George Ostertag/ASP; 32 (LO RT), Maxontravel/SS; 33 (UP LE), Kongsak Sumano/SS; 33 (UP RT), Ondrej Prosicky/SS; 33 (CTR LE), Flpa/ASP; 33 (CTR RT), Andrzej Kubik/SS; 33 (LO LE), Richardernestyap/SS

SPITZ-TYPE DOGS

34-35 (RT), Everita Pane/SS; 36 (UP LE), Flpa/ASP; 36 (LO RT), Dorling Kindersley Ltd/ASP; 37 (UP LE), Joppo/SS; 37 (CTR RT), Victor Gomez/ASP; 37 (LO LE), Natalya Rozhkova/SS; 38 (RT), Eric Isselee/SS; 38 (LO LE), Jun Sato/GI; 39 (UP LE), Africa Studio/SS; 39 (LO RT), Julie Poole/Animal Photography Stock; 40 (CTR RT), Roger Tillberg/ASP; 40 (LO LE), Capture Light/SS; 41 (UP RT), Juha Saastamoinen/SS; 41 (UP RT), Jogadka/SS; 41 (CTR RT), Northsweden/SS; 41 (LO LE), Dorling Kindersley Ltd/ASP; 42 (LO RT), George Rinhart/GI; 43 (CTR RT), Dmitry Kalinovsky/SS; 44 (UP LE), Eric Isselee/SS; 44 (CTR RT), USA Network/GI; 45 (UP RT), Alexis84/GI; 45 (LO RT), Barbara O'Brien/Animal Photography Stock; 46 (CTR RT), Erik Lam/SS; 46 (LO LE), Alice Van Kempen; 47 (UP RT), Cynoclub/SS; 47 (CTR LE), Sam Clark/Animal Photography Stock; 47 (LO RT), Roger Tillberg/ASP; 48 (LO RT), Wenn Ltd/ASP; 49 (CTR), Pattarawat/SS; 50 (UP LE), Globalp/SS; 50 (LO RT), Virgonira/GI; 51 (UP LE), Bidaoleksandr/SS; 51 (CTR RT), Degtyaryov Andrey/SS; 51 (LO LE), Pontus Schroder/SS; 51 (LO LE), Cynoclub/SS; 52 (UP RT), Landon Ginn/SS; 52 (CTR LE), Sally Anne Thompson/Animal Photography Stock; 52 (LO RT), Qngiw/SS; 53 (UP LE), Pardoy/SS; 53 (CTR RT), S.s.b/SS; 53 (LO LE), Arco Images Gmbh/ASP; 54 (LO LE), Isselee/DT; 54 (LO RT), Cowardlion/SS; 55 (UP RT), Erik Lam/SS; 55 (LO LE), Liliya Kulianionak/SS

HERDING DOGS

56-57 (RT), Wayne Hutchinson/GI; 58 (RT), Eric Isselee/SS; 59 (UP RT), Alf Manciagli/SS; 59 (LO LE), Flpa/ASP; 60 (CTR RT), Jagodka/SS; 60 (CTR RT), Callie Broaddus; 61 (UP LE), Rolf Klebsattel/SS; 61 (CTR RT), Thka/SS; 61 (LO RT), Cynoclub/SS; 62 (LO RT), Csanad Kiss/SS; 63 (UP RT), Darcy Kiefel for Balto Farms LLC; 63 (LO RT), Boston Globe/GI; 64 (UP LE), Eric Isselee/SS; 64 (LO RT), Ognjeno/GI; 65 (UP LE), Domagoj/GI; 65 (CTR RT), Eva-Maria Kramer/Animal Photography Stock; 65 (LO LE), Charalambos Andronos/GI; 65 (LO RT), Michael Kraus/SS; 66 (LO CTR), Shchipkova Elena/SS; 67 (UP LE), Hoang Dinh Nam/GI; 67 (UP RT), Behrouz Mehri/GI; 67 (LO LE), Lwa/Dann Tardif/GI; 67 (LO RT), Africa Studio/SS; 68 (UP LE), Eric Isselee/SS; 68 (LO LE), Vera Zinkova/SS; 69 (LO RT), Dora Zett/SS; 69 (CTR RT) (LO LE), Alice Van Kempen; 70 (UP LE), Erik Lam/SS; 70 (LO RT), Cbs Photo Archive/GI; 71 (LO RT), Pavel Hlystov/SS; 71 (LO LE), Kazlouski Siarhei/SS; 72 (CTR RT), Helenaqueen/SS; 72 (LO LE), Grisha Bruev/SS; 73 (UP LE), Vivienstock/SS; 73 (CTR RT), Reva Vera/SS; 73 (LO LE), Everydoghasastory/SS; 74 (CTR RT), Sasastock/SS; 74 (LO RT), Everita Pane/SS; 75 (UP LE), Joe Barti/SS; 75 (CTR RT), Borina Olga/SS; 75 (LO RT), Jne Valokuvaus/SS; 76 (LO RT), Eric Isselee/SS; 77 (CTR RT), Jogodka/SS; 77 (LO RT), Shanna Wilkenson; 78 (UP RT), Monica Martinez Do-Allo/SS; 78 (CTR LE), Dorling Kindersley Ltd/ASP; 78 (LO RT), Tierfotoagentur/ASP; 79 (UP LE), Callipso/SS; 79 (CTR RT), Capture Light/SS; 79 (LO LE), Degtyaryov Andre/SS; 79 (LO RT), Nikolayn/SS; 80 (RT), Eric Isselee/SS; 81 (UP RT), Cynoclub/SS; 81 (LO RT), Jpc-Prod/SS; 82 (UP CTR), Zoonar Gmbh/ASP; 82 (CTR RT), Photocreo Michal Bednarek/SS; 82 (LO LE), Eva-Maria Kramer/Animal Photography Stock; 83 (UP LE), Eva-Maria Kramer/Animal Photography Stock; 83 (UP RT), Aquariagirl1970/SS; 83 (CTR RT), Joachim Bartoll/SS; 83 (LO LE), Lenkadan/SS; 84 (CTR), Alexei_tm/SS; 85 (CTR LE), Juniors Bildarchiv Gmbh/ASP; 85 (CTR LE), Josh Schutz/SS; 85 (LO RT), Pilley Bianchi; 86 (UP LE), Eric Isselee/SS; 86 (UP RT), Jagodka/SS; 86 (CTR RT), Eva-Maria Kramer/Animal Photography Stock; 86 (LO LE), Diyanski/SS; 87 (UP LE), Ricantimages/SS; 87 (CTR RT), Gloverk/SS; 87 (LO RT), Eric Isselee/SS

MOUNTAIN DOGS & MASTIFFS

88-89 (RT), Alfaguarilla/SS; 90 (CTR), Eve Photography/SS; 91 (LO RT), Daniel Clarke; 92 (UP LE), Schubbel/SS; 92 (UP RT), Tetsu Yamazaki/Animal Photography Stock; 92 (LO RT), Nadiia Diachenko/SS; 93 (UP LE), Margarita Zhuravleva/SS; 93 (CTR RT), Myimages - Micha/SS; 93 (LO LE), Ricantimages/SS; 93 (LO RT), Photostockimage/SS; 94 (LE), Vivienstock/SS; 94-50 (RT), Robin Burkett/Animal Photography Stock; 95 (UP RT), Eric Isselee/SS; 95 (LO LE), Erik Lam/SS; 96 (UP RT), Peter Josto/SS; 96 (CTR LE), Tierfotoagentur/ASP; 96 (LO RT), Farlap/ASP; 97 (UP LE), Dorling Kindersley Ltd/ASP; 97 (CTR RT), Daria Chichkareva/SS; 97 (LO LE), Sergey Lavrentev/SS; 98 (UP RT), Eric Isselee/SS; 98 (LO RT), Anton_ivanov/SS; 99 (CTR), Isselee/DT; 99 (LO RT), Chronicle/ASP; 100 (CTR RT), Borchee/GI; 100 (CTR LE), Anetapics/SS; 100 (LO RT), Olegganko/SS; 101 (UP LE), Degtyaryov Andrey/SS; 101 (CTR RT), Dorling Kindersley Ltd/ASP; 101 (LO RT), Svetography/SS; 102 (CTR), Elbud/SS; 103 (Freestyle), Ivanova N/SS; 103 (Agility), Cunfek/GI; 103 (Conformation), Apple Tree House/GI; 103 (Flyball), Jon Freeman/ASP; 103 (Nose Work), Bon9/SS; 103 (Rally), Juha Saastamoinen/SS; 104 (UP RT), Koraysa/SS; 104 (CTR LE), Papilio/ASP; 104 (LO RT), Hsbortecin/SS; 105 (UP RT), Subertt/SS; 105 (LO LE), F8grapher/SS; 105 (LO RT), Erik Lam/SS; 106 (CTR RT), Eric Isselee/SS; 107 (CTR RT), Jagodka/SS; 107 (LO RT), Cynoclub/SS; 108 (UP LE), Tatiana Dyuvbanova/SS; 108 (CTR RT), Eva-Maria Kramer/Animal Photography Stock; 108 (LO LE), Eric Isselee/SS; 109 (UP RT), Egon Zitter/SS; 109 (CTR LE), Roger Tillberg/ASP; 109 (LO LE), Luisa Leal Photography/SS; 109 (LO CTR), Viorel Sima/SS; 110 (LO RT), Photo Spirit/SS; 111 (CTR), Alberto Clemares Exposito/SS; 112 (LO RT), Willeecole Photography/SS; 113 (UP LE), Joao Roda/SS; 113 (CTR RT), Little Moon/SS; 113 (LO LE), Dorling Kindersley Ltd/ASP; 113 (LO RT), Hurst Photo/SS; 114 (LO), Cynoclub/SS; 115 (LO RT), Photology1971/SS; 116 (UP LE), Eric Isselee/SS; 116 (CTR RT), Tsik/SS; 116 (LO RT), Forget Patrick/ASP; 117 (UP LE), Alice Van Kempen; 117 (CTR RT), Tsik/SS; 117 (LO LE), Vivien Stock/DT; 117 (LO RT), Sandra Van Der Steen/SS

SIGHT HOUNDS

118-119 (RT), Angel Sallade/SS; 120 (LO RT), Aneta Jungerova/SS; 121 (UP RT), Kuznetsov Alexey/SS; 121 (LO LE), Otsphoto/SS; 122 (LO LE), Artsilense/SS; 122 (LO RT), Kim Christensen/SS; 123 (UP LE), Dora Zett/SS; 123 (CTR LE), Daniel Heighton/SS; 123 (CTR RT), Mega Pixel/SS; 123 (LO RT),

Eric Isselee/SS; **124** (UP RT), Tracy Morgan/GI; **124** (CTR LE), Fotojagodka /GI; **124** (LO RT), Debra Bardowicks /GI; **125** (UP LE), Morgan Animal Photography/GI; **125** (UP RT), Tsik/SS; **125** (LO RT), Tracy Morgan/GI; **125** (LO RT), Isselee/DT

SCENT HOUNDS
126-127 (RT), Emmanuel Lattes/ASP; **128** (CTR LE) (LO RT), Alice Van Kempen; **129** (UP LE) , Arterra Picture Library/ASP; **129** (UP LE), Alice Van Kempen; **129** (LO RT), Alexey Stiop/SS; **130** (UP RT), Alice Van Kempen; **130** (CTR LE), Eva-Maria Kramer/Animal Photography Stock; **130** (LO RT), Arco Images Gmbh/ASP; **131** (UP LE) (CTR RT) (LO LE), Arco Images Gmbh/ASP; **132** (UP RT), Sally Anne Thompson/Animal Photography Stock; **132** (CTR LE), Arco Images Gmbh/ASP; **132** (LO RT), Gerard Lacz/ASP; **133** (UP LE), Dorling Kindersley Ltd/ASP; **133** (UP RT), Versusstudio/SS; **133** (CTR RT), Farlap/ASP; **133** (LO LE), Christian Mueller/SS; **134** (LO RT), Waterbury Publications, Inc.; **135** (CTR), Lori Epstein; **136** (UP RT), Everydogasastory/SS; **136** (CTR LE), Don B. Stevenson/ASP; **136** (LO RT), Eichenluft/DT; **137** (UP LE) (CTR RT), William Wise/DT; **137** (LO LE), Eva-Maria Kramer/Animal Photography Stock; **137** (LO RT), Gillma/SS; **138** (UP LE), Arco Images Gmbh/ASP; **138** (CTR LE), Tierfotoagentur/ ASP; **138** (LO RT), Jbouma09/GI; **139** (UP LE), Eudyptula/SS; **139** (CTR RT), William Wise/DT; **139** (LO LE), Susan Schmitz/SS; **139** (LO RT), Zuma Press, Inc./ASP; **140** (UP RT), Capture Light/SS; **140** (CTR LE), Zoonar Gmbh/ASP; **140** (LO RT), Radomir Rezny/DT; **141** (UP LE), Imagebroker/ ASP; **141** (CTR RT), Grossemy Vanessa/ASP; **141** (LO LE), Plotitsyna Nina/ SS; **141** (LO RT), Annette Shaff; **142** (CTR), Luminoisty-Images.com/ SS; **143** (UP LE), Dimedrol68/SS; **143** (UP RT), Erik Lam/SS; **143** (LO LE), 826A Ia/SS; **143** (LO RT), Purino/SS; **144** (UP RT), Ricantimages/SS; **144** (CTR LE), Imagebroker/ASP; **144** (LO LE), Eric Isselee/SS; **145** (UP LE), Dorling Kindersley Ltd/ASP; **145** (CTR RT), F8grapher/SS; **145** (LO LE), Eva-Maria Kramer/Animal Photography Stock; **146** (UP RT), Capture Light/SS; **146** (CTR LE) (LO RT), Dorling Kindersley Ltd/ASP; **147** (UP LE), F8grapher/ASP; **147** (CTR RT), Eva-Maria Kramer/Animal Photography Stock; **147** (LO LE), Roger Tillberg/ASP; **147** (LO RT), Victoria Brassey/SS; **148** (CTR), Leoba/GI; **149** (LO RT), Fatcamera/GI; **150** (UP RT) (CTR LE), Roger Tillberg/ASP; **150** (LO RT), Dorling Kindersley Ltd/ASP; **151** (UP LE) (CTR RT), Dorling Kindersley Ltd/ASP; **151** (LO RT), Roger Tillberg Stock Photo/ASP; **151** (LO RT), Susan Schmitz/SS; **152** (UP RT), Farlap/ASP; **152** (CTR LE), Cynoclub/SS; **152** (LO LE), Tierfotoagentur/ASP; **153** (UP LE), Radomir Rezny/ASP; **153** (CTR RT), Cynoclub/SS; **153** (LO RT), Eva-Maria Kramer/Animal Photography Stock; **154** (LO RT), Af Archive/ASP; **155** (CTR), JIsphotos/SS; **156** (UP RT), Arco Images Gmbh/ASP; **156** (CTR LE), Eva-Maria Kramer/Animal Photography Stock; **156** (LO RT), Radomir Rezny/DT; **157** (UP RT), Capture Light/SS; **157** (CTR LE), Dorling Kindersley Ltd/ASP; **157** (LO RT), Marka/ASP; **158** (UP LE), Perky Pets/ASP; **158** (CTR RT), Arco Images Gmbh/ASP; **158** (LO LE), Tierfotoagentur/ASP; **159** (UP LE), Capture Light/SS; **159** (CTR RT), Petra Wegner/ASP; **159** (LO RT), Eric Isselee/SS; **160** (LO RT), Waterbury Publications, Inc.; **161** (UP RT), Oldaovcharenko/ SS; **161** (CTR), Otsophoto/SS; **162** (CTR LE), Dorling Kindersley Ltd/ASP; **162** (LO RT), Corrina Bernsdorff; **163** (UP LE) (LO LE), Eva-Maria Kramer/ Animal Photography Stock; **163** (CTR RT), Jane Maddern; **163** (LO RT), Rena Mark/SS; **164** (CTR), Marry Kolesnik; **165** (LO RT), Rob Byron/SS; **166** (UP RT), Alice Van Kempen; **166** (CTR LE), Eva-Maria Kramer/Animal Photography Stock; **166** (LO RT), Spanic/GI; **167** (UP LE), Roger Tillberg/ Asp; **167** (CTR RT), Tierfotoagentur/ASP; **167** (LO LE), Dorling Kindersley Ltd/ASP; **167** (LO RT), Alexander Raths/SS; **168** (LO RT), Patti Mcconville/ ASP; **169** (CTR), Vladimir Picdeal Svanda/SS

POINTERS
170-171 (RT), Ivanova N/SS; **172** (UP CTR), Craig Koshyk; **172** (CTR LE), Eric Isselee/SS; **172** (LO CTR), Grossemy Vanessa/ASP; **173** (UP LE), Zuzule/ SS; **173** (CTR RT), Tierfotoagentur/ASP; **173** (LO LE), Petit Philippe /GI; **173** (LO RT), Irin-K/SS; **174** (UP LE), Tomprout/GI; **174** (LO RT), Mirrorpix/The Image Works; **175** (RT), Sikorskifotografie/GI; **176** (UP RT), Tetsu Yamazaki/ Animal Photography Stock; **176** (LO LE), Juniors Bildarchiv Gmbh/ASP; **177** (LO LE), Zuma Press, Inc./ASP; **177** (LO RT), Otsphoto/SS; **178** (LO), Olena Brodetska/SS; **179** (I'm on Alert), Daniel Kay/SS; **179** (What's That), David Porras/SS; **179** (Let's Play), Mary Swift/SS; **179** (Please Don't Be Mad), Lightfieldstudios/GI; **179** (I'm Scared), Bambara/SS; **180** (UP RT), Roger Tillberg/ASP; **180** (CTR LE) (LO RT), Farlap/ASP; **181** (UP LE), Eva-Maria Kramer/Animal Photography Stock; **181** (CTR RT), Pedro Monteiro/ SS; **181** (LO RT), Perky Pets/ASP; **182** (UP RT), Nataliya Kuznetsova/SS; **182** (LO RT), Waterbury Publications, Inc.; **183** (RT), Erik Lam/SS; **184** (UP RT), Gerard Lacz/ASP; **184** (CTR LE), Labat / Vwpics/ASP; **184** (LO RT), Alice Van Kempen; **185** (UP LE), Arco Images Gmbh/ASP; **185** (UP RT), Steve Collender/SS; **185** (CTR RT), vÖystein Engan/ASP; **185** (LO LE), Eric Isselee/ SS; **186** (LO RT), Csa Images/GI; **187** (CTR), Tierfotoagentur/ASP; **188** (UP RT),

CREDITS AND ACKNOWLEDGMENTS

Copyright © 2019 National Geographic Partners, LLC

Published by National Geographic Partners, LLC. All rights reserved. Reproduction of the whole or any part of the contents without written permission from the publisher is prohibited.

Since 1888, the National Geographic Society has funded more than 12,000 research, exploration, and preservation projects around the world. The Society receives funds from National Geographic Partners, LLC, funded in part by your purchase. A portion of the proceeds from this book supports this vital work. To learn more, visit natgeo.com/info.

NATIONAL GEOGRAPHIC and Yellow Border Design are trademarks of the National Geographic Society, used under license.

For more information, visit nationalgeographic.com, call 1-800-647-5463, or write to the following address:

National Geographic Partners
1145 17th Street N.W.
Washington, D.C. 20036-4688 U.S.A.

Visit us online at nationalgeographic.com/books

For librarians and teachers: ngchildrensbooks.org

More for kids from National Geographic: natgeokids.com

National Geographic Kids magazine inspires children to explore their world with fun yet educational articles on animals, science, nature, and more. Using fresh storytelling and amazing photography, *Nat Geo Kids* shows kids ages 6 to 14 the fascinating truth about the world— and why they should care. kids.nationalgeographic.com/subscribe

For information about special discounts for bulk purchases, please contact National Geographic Books Special Sales: specialsales@natgeo.com

For rights or permissions inquiries, please contact National Geographic Books Subsidiary Rights: bookrights@natgeo.com

Designed by Waterbury Publications, Inc.

National Geographic supports K-12 educators with ELA Common Core Resources. Visit natgeoed.org/commoncore for more information.

Hardcover ISBN: 978-1-4263-3445-0

Reinforced library binding ISBN: 978-1-4263-3446-7

The publisher would like to thank everyone who worked to make this book come together: T. J. Resler, writer; Priyanka Lamichhane, senior editor; Jen Agresta, project manager; Dr. Gary Weitzman and Amanda Kowalski, expert reviewers; Callie Broaddus, art director; Sarah J. Mock, senior photo editor; Mike McNey, map production; Sally Abbey, managing editor; Sean Philpotts, production director; and Anne LeongSon and Gus Tello, design production assistants.

For the furry friends who stole my heart: Laddie, Tuffy, Pablo, and especially Murphy, who keeps me company while I write and insists I take breaks for walks and games of fetch —T.J.R.

Printed in China
19/RRDS/1

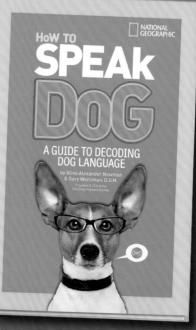

Ever wonder
WHAT'S UP WITH YOUR PUP?

Discover how to decode dog language in this fun and fascinating guide, full of quizzes, activities, training tips, and more!

NATIONAL GEOGRAPHIC

HoW TO SPEAk DOG

A GUIDE TO DECODING DOG LANGUAGE

by Aline Alexander Newman & Gary Weitzman, D.V.M. President & CEO of the San Diego Humane Society

NATIONAL GEOGRAPHIC KiDS

AVAILABLE WHEREVER BOOKS ARE SOLD
Discover more at natgeokids.com

© 2019 National Geographic Partners, LLC